Recent Developments in Artificial Intelligence and Communication Technologies

Edited by

Vikash Yadav

Government Polytechnic Bighapur Unnao
Board of Technical Education
Uttar Pradesh
India

Parashu Ram Pal

SAGE University, Bhopal
Madhya Pradesh
India

&

Chuan-Ming Liu

National Taipei University of Technology
Taiwan

Recent Developments in Artificial Intelligence and Communication Technologies

Editors: Vikash Yadav, Parashu Ram Pal and Chuan-Ming Liu

ISBN (Online): 978-1-68108-967-6

ISBN (Print): 978-1-68108-968-3

ISBN (Paperback): 978-1-68108-969-0

Published by Bentham Science Publishers Pte. Ltd. Singapore. All Rights Reserved.

First published in 2022.

need for a court order if at any point you breach any terms of this License Agreement. In no event will any delay or failure by Bentham Science Publishers in enforcing your compliance with this License Agreement constitute a waiver of any of its rights.

3. You acknowledge that you have read this License Agreement, and agree to be bound by its terms and conditions. To the extent that any other terms and conditions presented on any website of Bentham Science Publishers conflict with, or are inconsistent with, the terms and conditions set out in this License Agreement, you acknowledge that the terms and conditions set out in this License Agreement shall prevail.

Bentham Science Publishers Pte. Ltd.
80 Robinson Road #02-00
Singapore 068898
Singapore
Email: subscriptions@benthamscience.net

CONTENTS

PREFACE

Imparting intelligence has become the focus of various computational paradigms. Thanks to evolving soft computing and artificial intelligence methodologies, scientists have been able to explain and understand real-life processes and practices that formerly remained unexplored by dint of their underlying imprecision, uncertainties and redundancies, as well as the unavailability of appropriate methods for describing the inexactness, incompleteness and vagueness of information representation. Computational intelligence tries to explore and unearth intelligence embedded in the system under consideration.

This book aims to discuss computational intelligence approaches, initiatives, and applications in engineering and science fields (including Machine Intelligence, Mining Engineering, Modeling and Simulation, Computer, Communication, Networking and Information Engineering, Systems Engineering, Innovative Computing Systems, Adaptive Technologies for Sustainable Growth, and Theoretical and Applied Sciences). This collection should inspire various scholars to contribute research on intelligence principles and approaches in their respective research communities while enriching the body of research on computational intelligence.

Vikash Yadav
Department of Technical Education
Uttar Pradesh
India

Parashu Ram Pal
SAGE University, Bhopal
Madhya Pradesh
India

&

Chuan-Ming Liu
National Taipei University of Technology
Taiwan

List of Contributors

Ankita Gupta	G.B. Pant Engineering College, New Delhi, India
Ankit Srivastava	G.B. Pant Engineering College, New Delhi, India
Alok Kumar	Motilal Nehru National Institute of Technology Allahabad, Prayagraj Uttar Pradesh, India
Avjeet Singh	Motilal Nehru National Institute of Technology Allahabad, Prayagraj Uttar Pradesh, India
Anoj Kumar	Motilal Nehru National Institute of Technology Allahabad, Prayagraj Uttar Pradesh, India
Anita Yadav	Department of Computer Science and Engineering, Harcourt Butler Technical University, Kanpur, Uttar Pradesh, India
Dharmendra Kumar Yadav	Motilal Nehru National Institute of Technology, Prayagraj, Uttar Pradesh, India
Etika Rastogi	Department of Computer Science and Engineering, Meerut Institute of Engineering and Technology, Meerut, Uttar Pradesh, India
Harishchandra A. Akarte	Motilal Nehru National Institute of Technology, Prayagraj, Uttar Pradesh, India
Hardik Sharma	Department of Computer Science and Engineering, Meerut Institute of Engineering & Technology, Meerut, U.P., India
Kajal Gupta	Department of Computer Science and Engineering, Meerut Institute of Engineering and Technology, Meerut, Uttar Pradesh, India
Lipika Goel	Gokaraju Rangaraju Institute of Technology, Hyderabad, India
Lekhraj	Motilal Nehru National Institute of Technology Allahabad, Prayagraj Uttar Pradesh, India
Mukesh Rawat	Department of Computer Science and Engineering, Meerut Institute of Engineering and Technology, Meerut, Uttar Pradesh, India
Manish Dixit	Department of CSE & IT, Madhav Institute of Technology and Science, Gwalior, M.P., India
Mohammed Abdul Wajeed	Vasavi College of Engineering, Ibrahimbagh, Telangana, India
Mahendra Pratap Yadav	SRMIST NCR Campus, Modinagar, Ghaziabad, UP-201204, India
Mukesh Rawat	Department of Computer Science and Engineering, Meerut Institute of Engineering & Technology, Meerut, U.P., India
Manan Gupta	Department of Computer Science and Engineering, Meerut Institute of Engineering & Technology, Meerut, U.P., India
Pooja Gupta	Meerut Institute of Engineering and Technology, Meerut, Uttar Pradesh, India
Preksha Pratap	Department of Computer Science and Engineering, Meerut Institute of Engineering & Technology, Meerut, U.P., India
Rohit Anand	G.B. Pant Engineering College, New Delhi, India

Rohit Vashisht ABES Engineering College, Ghaziabad, India

Ruchi Jayaswal Department of CSE & IT, Madhav Institute of Technology and Science, Gwalior, M.P., India

Sonam Gupta Ajay Kumar Garg Engineering College, Ghaziabad, India

Urvashi Saraswat Department of Computer Science and Engineering, Harcourt Butler Technical University, Kanpur, Uttar Pradesh, India

Vimal Kumar Meerut Institute of Engineering and Technology, Meerut, Uttar Pradesh, India

CHAPTER 1

Automatic Suggestion Model for Tourist Using Efficient BST Searching

Etika Rastogi[1,*]**, Kajal Gupta**[1] **and Mukesh Rawat**[1]

[1] *Department of Computer Science and Engineering, Meerut Institute of Engineering and Technology, Meerut, Uttar Pradesh, India*

Abstract: The traditional artificial guide service can be substituted by the advanced intelligent tourism guide system, which can help many developing tourism industries as the demand for tourism is going higher in today's world. An intelligent tourism guide system can create automatic recommendations according to the preferences [1]. With the instantaneous evolution of computer technology and electronic information technology as the basis, this chapter combines the tree-based algorithm and associated knowledge of tree theory to implement an algorithm and processing plan. The objective of our approach is to build a relationship between the user and the system. The application provides many services to the user meeting their needs and the purpose of gaining information about the places. The application mainly represents a mobile tour guide system with augmented reality. The main objective of the application is to make a system that runs on most of the mobile devices and becomes helpful to the user while visiting new places. The system should find a place using user preferences, like beaches, historical monuments, hill stations, temples, adventurous places, *etc*. The system should show recommendations about those places along with the description and images. This application will help the people who love to travel and want to travel to new places without having previous information about the place. This model [2-5] makes the use of efficient BST Searching as compared to the database. The information about various places is stored in the tree data structure, and it becomes easy to store a lot of data in the tree as compared to the database because it requires more memory and time to store lots of information into the database. The main advantage of using the system is to make the searching process easier and to ease the process of storing the data in the tree rather than the database. The tree-based algorithm is efficient in terms of storage and retrieval of data so that the performance of the system is enhanced. The application takes less time to fetch the data using a tree-based algorithm according to added preferences by the user as compared to the database, which takes more time to fetch the data and to display it as required.

Keywords: Algorithm, Binary search tree, Deserialization, Efficient searching, Intelligent tourism guide, Retrieval, Serialization, Traversal.

* **Corresponding author Etika Rastogi:** Department of Computer Science and Engineering, Meerut Institute of Engineering and Technology, Meerut, Uttar Pradesh, India; E-mail: etikarastogi101@gmail.com

Vikash Yadav, Parashuram Pal & Chuan-Ming Liu (Eds.)

INTRODUCTION

Tourism is an industry that influences millions of people. With the help of tourism, people expand their scope, explore their beliefs and interests. It provides proliferation, increasing hospitality among many countries and regions [6, 7]. It unites every individual with one another, enables creation of new traditions and meets the demands of various researchers. Tourism is not only about the places of choice, but it is also about culture, traditions, historical beliefs, climate enjoyment, economic advantages, solid perspectives and scientific discoveries. Tourism is used as a gateway for development and, gradually, has become a common development focus for various countries. Tourism is a social, economical and a cultural fact that enlightens the activity of individuals to various places instead of their usual environment either because of their personal or professional work. Tourists are usually called visitors and they can be residents or non-residents, involved in either tourism or sight-seeing. Tourism attracts them towards the beautiful places to visit, and it contributes to the expenditure of the tourism industry. With the rapid evolution of the national economy and the origination of a new life theory and excellence of the tourism system, the tourism system has become more popular and most preferred during the vacations. With the developing demands from tourism, the previous system providing these facilities cannot fulfill the current demand scenario. The way that we are using to fulfil the current requirements involves many limitations. The traditional tourism system does not implement the suggested and recommended models into it, and it is not much efficient because it uses the database for storing and retrieving the information about various visiting places around the world [8]. There is a need to make the tourism guide system more efficient and to create a valuable recommendation model to ease the process of getting information about the best-suited visiting places around the world. As we know that tourists are the key to guide services, we should lay out a conceptual study and practical design of intelligent tourism guide systems based on the demands of tourists. The main objective of our approach is to implement a system that will operate on phones and other devices and will be very helpful while visiting various new places and cities. This system must be capable of finding a route according to user criteria. According to our approach, the users will have to actuate this application and then by specifying certain criteria according to the requirements, they can get important information that is related to the place they want to visit, or they are travelling now or will travel to in the future. The user when will register for the first time, will have to fill the details like name, email, and preferences in the form of tags. Next time, when the user will login with the registered email id, the user will get automatic suggestions and recommendations according to the added preferences by the user at the time of registration. The user can also edit his preferences and update his choice. The criteria must be straightforward and ordinary, for example, theu user can make a list of museums, the famous historical monuments, and restaurants to visit. The traditional artificial tourism guide service can be substituted with the advanced intelligent tourism guide system, which can help many developing tourism industries as the demand for tourism is increasing in today's world. The intelligent tourism guide system can create automatic suggestions and recommendations according to the preferences of the user. The automatic recommendations based on the information of the tourist places that are most visited by various visitors and the places that are reviewed as good and interesting places to visit again are given to the users in this application. The main objective of this system is to implement an automatic suggestion and recommendation model into a single system so that the user can get a unified view of the system in a single place. The system should have a user registration form that accepts users' input and asks for their preferences, like historical places, hill stations, beaches, adventurous places, *etc.*; thus, those preferences are used to ease the searching process and to give a better suggestion for visiting places to the tourists who are willing to visit various places based on the added preferences. The main advantage of using this system is that it increases the efficiency of the application because database accessing and retrieval slow down the performance of the overall application. To increase the efficiency of the system, a tree data structure is used to store and retrieve information about various visiting places around the world. The system is basically used for providing automatic recommendations suggesting information about visiting places to the users according to their added choices and generate automatic recommendations by analysing the reviews given by various people of the places majorly visited and highly recommended by others. As it is known that the place that is mostly reviewed by the people is a better choice than the place that is less reviewed. The main advantage of using this system is that the user can get all the functionalities into a single system. This Intelligent Tourist Information System, along with the recommendation model, will help the people who love to travel or want to travel to a new place without any previous information about that place. As of now, if we take both things, automatic suggestion and recommendation model, into consideration, the system is not available yet that satisfies both the requirements. The main aim of implementing the application is to make tourism a better service for the users.

Study of the Existing System

Tourism is a business that influences thousands of people, and with the help of which many people expand their scope, earn money and keep themselves entertained. Tourism has a great demand in today's world. Tourism has been a widespread concern in the past and so is today. Ancient tourism is important for many reasons. Ancient tourism has a precise economic and social effect. It initiates and strengthens identity, helps form image, helps conserve the societal and historical legacy, and with customs as a tool, it facilitates peace, harmony, and builds understanding among the people.

There are many traditional systems that provide travel and tourism services to the users and have various advance and interesting features as well as various shortcomings. Many websites are available over the internet that provide great content about the various tourism services and those mostly used by the visitors. The proposed system has some additional features that are not available in the existing system yet. The feature of providing automatic suggestion about visiting places and recommending various visiting places according to the reviews that were previously added by various visitors is not available in a single unified system. Some features are available in one application, and some features are available in another. The users prefer to have a unified view of all the features in a single application and this paper proposes the idea of implementing all the functionalities into a single application. Before talking about the proposed system, let's review the existing systems and take a look at the functionality of these systems and understand the working of these systems.

For instance, we consider Trip advisor website as an example from Figs. (**1** and **2**).

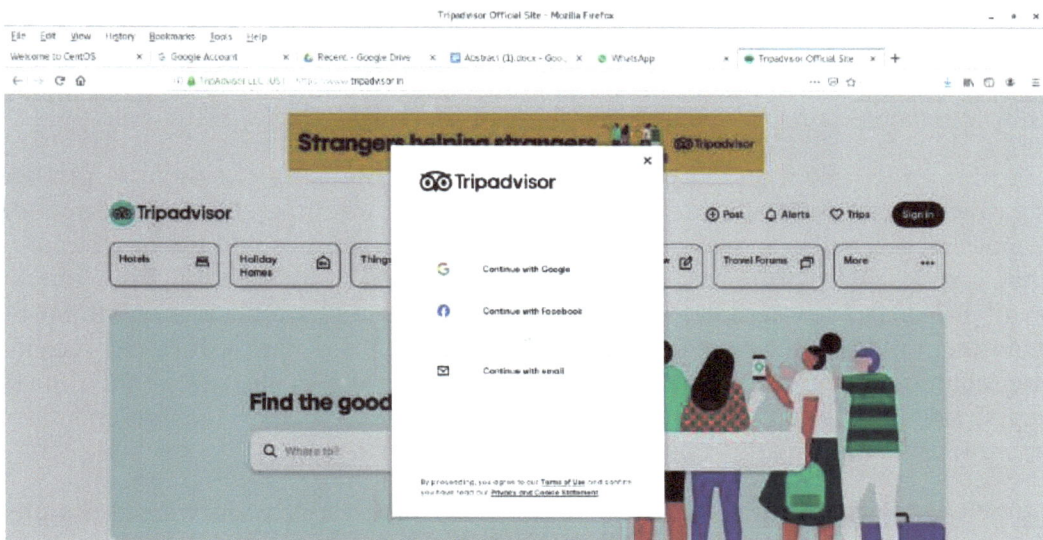

Fig. (1). Trip advisor website - Home Page.

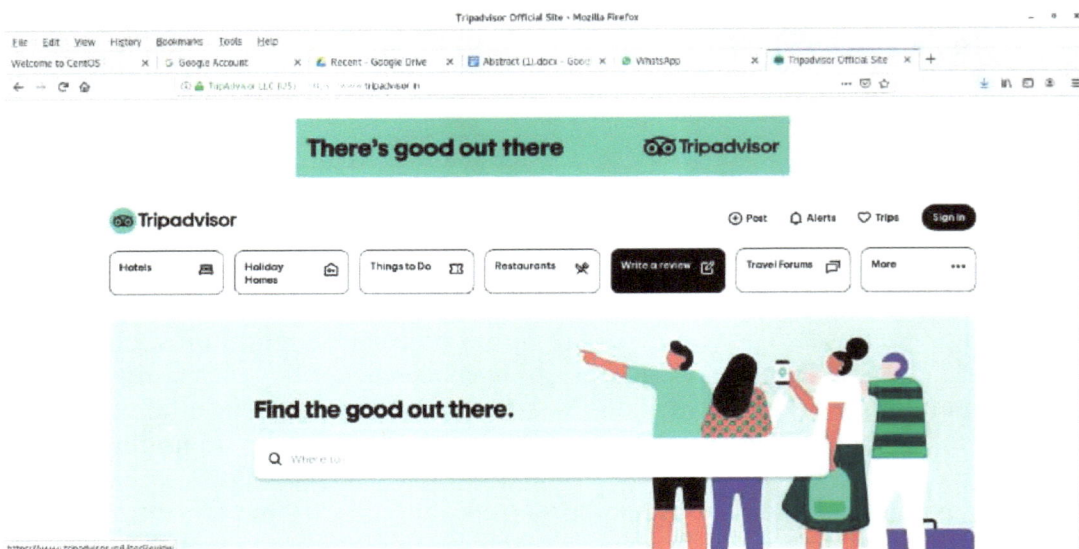

Fig. (2). Trip advisor website - Home Page.

This website contains a lot of information about various places around the world, but it does not contain the feature that our system provides, which is to add the preferences at the time of registration, like Do you want to go to Beach? Do you want to go to Hill Station? *etc.*, is not available in the existing system yet. This website provides a feature to write a review after the website has been visited by the user. On the other hand, our system has another added functionality according to which the system will recommend the most reviewed places.

Various government and non-government tourism websites are there to provide services to users who wish to visit a new place and want to get some information about that place. These websites have various functionalities, but the functionality that our research proposes is not implemented yet. It is unique from all the available ones; for example, if we consider the website Incredible India, it has all the functionalities for providing suggestions to the users, but it does not provide the recommendation according to the added preferences by the user at the time of registration. The functionality to provide the automatic recommendations according to the mostly reviewed place is not present in it.

Some previously existing websites, such as Airbnb.com, provide various features that are not available in other applications. It has a feature like online experiences where the user can view all the online experiences of the other users and their reviews. The feature of providing automatic suggestions according to the preferences of the user is not available in it.

There are various websites serving a good purpose to help the visitors in providing information about the best suited places to visit. They have several advantages and various shortcomings too. To overcome these shortcomings, we have come up with an idea to provide both the features to the user and improve the user experience.

Let's take another example of the most popular website, airbnb, shown in Fig. (**3**). This website serves various users all over the world and provides various functionalities to the visitors.

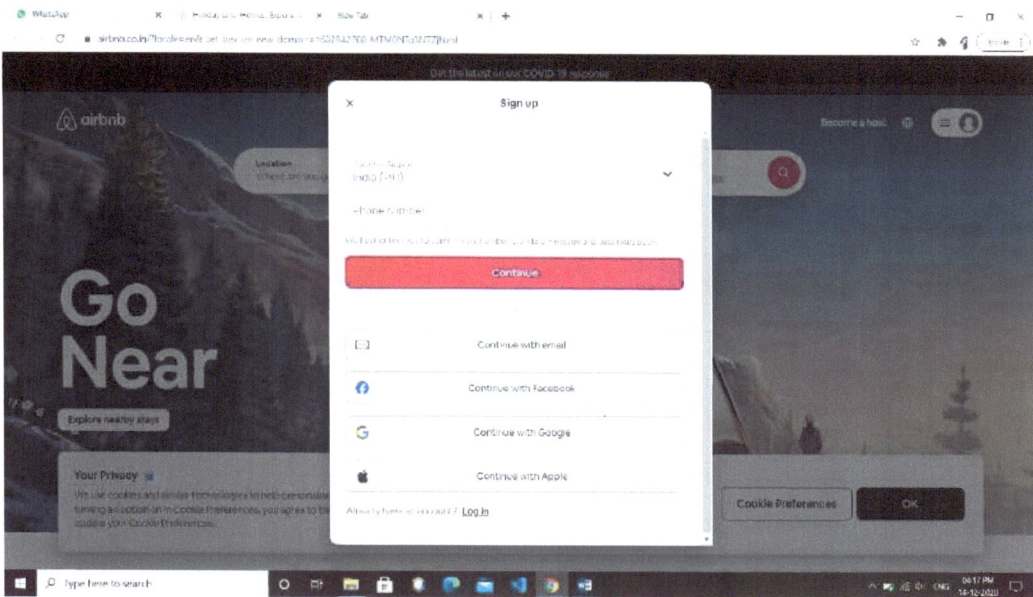

Fig. (3). Airbnb website – Home Page.

Design and Implementation of the Proposed System

The project proposes an intelligent tourism guide system that will take user preferences as input and will generate automatic suggestions for visiting places for tourists based on the added preferences by the user, as shown in Fig. (**4**).

The system will prompt the user to add the preferences at the time of registration so that the next time when the user logins into the system, the system will run a tree algorithm in the backend and will give the recommendations according to the added preferences by the user [9].

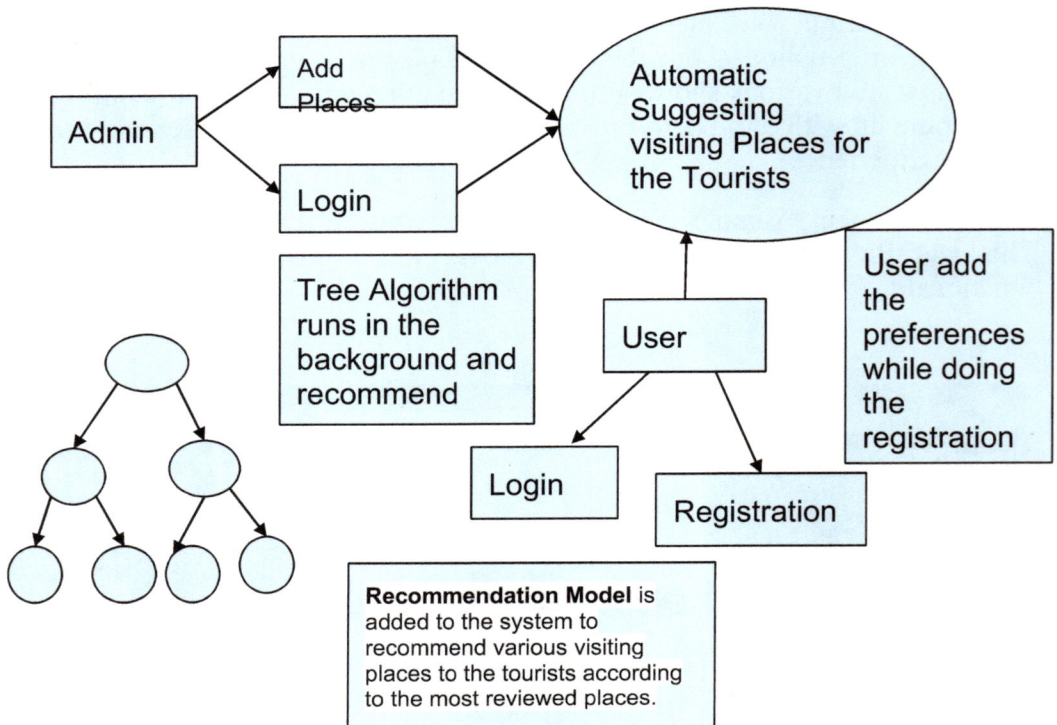

Fig. (4). Workflow of the system.

Module Description

1. **Tree creation-** This is the module in which we used a tree data structure to store the information about various places around the world, and the information about the places is to be stored in a hierarchical tree-like structure. The root node of the tree is Places. The various places are stored as the child of this root node along with their tags. These tags are basically used to filter out the searching process. The child of the root node is added using the user-defined function; add Child, and it will add all the places as the child of the root node along with their description and images. The various children, like Monuments, Temples, Beaches, Adventurous places, *etc.*, will be added. The tree will grow further when the child of these nodes is added. The main advantage of using the tree data structure is that it will make our application fast because the tree algorithm runs faster than other program used for fetching data from the database.

2. **Serialization of tree-** This module consists of the serialization process of the tree node. Serialization is the process by which an object is converted into a stream of bytes that store the object or transmit it to memory, a database, or a file.

The main purpose of serialization is to save the state of an object in order to be able to recreate it whenever required. The main idea to implement the serialization in the project is to save the tree node object into a txt file, and rather than making the tree again every time when the application runs, it will use the content of that txt file to perform further operations by desterilizing it. It will help to increase the performance of the application.

3. **Deserialization**- This module consists of the deserialization process of the file in which the content of the tree node object is stored. Deserialization is the process by which the data from a file, stream or network is taken out, and it rebuilds it into an object. The main idea of implementing deserialization in the project is to use the data from the file and rebuild it into an object for further processing.

4. **Traversal of tree**- This module consists of the traversal algorithm for the tree. When the user logins into the system, the preference of the respective user is fetched from the database, and it starts searching from the tree root and then compares those preferences with the first level of the tree; when the preference matches with the tree node, the user-defined function traverseNode executes and generates the output with respect to all the matching preferences. The tree algorithm is efficient in searching and traversing the tree node and will generate quick and accurate results.

Algorithm Used

Step 1:- Root Node Creation (Places)

Class TreeNode<T>

TreeNode menu=new TreeNode ("Places");

Step 2:- Adding various places along with its description and image.

publicTreeNodeaddChild (T place, T description, T image)

Step 3:- Adding children of the root node

TreeNode item1=menu. addChild ("Monuments");

TreeNode item2=menu.addChild("Beaches");

TreeNode item3=menu.addChild("Temples");

TreeNode item4=menu.addChild("Hill Stations");

Step 4:-

Add children of the node item1 as:-

TreeNode item11= (TreeNode)

item1.addChild ("TajMahal");

item11=item11.addChild (place, description, image);

TreeNode item21= (TreeNode) item2.addChild ("Varkala");

item21=item21.addChild (place, description, image);

Step 5:- Addition of various places to the tree.

Step 6:- Tree Node Object is Serialised.

Step 7:- Fetch the preferences of the respective user from the database using

SQL statement

Step 8:- Traverse the tree from the root node to the first level nodes and compare the preference with the tree nodes.

voidtraverseNode(TreeNodeobjectj) { if (object != null) {

for (intj = 0; j<object.childCounts; j++) {

if(object.childrens[j].description!=null)

println(object.childrens[j].place,object.childrens[j].descrip tion,object.childrens[j].image); else

println(object.childrens[j].value); traverseNode(object.childrens[j]);

}

}

Step 9:- Tree Node Object is Deserialised.

Step 10:- Whenever the preference matches with the tree node traverseNode functions get executed.

If ((treeNode.value).equals (res.value)){ voidprintTreeNode(TreeNode object) {

print(object.value); traverseNode(object);

}}

Design and Implementation of the Recommendation Model

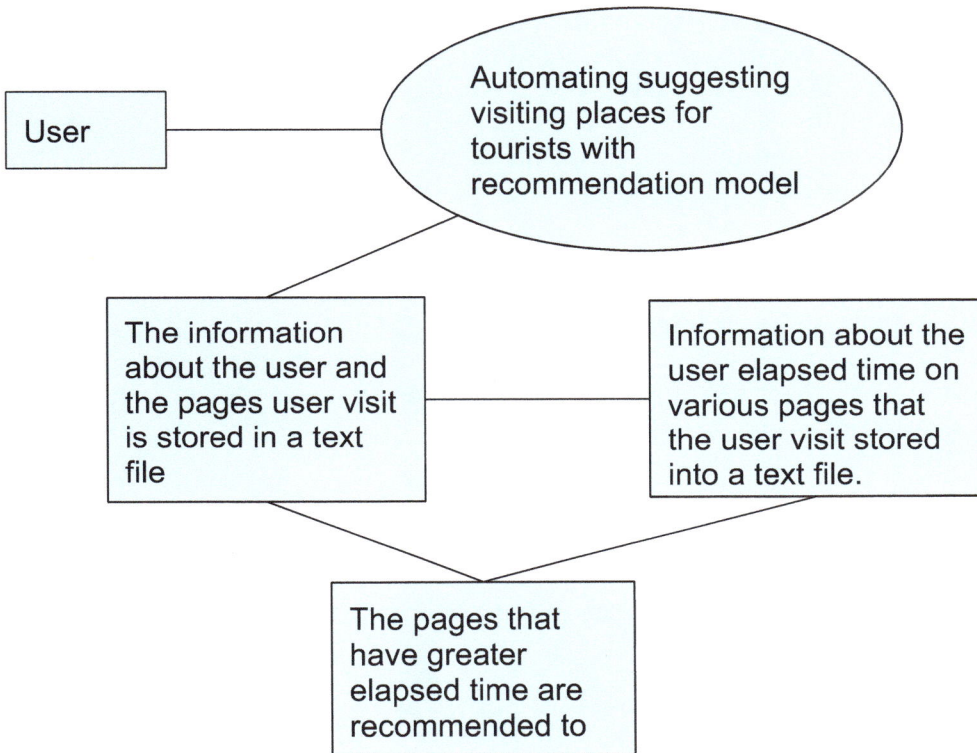

Fig. (5). Workflow of the system with recommendation model.

Module Description

Fig. (5) shows the workflow of the system with the recommendation model. Following are the modules:

1. **Information stored in the text file:-**This module consists of storing the user information in the text file. It monitors all the activity of the user on various pages that are displayed on the website. After successfully logging into the system, the user will have various automatic suggestions according to his added

preferences at the time of registration. The information about the user, like when he visited the pages on the website and the time he spent on every single page containing the information about various tourism places, is stored in a text file. FileInputStream class is used to store the information from log file into the text file for each page. It reads the single character at a time and write the data into the text file. These text files are further evaluated to generate automatic recommendations to the users according to their choice or preference.

2. **Parsing of text file:-**This module consists of parsing the text files and generating the required result to be shown to the user. In this module, all the text files are taken into consideration, and the time that the user spent on each page is taken into account, and this elapsed time is compared to the threshold time, say 10ms, and if the elapsed time is greater than the threshold time, then the user is considered to be interested in visiting the places whose information is displayed on that page.

3. **Recommendations to the user:-** This module provides automatic recommend-ations to the user. The system will parse the text file and generate the recommendation accordingly by elapsed time. The pages which have greater elapsed time, say threshold-10ms, recommend those places to the users. The user will have these automatic recommendations based on his preferences and his interest in visiting that place.

Algorithm Used

Step 1:- When a user enters the application and visits a web page, the init() method of the servlet gets executed and calculates the current time of the system [10].

Step 2:- Current time of the system is calculated as:

import java.time.format.DateTimeFormatter;

importjava.time.LocalDateTime;

DateTimeFormatterdt

DateTimeFormatter.ofPattern("yyyy/MM/ddHH:mm:ss");

currentTime1 = LocalDateTime.now();

Step 3:- When a user exits a web page, the destroy () method of the servlet gets executed and calculates the current time of the system.

Current time of the system is calculated as:

importjava.time.format.DateTimeFormatter;

importjava.time.LocalDateTime;

DateTimeFormatterdt=

DateTimeFormatter.ofPattern("yyyy/MM/ddHH:mm:ss");

currentTime2 = LocalDateTime.now();

Step 4:- Elapsed time for a web page is calculated as:-

elapsed Time = currentTime2-currentTime1;

Step 5:- FileInputStream class is used to input all the information from the log file into the text file for each page.

FileInputStream fin1=**new**FileInputStream("D:\\testout.txt");

int j=0;

while((j=fin1.read())!=-1){

System.out.print((**char**)j);

} fin1.close(); }

Step 6:- Set threshold time, say 10ms.

Step 7:- Parsing of each text file is done, and the required result is taken out.

Step 8:- If elapsed time>=threshold time

{recommend the place whose information is contained in the

respective page; } else

{continue; }

Execution of the Recommended Model

a. User login to the system: Fig. (6) shows the login page of the proposed recommender system.

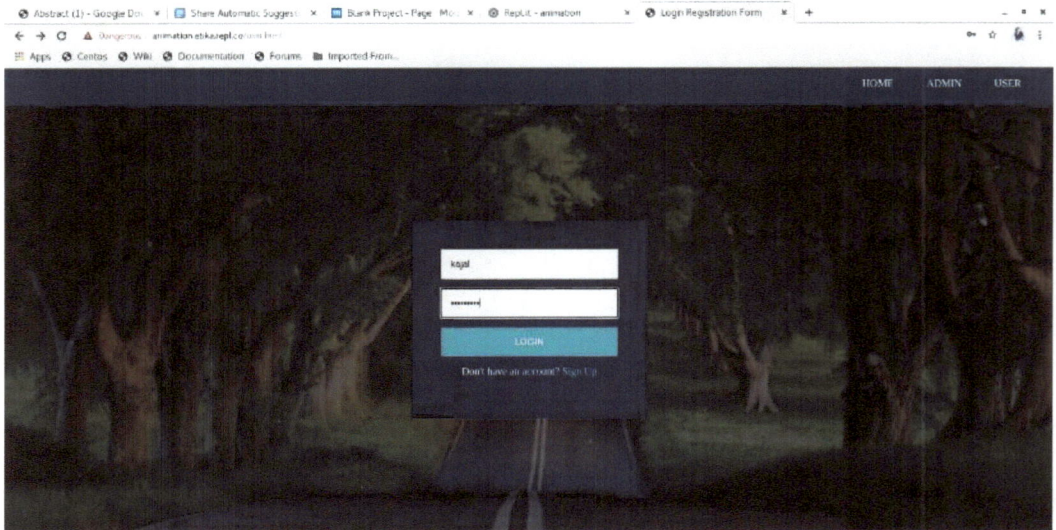

Fig. (6). User login to the system.

b. Information about the user is stored in the text file:-This module consists of storing the user information in the text file. It monitors all the activity of the user on various pages that are displayed on the website, as shown in Fig. (**7**). After successfully logging into the system, the user will have various automatic suggestions according to his added preferences at the time of registration. The information about the user, like when he visited the pages on the website and the time he spent on every single page containing the information about various tourism places, is stored in a text file. FileInputStream class is used to store the information from log file into the text file for each page. It reads the single character at a time and write the data into the textfile. These text files are further evaluated to generate the automatic recommendations to the users according to their choice or preference.

c. Parsing of the file:-This module consists of parsing of the text files and generating the required result to be shown to the user. In this module, all the text files are taken into consideration and the time that the user spent on each page is taken into account and this elapsed time is compared with the threshold time, say 10ms, and if the elapsed time is greater than the threshold time, then the user is considered to be interested in visiting the places whose information is displayed on that page.

Recommend various places according to the elapsed time of the user on various pages, as shown in Fig. (**8**).

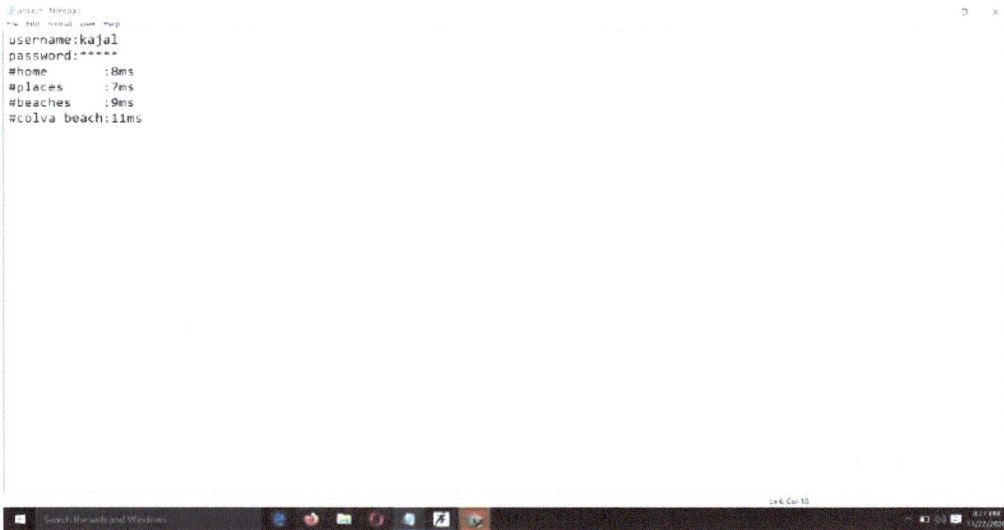

Fig. (7). Information about the user is stored in a text file.

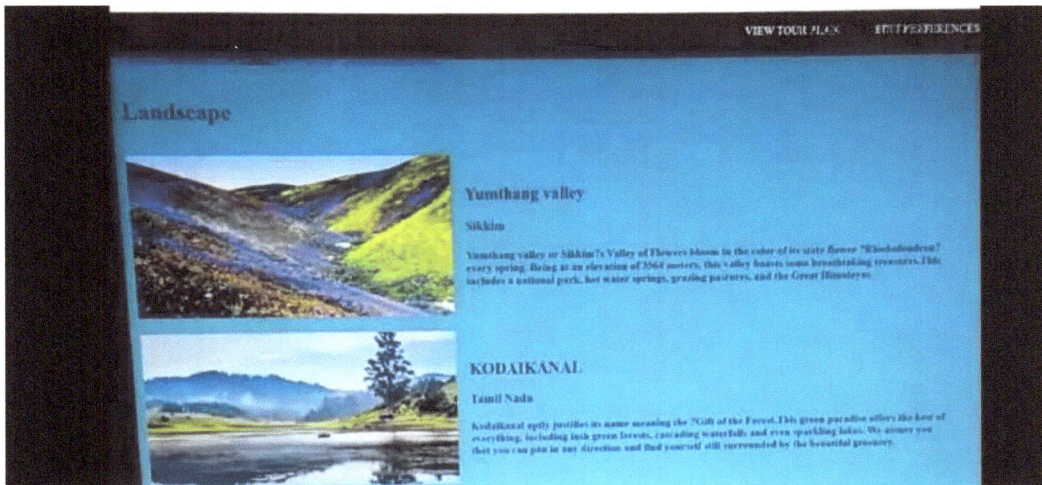

Fig. (8). Recommend various places according to the elapsed time of the user on various pages.

Performance Analysis

In this section, we apply our proposed scheme to achieve the optimal time taken by various phases of the application. So we have evaluated the time taken by the system to fetch the data when it runs a tree algorithm in the backend and traverses the tree node if the user preference matches with tree node value. The results are shown in Table **1**.

Table 1. Tabular representation of the performance (Number of entries *vs.* Time taken).

Number of Entries	Time Taken to Fetch the Data When it Runs Tree Algorithm (in Sec)
50	2
100	2
150	2.1
200	2.1
250	2.2
300	2.2
350	2.3

In Fig. (**9**), the X-axis denotes the number of entries about the places stored in the tree data structure, and Y-axis denotes the time taken to fetch the data when the system runs a tree algorithm in seconds. There is a relationship between them as the number of entries in the tree increases; the time taken to fetch the data does not increase in the same manner.

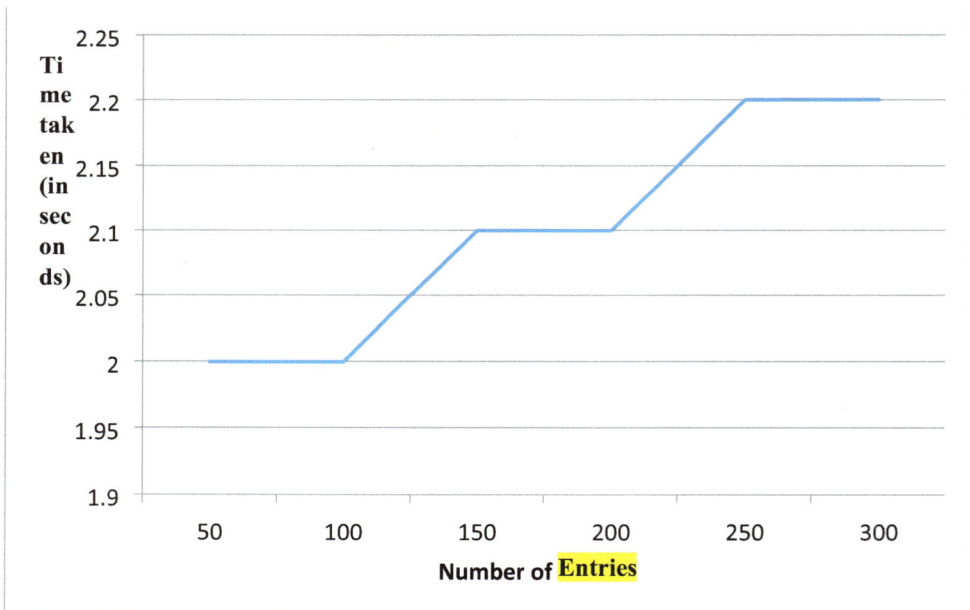

Fig. (9). Graphical representation of the performance (Number of entries *vs.* Time taken).

CONCLUSION

This work proposes an intelligent tourist guide system for the automatic recommendation of the places, and this system does not require the database for storing the information as we are using a tree data structure to store and retrieve the information about various places. The tree-based algorithm is efficient in storage and retrieval of data, which enhances the performance of the system. On the basis of the huge amount of information enclosed about various pleasing spots, this chapter considers the customized needs of the visitors. Also, considering it as a beginning point, this chapter has implemented an advanced intelligent tourism guide system to recommend automatic visiting places suggestions to the user. In addition to the automatic suggestion of the visiting places to the tourists, the paper proposes the recommendation model for automatically recommending the visiting places to the tourists based on their activity while visiting the application. This paper proposes a unique recommendation model, and this type of model has not been implemented yet. This model can handle multiple users and can work accurately. The recommendation model is really helpful for recommending new places to the user. We have seen various web server log files, which contain information about the errors during execution. Instead of the error information, the log files will contain the data about the user elapsed time in this system. This system provides the functionality by which it generates an automatic file and leaves the entry of the user elapsed time for the different web pages. The main goal of this chapter is that the final result can fulfill the practical needs. The author has constantly regulated the ideas to design and estimate the development technology of the system to design the efficient algorithm for generating recommendations to the user by using an advanced intelligent tourism guide system. The main goal of implementing the system is to make it automated, intelligent, more practical and compendious, thus reducing human efforts. The current stage of the proposed framework is completed.

CONSENT FOR PUBLICATION

Not applicable.

CONFLICT OF INTEREST

The author declares no conflict of interest, financial or otherwise.

ACKNOWLEDGEMENTS

Declared none.

REFERENCES

[1]   H.H. Owaied, H.A. Farhan, N. Al-Hawamde, and N. Al-Okialy, "A Model for Intelligent Tourism Guide System", *J. Appl. Sci. (Faisalabad),* vol. 11, no. 2, pp. 342-347, 2011.
        [http://dx.doi.org/10.3923/jas.2011.342.347]

[2]   Y. Yu, "Design and Evaluation of Intelligent Tourist Guide System Based on Mobile Devices", *2014 Sixth International Conference on Intelligent Human-Machine Systems and Cybernetics,* pp. 296-299, 2014.
        [http://dx.doi.org/10.1109/IHMSC.2014.79]

[3]   F. Rong, "Design of Tourism Resources Management Based on Artificial Intelligence", *2016 International Conference on Intelligent Transportation, Big Data & Smart City (ICITBS),* pp. 436-439, 2016.
        [http://dx.doi.org/10.1109/ICITBS.2016.97]

[4]   V. Yadav, "A New Approach for Movie Recommender System using K-means Clustering and PCA", *Journal of Scientific and Industrial Research (JSIR),* vol. 80, Scientific Publishers, no. 2, pp. 159-165, 2021.

[5]   K. Srinivasan, R. Kumar, and S. Singla, "Robust and efficient algorithms for storage and retrieval of disk based data structures", *2017 International Conference on Applied System Innovation (ICASI),* pp. 934-937, 2017.
        [http://dx.doi.org/10.1109/ICASI.2017.7988595]

[6]   C. Ho, K. Pak, S. Pak, M. Pak, and C. Hwang, "A Study on Improving the Performance of Encrypted Database Retrieval Using External Indexing System of B+ Tree Structure", *Procedia Comput. Sci.,* vol. 154, pp. 706-714, 2019.
        [http://dx.doi.org/10.1016/j.procs.2019.06.110]

[7]   H. Dewan, R. Hansdah, and P. Singh, "Sigma-Tree:Design of a Data Structure for Storing File Data Allocation Map in a Distributed File System", *2018 IEEE International Conference on Smart Cloud (SmartCloud),* pp. 90-98, 2018.
        [http://dx.doi.org/10.1109/SmartCloud.2018.00023]

[8]   A.S. Badashian, M. Najafpour, M. Mandavi, M.A. Deichen, and I. Khalkhali, "FTS: An efficient tree structure based tool for searching in large data sets", *2nd IEEE International Conference on Information Management and Engineering,* pp. 294-298, 2010.
        [http://dx.doi.org/10.1109/ICIME.2010.5477555]

[9]   Herbert Schildt, "Java", *McGraw Hill Education "The Complete Reference" (11th Edition),* 2009.

[10]   R. Lafore, *Data Structure and Algorithm in Java.* 2nd ed. , 2003.

CHAPTER 2

Internet Protocols: Transition, Security Issues and the World of IoT

Ankita Gupta[1], **Ankit Srivastava**[1] and **Rohit Anand**[1,*]

[1] *G.B. Pant Engineering College, New Delhi, India*

Abstract: With the tremendous increase in the use of internet in almost every sector of society, assigning addresses has appeared to be inefficient. The previous Internet Protocol version 4 (*i.e.* IPv4) failed to fulfill the highly growing demand. Though previous Internet Protocol Version 4 was used for assigning addresses, it could not sustain the high demand resulting in the downfall of IPv4. The chapter outlines the various advantages and disadvantages of the shift from IPv4 to IPv6. It also highlights the security threats of both the protocols and security issues due to which the coexistence of the two protocols was thought of as the solution. This chapter overall covers the transition from IPv4 to IPv6, their uses and management, followed by the analysis of IPv6 in terms of security issues. It further takes into account the effect of IPv6 on the world of Internet of Things (IoT). The eventual objective of this framework is to give comprehensive and detailed knowledge about the internet protocols in the Internet-of-Things world.

Keywords: Coexistence of IPv4 and IPv6, Internet protocols, IoT, IPv4, IPv6, Security issues.

INTRODUCTION

Internet protocols, known as the TCP/IP protocols, are the most important protocols involved directly in the technological enhancement of wireless communication, enabling the devices to access and connect through the internet from anywhere around the world. The network layer is responsible for the internet working in the form of the transfer of packets from the source to the destination host [1, 2].

IPv4, also known as Internet Protocol Version 4, is the first generation of IP to be widely used. With the tremendous advancement in the internet connection and the

* **Corresponding author Rohit Anand:** G.B. Pant Engineering College, New Delhi, India; E-mail: roh_anand@rediffmail.com

Vikash Yadav, Parashuram Pal & Chuan-Ming Liu (Eds.)

communication between the devices over the internet, IPv4 was pushed to its limits. It was then that the need for a much newer advanced IP version was thought of. IPv4 failed to provide the much-needed scalability to the internet with time. All these reasons led to the development of IPv6, a 128-bits length IP address. IPv6 had its advantages and disadvantages. There came a transition from IPv4 to the new Internet Protocol version IPv6. Later, the Internet Protocol domain witnessed the coexistence of the two internet protocols because of some security reasons.

To understand the complete working of Internet protocols and to further discuss the threats and their application in the world of IoT, it is required to have a basic understanding of "how an IP address works?" IP stands for Internet Protocol, where a protocol is a set of rules on which the movement of data packets across the internet is dependent. Each device connected to the internet has a unique address assigned to it. This is the IP address that makes it different from others and helps in communication. The communication between two computers over a network is the communication set up between the two respective IP addresses of the computers. The transfer of data between the two devices occurs in the form of encapsulated bits known as data packets. The process known as the datagram is responsible for the flow of data across the internet. In the datagram, the data packet consists of the information and the internet protocol (IP).

It is not just the internet protocol that is employed in the transfer of data across any network. An entirely connected complex network stack is required to transfer information, of which IP is just a small part. The network stack is divided into four layers: the Application layer, the Transport layer, the Networking layer, and the Data Link layer. In terms of users, the most familiar layer is the application layer, the layer with which we interact daily.

In this chapter, we will discuss the co-existence of both the internet protocols after discussion of these protocols. Further, we will discuss the security issues, their after-effects, their solutions, and the use of internet protocols in the world of IoT.

Next section deals with the existing related work. Section 3 deals with the description of IPv4 and IPv6. Section 4 discusses the transition from IPv4 to IPv6 and the co-existence of both the protocols. Section 5 describes the security threats related to IPv4, IPv6, and the transition. Section 6 explains the relation of IPv6 to the world of IoT. At last, the conclusion is drawn.

RELATED WORK

The related research is discussed in this section.

The authors in a study [1] compared the performances in terms of response time and throughput for two Internet Protocol Versions, IPv4 and IPv6, and proposed a system with the co-existence of both the protocols. The resulting system resulted in the need for a dual-stack system with the concept of tunnelling. In another research work [2], a comparative analysis was performed between IPv4 and IPv6 by the measurement of packet loss and throughput with the User Datagram Protocol (UDP). The study shows that IPv6 is more robust than IPv4 for video traffic as well as audio traffic. Doshi *et al.* [3] suggested that both the protocols, IPv4 and IPv6, must be supported together. Network Address Translation (NAT64) may also be used as a transition technology as an alternative to IPv6. NAT444 may also be used for running the various services of IPv4 after all the addresses of IPv4 are consumed. In one of the research works [4], the authors discussed the IPv6 security issues. First, the differences between IPv4 and IPv6 were discussed, followed by their vulnerabilities. IPv6 is considered a new protocol version currently, even after so many years of its existence, mainly because of its security issues. The authors in another study [5] explained that IPv6 has so many important features, like Quality of Service (QoS), mobility, more address space, and automatic configuration capability. The security threats common to IPv4 and IPv6 and those introduced by the transition from IPv4 to IPv6 and have been discussed in detail by the authors. The brief discussion of the security concerns and threats in all the layers and also all the protocols in each layer of TCP/IP model have been presented earlier [6]. Data security is of prime significance for most industries and organizations today. Joon and Yadav [7] presented a brief survey of the various detection methods for the critical distributed denial of service (DDoS) attack that slows a web server that results in the disruption and failure of all the webtechnologies and services running on hyper text transfer protocol (HTTP). H. Dawood [8] discussed the main vulnerabilities related to IPv6 threats and security. IPv6 is deployable only after considering its security issues. That is why, most industries are not ready for the transition to IPv6, although this protocol can easily be supported by the framework of the network. The authors in a paper [9] discussed the overview of the Internet Control Message Protocol (ICMP) and its vulnerabilities issues. ICMP was earlier used for flow control in IPv4, but the security issues led to the exploitation of ICMPv4. The security concerns in ICMPv4 led to the security issues in the expanded version, *i.e.*, ICMPv6. The authors discussed the smooth transition from IPv4 to IPv6 in a secured manner [10]. Tunnel mechanism is the focus of the research discussed by the authors. But there are some vulnerabilities and threats associated with this tunnel mechanism. The approach to overcome these vulnerabilities and attacks to yield a new secure tunnel mechanism is also discussed. F. A. Ghumman [11] provided a brief overview of the comparison between the various IPv6 transition approaches in Internet of Things (IoT). The approaches, like tunneling, dual-stack, *etc.*, were compared in terms of transition. In another work [12], the authors provided a brief introduction to OSI and TCP/IP model. Afterwards, the internet protocol IPv4 has been compared with IPv6. Finally, the network routing based on IoT was discussed in detail and then compared with the traditional protocols of routing. In another study [13], the authors suggested a technique to reduce the power consumption in IoT devices and to handle the security concerns in the data.

IPV4 AND IPV6

IPv4

IPv4 is the fourth version of the internet protocol. It is still used widely despite the newer IPv6 version. IPv4 was the first internet protocol version that enabled internetworking at the Internet layer. It is represented as a 32-bit integer-valued address separated by dots after every octet. It consists of four octets. When IPv4 was realized, 32 bits served enough for all the communications between devices. But with the technological advancements and increase in the number of devices over the internet, IPv4 faced a few limitations. With IPv4 in use, the internet address became short in demand [14].

Some of the terms related to IPv4 are as follows:

- Internet Header Length (IHL): The internet header length consists of 4 bits. The smallest size of the field is 5, as the minimum size of the IPv4 header is at least 20 bytes. In case the header does not use all 4 bytes, the left bytes are padded with 0s.
- Type of Service (ToS): This field indicates the service type. For example, Voice over Internet Protocol (VoIP) may be used for services related to interactive audio calling.
- Total length: The total length of the IPv4 is the length of the IPv4 header, and the IPv4 payload makes up the size of the field as 16 bits.
- Identification: It is used to uniquely recognize the fragments of a datagram.
- Flags: Flags field has a size of 3 bits with 2 bits in current use. Specifically, there are two flags, one of them tells whether IPv4 is fragmented while the other tells if more fragments can follow.
- Fragment offset: The size of the fragment offset field is 13 bits to indicate the position of the fragment concerning the payload.

- Time to Live (TTL): The size of the field is 8 bits, and it tells about the highest number of links an IPv4 data packet will cover before being discarded.
- Protocol: Protocol field is 8-bit and is used to demultiplex the data packet with a protocol, such as Transmission Control Protocol (TCP), User Datagram Protocol (UDP) or Internet Control Message Protocol (ICMP).
- Header Checksum: The header checksum is a 16-bit field and is used in the data verification process. If the IPv4 data packet checksum does not validate with the header checksum, the data packet is not considered.
- Source Address: This 32-bits field stores the address of the originating host.
- Destination Address: This is also a 32-bits file that stores the address of the destination host.

IPv6

As already discussed, it is clear that IPv4 has many shortcomings and limitations with the increasing number of devices connected through the internet. IPv6 was thought of as the solution. It was in 1991 when the development of this version started, which was completed in 1997 by the Internet Engineering Task Force (IETF) [2, 15]. The data transfer process is based on the addressing scheme, *i.e.*, the packets of data require the address of the source and the destination for the transfer of information from one device to another. To fulfill the need, each device must be assigned a unique address. IPv6 was developed because IPv4 had a limit of the unique addresses that in turn had a limit on the number of devices that could be connected [16].

The fields of IPv6 [14] are:

- Traffic Class (Prior): It is a field of 8 bits used to indicate the priority of the data packet.
- Flow Label: It is a field of 20 bits and is used to indicate the flow of the sequence of data packets from the source to the destination. The flow is done by IPv6 routers.
- Payload Length: It is a 16-bit field used to show the IPv6 payload length. It can show up to 65,535 bytes, and for a payload of length greater than that, the field is set to 0. In that case, Jumbo Payload option is used.
- Next Header: It is an 8-bit field used to indicate either the extension or the protocol in the upper layer.
- Hop Limit: It is a field of 8 bits. It is similar to the IPv4 version that shows the maximum number of links over which IPv6 packet can travel before being discarded. It also has no time limit attached to it as of the IPv4 TTL field.
- Source Address: This field is of 128 bits and stores the IP address of the source.

- Destination Address: This field is also of 128 bits. It is used to store the IP address of the destination.

Fig. (1) shows the IPv4 and IPv6 protocol versions [17].

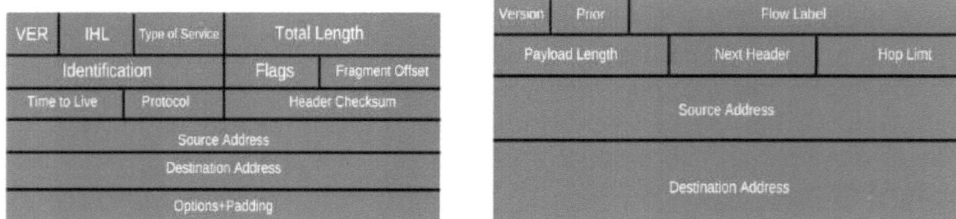

Fig. (1). IPv4 and IPv6 protocol versions (left = IPv4, right = IPv6).

Shortcomings of IPv4

Some of the drawbacks associated with IPv4 are mentioned below:

- *Scarcity of IP addresses for the growing devices*: As discussed above, IPv4 version was insufficient to meet the needs of the growing devices that would connect over a network for communication. The IPv4 version was capable of accommodating only 4 billion hosts [1].
- *Security*: IPv4 failed to provide any kind of security to the information being transferred in the form of the data packet or the encryption of data [18].
- *Quality of Service*: IPv4 provided poor quality as it relied totally on 8 bits of service field and on the payload identification that sometimes fails due to packet payload encryption [14].
- *Network Congestion*: Because of the feature of the broadcast that is sending the data packets to all the addresses of the network, it created congestion and overloading.
- *Packet Loss*: Data may be delayed, and following multiple requests from the other end can cause the data to be lost completely, which can affect the real-time data like video streaming. The data loss occurs at the set expiry time of the Time to Live (TTL) field of the header of an IP address.

NEED TO TRANSITION FROM IPV4 TO IPV6

With this entire internet around and with the concept of connection using IoT and other technologies like artificial intelligence and machine learning surfacing, the need to have more IP addresses arose. The need for more IP addresses was merely because the IP addresses provided by the IPv4 version were exhausting at a tremendous rate.

The Internet opened new paradigms to technology and changed the concept of connectivity from wired to wireless at much more affordable rates. It led to the production of more handheld devices like mobile phones, computers, tablets, iPods, and other things. Earlier there were a limited number of computer users. So, the need for unique IP addresses per device was much lesser than today. These all were the reasons at the core of the need for the transition from IPv4 to IPv6 [19].

It was in 2011 that Internet Corporation for Assigned Names and Numbers (ICANN) released the last set of IPv4 addresses. With the expanding companies with technology being the prominent part of growth and success, the need for new addresses for the new large set of devices was felt.

IPv6 was not thought of as the direct solution to the problem at the time of IPv4 addresses getting exhausted. Some technologies like the Network Address Translation (NAT), dynamic IPv4 address assignment (DHCP), Dynamic Host Configuration Protocol (DHCP) and Classless Inter-Domain Routing (CIDR) were used as an immediate solution to further shift the timeline of IPv4 addresses. NAT was a popular method in which multiple private IPv4 addresses were mapped directly to a single public IP address.

The speedy transition from IPv4 to IPv6 can be better understood with the help of statistics. Fig. (**2**) shows the data taken from the Google's IPv6 statistics page. It clearly shows how from just 2% in 2013, the use of IPv6 has increased to 22.06% [17]. The entire transformation from IPv4 to IPv6 is yet to finish.

IPv4 and IPv6 Coexistence

With IPv4 at the core of communication, the adoption of IPv6 at a large scale will take time and will also have some obstacles to be addressed. But IPv6 needs to be used because of the benefits such as a larger number of IP addresses, efficiency in routing, faster packet transfer, overpowering the difficulties of broadcasting packets, and avoiding network address translation (NAT). The above-mentioned needs and benefits related to IPv6 led to the coexistence of IPv4 and IPv6 at the initial stage [3].

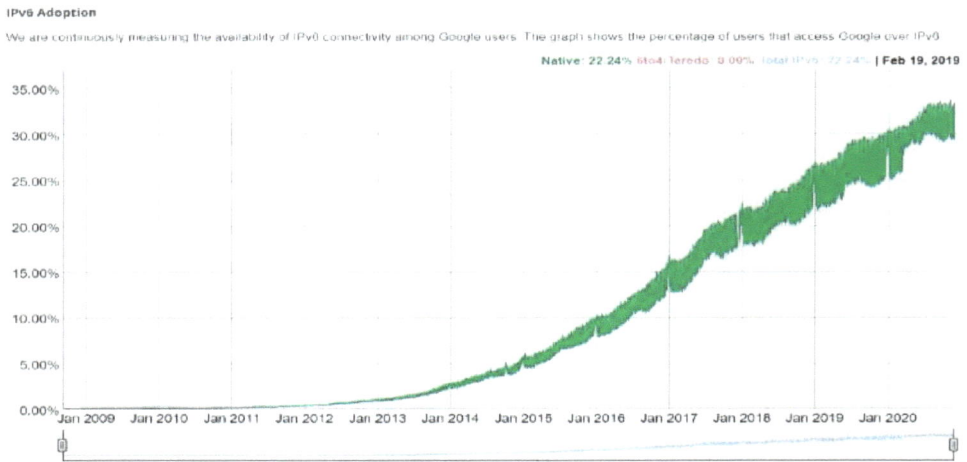

Fig. (2). IPv6 Connectivity of Google Users [17].

SECURITY THREATS

IPv6 has its numerous advantages over IPv4, but it also has some new security issues [4] apart from the security issues that rolled over to the IPv6 from the IPv4 usage [5]. It is expected that over 1000 unique addresses per individual would be made available due to the increase in the use of the internet. With such a large amount of IP addresses floating in the environment, security concerns are bound to increase.

IP security in broad terms means the security of data is being transferred from source to destination over a network. IP security deals with both the data travelling among the private as well as the public network. IP security can be divided into five major groups [5], as shown in Fig. (3).

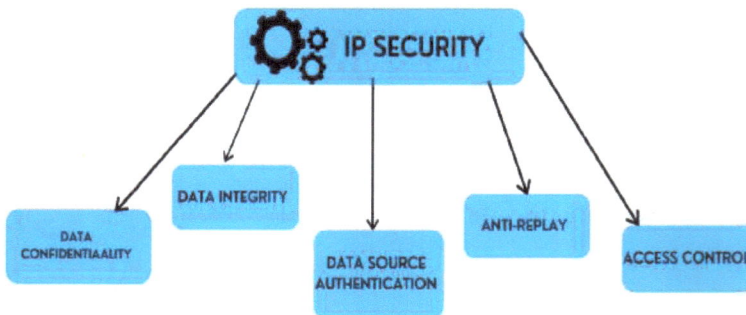

Fig. (3). IP security threats.

- *Data Confidentiality*: It refers to the encryption of data packets before the transmission from the source.
- *Data integrity*: It ensures that data packets are free-altered and are changed during transmission.
- *Data Source Authentication*: In this, the source address is authenticated.
- *Anti-replay*: The focus of anti-replay is to detect and reject the duplicated data packets (if any).
- *Access Control*: It ensures the control of access to a system or service.

IP security consists of two protocols. The first protocol is the authentication header (AH), which provides data integrity, authentication, and anti-replay service. The authentication header must be placed before all headers. The second protocol is the Encapsulation Service Payload (ESP) that provides data integrity, anti-replay, data confidentiality, and authentication. ESP needs to be placed at the last of the headers that need to be processed by intermediate nodes. It protects only the data packet which is delivered.

Further, IP security has two traffic modes (Fig. **4**) to achieve the security of data packets.

- Transport mode
- Tunneling mode

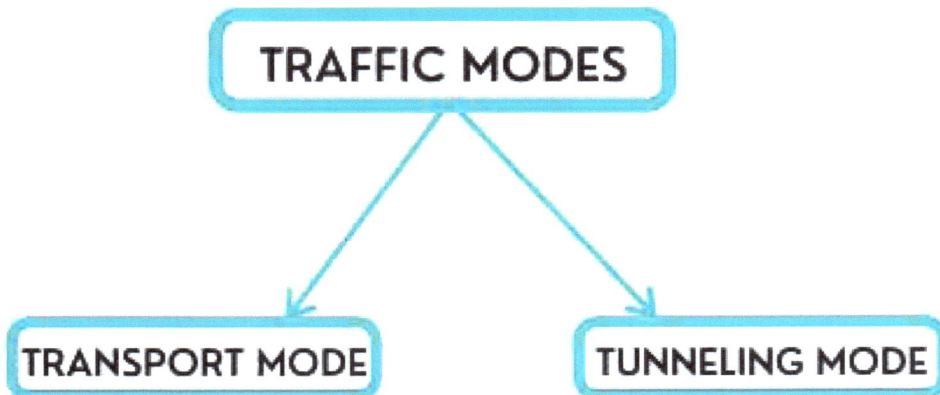

Fig. (4). Traffic modes.

The transport mode is used to communicate between two servers or clients. It uses both the AH and ESP headers for the encryption of the payload. The tunneling mode encrypts the payload and the IP headers [5]. It can use either AH or ESP header to protect the IP data packet. Tunneling mode can only be used after the transport mode.

To establish the secure communication between devices, the two devices use Security Association (SA) to decide how the data packet needs to be protected. Both AH and ESP contain a 32-bit number known as Security Parameter Index (SPI) that identifies SA [20].

Most common security threats are shown in Fig. (**5**).

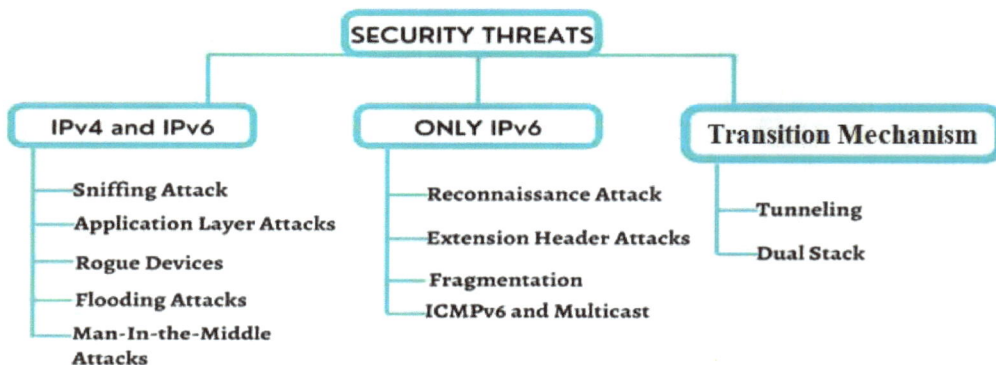

```
                        ┌─────────────────┐
                        │ SECURITY THREATS │
                        └─────────────────┘
        ┌───────────────────────┼────────────────────────┐
┌──────────────┐        ┌──────────────┐         ┌──────────────────────┐
│ IPv4 and IPv6 │        │  ONLY IPv6   │         │ Transition Mechanism │
└──────────────┘        └──────────────┘         └──────────────────────┘
  ─Sniffing Attack         ─Reconnaissance Attack      ─Tunneling
  ─Application Layer Attacks ─Extension Header Attacks  ─Dual Stack
  ─Rogue Devices           ─Fragmentation
  ─Flooding Attacks        ─ICMPv6 and Multicast
  ─Man-In-the-Middle
   Attacks
```

Fig. (5). Classifications of security threats.

Security Threats Common to IPv4 and IPv6

In this section, we will discuss the common security threats for both IPv4 and IPv6.

1. *Sniffing Attack:* It is similar to a physical spy. It is mainly the interception of data by the sniffers while data packets are transferred from one end to another. The data packets may contain important information like passwords, account ID, banking details that can be used illegitimately by the attackers [6].

There are two types of sniffing. Passive switching takes place at the hub. The attackers keep the sniffing device at the hub, and all the network traffic or data packets can then be easily accessed by the sniffer. Next comes the active sniffing, in which the attackers fill the Content Addressable Memory (CAM) table of the switch, after which the switch loses the link of where to send which data packet and sends it to all the network ports.

The best way to get rid of sniffing is the encryption of every data packet that leaves the user system.

2. *Application Layer Attacks:* Application layer attacks are the most common security concerns faced by both the internet protocol versions. In this, the attacker makes a fault in the operating system of the user device, after which he can easily change, add, delete, or get access to any information stored on that device [6].

The two common application layer attacks are HTTP flood and Slowloris attack. In HTTP flood, the attackers use the HTTP link to fetch the information. They send a GET or POST request to the web server after which it follows all the hidden links of the corrupt HTTP link in a recursive manner. In a Slowloris attack, the HTTP request sent monopolizes the device resources.

The best way to prevent application layer attacks is by using an Integrated Database Management System (IDMS) to detect the corrupt behavior.

3. *Rogue Devices:* This is a type of security issue faced by many organizations [21]. Rogue devices are unwanted devices that connect to the organization's network and access all the essential information of the company. They can easily connect either wirelessly through radio waves or using a wired connection. The major consequences of rogue devices are jamming, eavesdropping, and spoofing.

Rogue devices are mainly of two types: Bot and Sniffer. A bot is used to send repetitive emails or cause a denial of any service on the network, whereas a sniffer sits passively without any interaction and keeps a check on the traffic within the network.

The best ways to get rid of rogue devices are periodic scanning, continuous monitoring of the connected devices over a network, and immediate alerting for the device change as soon as any malpractice is noticed.

4. *Flooding Attacks:* A flooding attack is a type of active attack. In this, the attacker floods the network with messages and consumes all the bandwidth and energy. The flooding of devices with network traffic makes them non-responsive and unserviceable. Some of the types of flooding attacks are [22]:

- Hello Flooding: In this type, the attacker node keeps sending Hello messages to the other nodes connected on a network to befriend them. As a result, the other nodes carrying secure data packets forward them to the attacker node thinking it to be the high power node that is part of the network.
- Data Flooding: In this type, two attacker nodes get connected to a network and start sending each other a huge amount of fake data, hence consuming all the

energy of the in-between genuine nodes of the network. It is also known as Sleep Deprivation Attack.
• RREQ Flooding: RREQ flooding means that the attacker nodes keep sending Route Requests for non-existent nodes. The normal nodes take these requests and keep forwarding them to find the fake nodes.
• SYN Flooding: SYN flooding uses a huge amount of synchronization packets to hamper the system. In this, the attacker nodes consume the memory allotted to the normal nodes.
• Error Flooding: In this flooding method, the attacker nodes make their way in between the two communicating nodes and start sending error messages to all the nodes in their range. This process leads to interruptions in the normal communication between the nodes. As they receive error messages, the nodes start the discovery phase again, thinking that the message sent from the other node is unreadable.

The best way to get rid of this security issue is by following the Distributed Denial of Service (DDoS) attack-defence life cycle [7].

5. *Man-in-the-Middle (MIM) Attacks:* In this type of security attack, the attacker grabs the data which is sent without any data origin authentication from the source. He can read and manipulate the data, and corrupt data is sent to the user by the attacker [23]. The commonly used communication channels for MIM attacks are GSM, long-term evolution (LTE), UTMS, Wi-Fi, Radiofrequency, and even near-field communication (NFC).

There are different types of MIM attacks that attack different communication channels [24]. For the OSI layers, Address Resolution Protocol (ARP) spoofing affects the data links; Secure Sockets Layer (SSL) decryption and Certificate Authority (CA) decryption affect the presentation layer; IP spoofing affects the transport and network layers; and Dynamic Host Configuration Protocol (DHCP), Border Gateway Protocol (BGP) and Domain Name System (DNS) spoofing affect the application layer. In cellular networks, Fake Base Station (FBS) spoofing affects the GSM and UTMS. Spoofing, in simple terms, means that the attacker gets access to the confidential data being communicated between the two hosts without any notice.

The main approach involved in detecting the MIM attacks is Deep Packet Inspection and Deep Flow Inspection [25]. The Deep Packet Inspection method checks whether the traffic IP address matches the actual IP address, whereas the Deep Flow Inspection method classifies the traffic based on the network flow features like duration of flow, count flow, and average packet bytes flow, and packet count flow.

Table **1** summarizes all the common types of security issues faced in the IPv4 and IPv6, along with their explanation and prevention.

Table 1. Common security issues in IPv4 and IPv6.

S. No.	Security issue	Explanation	Prevention
1	Sniffing Attack	Interception of data while transmission of data packets between two nodes	Encryption of data
2	Application Layer Attack	The attacker makes a fault in the operating system	Integrated Database Management System
3	Rogue Devices	Unwanted attacker devices get connected to the network	Periodic scanning and monitoring of the connected devices
4	Flooding Attack	Attackers flood the network with messages like requests or error messages	Distributed Denial of Service (DDoS)Attack Defence life cycle
5	Man-in-the-Middle Attack	The attacker gets access to data, manipulates it, and then forwards it to the user	Deep Packet Inspection and Deep Flow Inspection

Security Threats Related to IPv6

Earlier we discussed the security issues that are common to both IPv4 and IPv6 [4, 5]. How the Internet Protocol version 6 interacts with the layers of the TCP/IP model gives rise to new security issues.

In this section, a list of IPv6 specific security threats is discussed in detail along with the best possible way to detect, prevent, and address them.

- *Reconnaissance Attack:* This attack [26] is one of the very first steps towards accessing the information by the attackers. Knowledge about the vulnerable and manipulative services along with reconnaissance helps in accessing any information easily. First, the attacker pings the probe to search for the targeted IP address and then starts a port scan. This step can be done easily with the help of software like Network Mapper (NMAP) and Strobe [5]. Some of the examples are packet sniffing, port scanning, phishing, social engineering, ping sweeping, and internet information query generations.

Typically network reconnaissance attack takes place in either a horizontal or vertical way. Attackers collect all the valuable information from the hosts and build a network map of the target network. Then it switches to investigate the vulnerabilities in specific services of their interests [26]. The information can be collected using various sources, like websites, domain name system (DNS) server data, search engines, or specialized tools like Maltego [27].

Further, reconnaissance attacks can be divided into logical and physical types. Logical reconnaissance means a security attack without the need for any manual guidance at the other end. The attack takes place completely in the digital spectrum with no human involvement. It can be done using the ping sweep and port scan methods which investigate whether the system is present and, if it is, then what it is searching for in the network. Additional queries can also be seen over the internet. Next comes physical reconnaissance that refers to getting control of the system to an extent that the network security remains intact. The attackers make use of the security elements, like location, door locks, and cameras that can never be fully protected and still play an important role in securing a network. It may also include noticing the entry and exit times of the employees in a company or a bank for instance, or examining how and where the paper is sent for recycling to find useful information. But, IPv6 is mainly associated with logical reconnaissance, which involves ports and pings.

There are only a few things one can do when it comes to protection from reconnaissance attacks. One method is to maximize the bandwidth allocation, and another can be network isolation. Also, regular checking, updating, and hardening of the connected devices are also protection methods against reconnaissance.

- *Extension Header Attacks:* Extension headers are inserted before the next layer protocol. Two such extension headers play a major role in IP security: Routing Header 0 and Routing Header 1. Routing header 0 refers to in-between nodes that the data packet traverses before reaching the destination from the source, while Routing Header 1 is used for mobile IPv6 [28].

Routing header causes a change in the destination address at each level-3 hop. Routing header attacks redirect the traffic from the genuine node to the attacking node to collect the valuable data packets. This is done by changing the destination address with the attacker node address making the router think that it has forwarded the traffic to the correct next destination. The routing header type 0 was deprecated because of the potential harm it caused. Earlier the extension headers did not have a standard format which was later introduced to reduce the security threats related to the headers. The extension header attacks mainly the routing header type 0. These attacks can be prevented by:

i. Blocking routing header type 0 as is the case in IPv4
ii. Prevention of processing at intermediate nodes
iii. Using the ACL blocking route header type-0
  ○ *Fragmentation:* During the transfer of information in the form of data packets from source to destination, it is appropriate and convenient to transmit a few larger packets than many small data packets. To keep a check on the size of the packet to be transmitted, the Maximum Transmission Unit (MTU) is defined. If the data packet is more than the set MTU, it would have to be broken into more data packets, a process known as fragmentation [5].

The security threat arises when the reassembly of the data packets is to be done from the fragments, and a popular security threat that can be manipulated is to evade firewalls. In IPv4, it is not present because IPv4 drops the fragments with an offset of one byte, which cannot be done in IPv6 as any number of extension headers can be placed before the next layer protocol header. Overlapping fragments may help the attack go undetected as the attacker can send the fragments along with some random data to which the operating system will respond by overwriting a part or whole of the data packets with other fragments in the reassembly. Another security threat related to fragmentation is IP fragment overrun. It occurs when the fragment length crosses the packet length, which leads to the denial of service attempt or makes the system crash [28].

One way to get rid of the fragmentation threat is through deep packet inspection with the help of routers, firewalls, proxy servers, or intrusion detection systems. Another way is to keep the operating system up to date with all the security patches installed. It is best to follow a multilayered approach for the prevention and protection against fragmentation attacks.

• *ICMPv6 and Multicast*: These two features could be easily filtered by the network administrator in the case of IPv4. But in IPv6, multicast and ICMP are the integral parts of its proper functioning. It can still be controlled by the network administrator by allowing only certain pre-checked Internet Control Message Protocol (ICMP) and multicast messages [8].

ICMP was developed to act as a link between the hosts and the gateways in the IP network by providing the query and error messages whenever and wherever necessary [9]. ICMP attacks can be further divided into ICMP sweep attack, inverse mapping, ICMP route redirects, Smurf attack, and ping of death. In the ICMP sweep attack, the attackers keep sending a range of echo requests to keep the host busy. It degrades the overall performance of the network. The inverse mapping is used by the attackers to target the devices protected using filtering devices like firewalls. It is also done by sending echo requests to the devices to which internal routers respond with a "Host Unreachable" message. This information helps the attackers to trace the path of the targeted devices. In Smurf, attacks spoofed ICMP echo requests are sent to multicast addresses which reach all nodes in turn [9].

Some of the best ways to protect against ICMP security threats are installing firewalls and intrusion detection systems. Another method is to use the tools with pre-installed mechanisms to protect the devices against IPv6.

Security Threats Caused Due to Transition Mechanism

The transition from IPv4 to IPv6, *i.e.*, deploying IPv6 devices to IPv4 networks, has given rise to security vulnerabilities in techniques, like dual-stack, traffic tunneling, and protocol translation. The tunneling and protocol translation are the most important ones.

Tunneling: Tunneling is another method of establishing a connection between two clouds working on different internet protocol versions. It requires each tunnel endpoint to support both the internet protocol versions, *i.e.*, IPv4 and IPv6. In general, all the tunnels do not possess all three essential security elements: authentication, integration, and confidentiality. Hence, IPv6 provides some major loopholes that can further lead to other interrelated security threats. If no perimeter firewall exists, then traffic can easily move inside and outside the IPv6 tunnels, which open the network for the attackers for tunnel sniffing, tunnel overload, and tunnel injection [10]. Tunnel works on the phenomenon that the packet arriving at the tunnel is sent by any of the genuine endpoints. But because of the lack of any authentication, the lack of knowledge about the endpoints can be misused by the attackers.

Some of the best ways to get rid of security threats related to tunnels are by denying the use of IPv6 tunnels by blocking the useless ports and protocols. Another can be to inspect the tunneled packets using firewalls. We can also use the IP Security (IPSec) mechanisms that do not allow any data packet without passing it through the mutual authentication phase.

Dual-Stack: Dual-Stack is known as the most commonly used mechanism for the migration from IPv4 to IPv6. It includes the involvement of both IP networks to exist in the same network. Dual-stack uses the mechanism of sending the request to the DNS server to connect a client to the server for which IPv6 is selected by default. The major cause of the security threats in dual-stack is IPv6. Also, since two internet protocol versions are used, the deployment of both requires the proper security precautions that come out to be quite expensive in terms of both time and material [5].

One way to prevent dual-stack security threats is to block, inspect, and control all the traffic from both the IP protocols with the help of host intrusion prevention, personal firewalls, and Virtual Private Network (VPN) clients.

IPV6 & THE WORLD OF IOT

Internet of things, in a broader sense, is a paradigm for new services and technological advancements and innovations. It provides the methods to connect the different machines, sensors, humans, and other devices to transfer the data from one place to another over a secure network. IoT [29 - 31] is based on the integration of network devices to include automation and reduce manual labour. All the sectors of society, from education, multimedia, business, and transport to even agriculture, have now started using the technology to utilize the attached benefits with the technology and to establish better connections and communications between all the devices.

At present, two types of internet protocol versions are currently being used to establish the communication between two devices and transfer data [32]. Due to the limited number of devices that can be connected using the IPv4, the need for IPv6 was felt. IPv6, being a 128-bit long address, can handle billions of devices by assigning different unique addresses to each device. Apart from communication establishment efficiency, it also provides an effective routing mechanism as compared to IPv4 [11, 22]. The main reason behind this is that, unlike IPv4, the fragmentation is handled by the source device in IPv6. Also, IPv6 helps save network bandwidth by sending the data packets using multicast, which is not supported in IPv4 as IPv4 uses broadcasting. Another advantage of IPv6 in IoT is that the IP addresses of the devices are auto-configurable (which is not the case in IPv4), and they need to be configured manually, which is hectic and time-consuming. These are some of the concerned factors because of which IPv6 is preferred over IPv4.

IPv6 over IPv4 for IoT

Some of the major reasons for choosing IPv6 over IPv4 are as follows [33]:

• Security: IPv6 data packets are more secured when compared to IPv4 data packets. This is because IPv6 works on end-to-end encryption, *i.e.*, data packet is encrypted before being transferred from one place to another, and it cannot be hacked easily. Moreover, it supports secure name resolution to use.

- Scalability: Second most important thing is the scalability that IPv6 offers. It can provide connectivity of the devices on a larger scale, hence enabling easy long-distance communication.
- Connectivity: Last but not the least, IPv6 can connect millions of devices and share data over a network. IPv6 offers about 4.3 billion unique IP addresses for a huge number of devices to connect without any ambiguity.

Internet protocol serves as an important component for internetwork routing, error reporting, and reassembly of data packets. IPv6, with its 4.3 billion unique IP networks, provides an effective and easier way to communicate with each other. For IP addressing, IPv6 is broadly classified into three categories [12]: Unicast, Multicast, and Anycast addresses, as shown in Fig. (**6**).

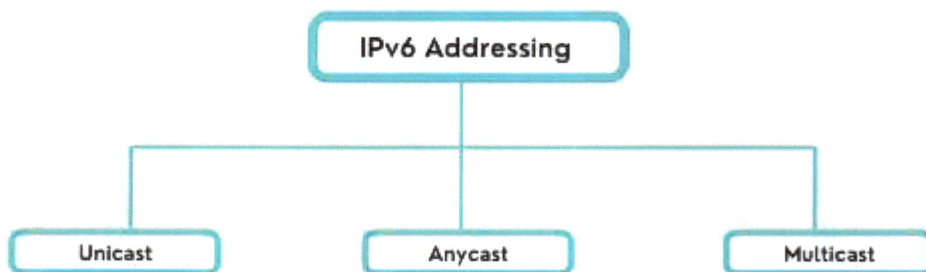

Fig. (6). IPv6 addressing modes.

Unicast: A unicast address is used to send the data to a single interface. The IPv6 packet is sent to only a single interface identified by that address.

Multicast: A multicast address is used to send the data to a group of interfaces that may or may not belong to the different nodes. In this, the IPv6 data packet is delivered to multiple interfaces.

Anycast: An anycast address is used to send the data to a set of pre-identified interfaces that belong to the different nodes. In this, IPv6 data packet is delivered to only a single interface.

Why IPv6 for IoT?

To understand why IPv6 is used widely for IoT, we first need to understand the network architecture of IoT. Fig. (**7**) shows the IPv6 network and the Low Power

Wireless Personal Area Network (collectively called 6LoWPAN). Routers are responsible for routing between the internal host, sub-host and external host. In this figure, the 6LoWPAN network is responsible for the generation of the data stream [13].

The 6LopWPAN was developed by Geoff Mulligan [34] to reduce the extra memory costs and increase the battery life of small devices and sensors. In this protocol, the 40 byte long IPv6 header is compressed to 1 byte, thus increasing the efficiency and increasing the battery life. Moreover, it helps small appliances to use the energy-harvesting technology that can ultimately eliminate the batteries. 6LoWPAN eliminates some of the unnecessary fields of the IPv6 header that are not required for the functioning of the sensor. Further, it also deletes some of the repetitive fields (if any). These are some of the features not available with IPv4.

Given a low-power network, IPv6 is more suitable for being able to satisfy the low-power characteristics of IoT devices. IPv4 fails to do so because of the lack of address space [35].

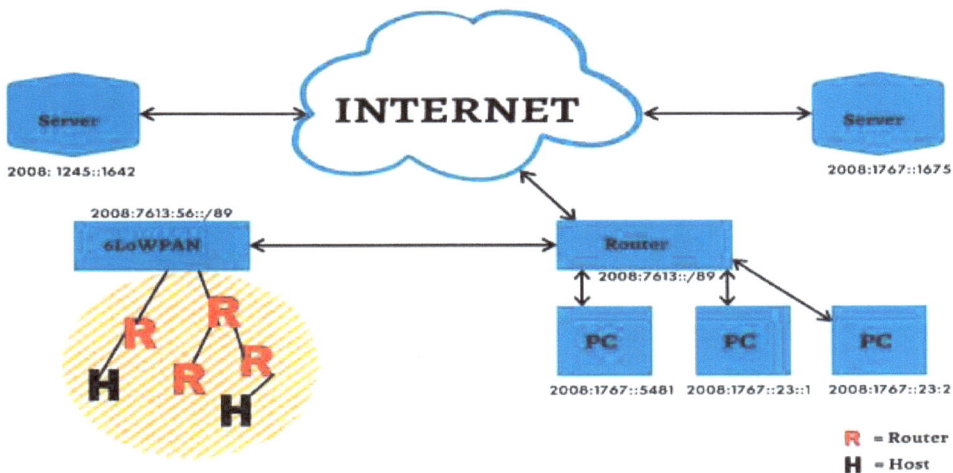

Fig. (7). IoT structure using IPv6 and LoWPAN.

Routing - IPv6 and the IoT Network

Routers use the routing charts to establish communication and exchange the data packets among themselves. TCP/IP specifically makes the IP packets travel one hop at a time. At each stop, the next hop is determined by using internal information by matching the destination address within the data packet with the entry in the current routing table. Some of the fundamentals of routing are discussed below:

Static and Dynamic routes: Static routes simply refer that the paths are defined manually between the two routers, whereas dynamic routing requires the software to find the routes. Static routes need manual up-gradation, while there are algorithms in dynamic routing to take care of any change in the network. Static routing is limited to small devices, while dynamic routing is used extensively in internet-based routing protocols.

Routing Tables: It is a table consisting of destination addresses and the next hop pairs.

Link-State Routing: In this, all the routers should be aware of each other's paths in the network. It involves the flooding of link-state data to the entire set of routers in autonomous systems. Autonomous systems are systems organized and managed by a single organization. This type of routing can degrade the network performance because of flooding the entire network.

Distance-Vector Routing: In this, the routes contain both the directions and distance to decide the path to a remote network using hop counts. In distance-vector routing, the exchange of information takes place only with neighbours and not with all the routers.

IoT Architecture Based on IPv6

IPv6-based architecture is capable of integrating the heterogeneous IoT components, and such a structure is known as IoT6 stack/architecture. It has IPv6/6LoWPAN in the network layer. The implementation of this architecture in various fields, like Gateway and Mobile phones, provides the functionalities of open service layer, hence enabling interoperability.

In IoT6, four major elements have been developed: the Global Digcovery, the Local Digrectory, Smart Object, and Mobile Digcovery. The global digcovery acts as a centralized platform to enable the clients to lookup IoT resources, such as HTTP. In the local digrectory, the fine-grained descriptions of the IoT services and resources, such as HTTP and Constrained Application Protocol (CoAP), following DNS to support the local queries, are defined. The smart object uses multicast DNS (mDNS) and CoAP protocols to enable machine-to-machine (M2M) access to the resources available for IoT Devices. Mobile digcovery refers to maximizing efficiency by offering a framework that allows the users to discover the available resources over a network through the mobile phone by registering their sensors into the common network framework. In this architecture, a heterogeneous description to support the interoperability in IoT domains is provided. Further to add to the functionalities, it is integrated with the search engine for scalable lookup based on geo-location. It also has communication interfaces to establish the connections between IoT and different clients.

Fig. (**8**) shows the IoT6 protocol architecture [36].

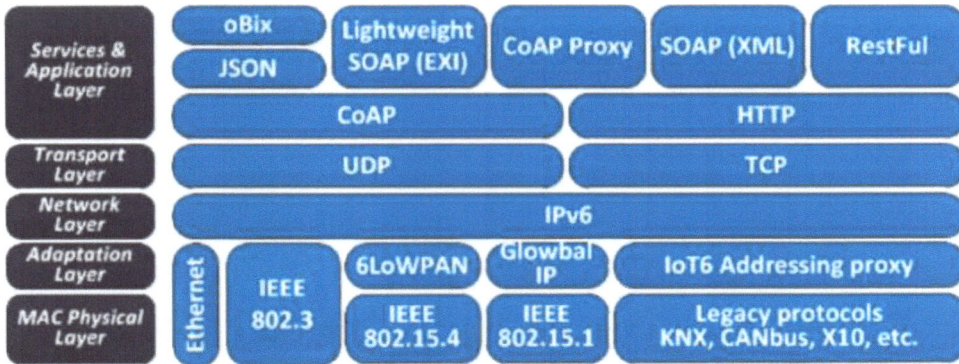

Fig. (8). IoT6 protocol architecture [36].

CONCLUSION AND FUTURE SCOPE

The chapter has discussed in detail the internet protocol versions and the security threats related to IPv4 and IPv6. Further, it has discussed the need for transition from IPv4 and IPv6. With IoT gaining so much popularity in all the sectors of the society, the need to connect more and more devices for the proper management is necessary. More connections mean more IP addresses, that is the reason why IPv6 is such a used concept in the field of IoT. IPv6 opens a new paradigm for the different sectors to establish connections much more easily and securely for the fruitful utilisation of IoT.

IPv6-based IoT architecture has now become the backbone of many prosperous companies. The vast use of IPv6 in IoT is an ongoing process, and the research would continue over many upcoming years for establishing the connections more securely and easily and also for exploring the newer ways of integration of the heterogeneous IoT system. Today, IPv6 is being mainly referred and deployed globally for the IoT functionalities and the large-scale machine to machine interactions at the networking layer. The study of the current state of IoT marks future research on the world-scale use of IPv6. The role of IPv6 in IoT and security is yet to reach new heights.

CONSENT FOR PUBLICATION

Not applicable.

CONFLICT OF INTEREST

The author declares no conflict of interest, financial or otherwise.

ACKNOWLEDGEMENTS

Declared none.

REFERENCES

[1]   H.C. Paul, and K.A. Bakon, "A study on IPv4 and IPv6: The importance of their co-existence", *International Journal of Information System and Engineering,* vol. 2, 2016. [http://dx.doi.org/10.24924/ijise/2016.11/v4.iss2/97.106]

[2]   A. Zakari, M. Musa, G. Bekaroo, S.A. Bala, I.A.T. Hashem, and S. Hakak, "IPv4 and IPv6 protocols: A comparative performance study", *IEEE 10th Control and System Graduate Research Colloquium (ICSGRC),* pp. 1-4, 2019. [http://dx.doi.org/10.1109/ICSGRC.2019.8837050]

[3]   J. Doshi, R. Chaoua, and S. Kumar, "A comparative study of IPv4/IPv6 co-existence technologies", *University of Colorado, Boulder,* pp. 1-13, 2012.

[4]   R.P. Van Heerden, I.M. Bester, and I.D. Burke, "A review of IPv6 security concerns", *Journal of Information Warfare,* vol. 11, no. 3, pp. 25-38, 2012.

[5]   A. Shiranzaei, and R.Z. Khan, *IPv6 security issues—A systematic review.* Springer: Next Generation Networks, Singapore, 2018, pp. 41-49.

[6]   A.M. Alotaibi, B.F. Alrashidi, S. Naz, and Z. Parveen, "Security issues in protocols of TCP/IP model at layers level", *International Journal of Computer Networks and Communications Security,* vol. 5, no. 5, p. 96, 2017.

[7]   K. Joon, and V. Yadav, "DDoS Attack Prevention protocol through Support Vector Machine and Fuzzy Clustering Mechanism on Traffic Flow with Harmonic Homogeneity Validation Technique", *International Workshop on Soft Computing Applications,* vol. 1221, pp. 197-214, 2018. [http://dx.doi.org/10.1007/978-3-030-51992-6_17]

[8]   H. Dawood, "IPv6 security vulnerabilities", *International Journal of Information Security Science,* vol. 1, no. 4, pp. 100-105, 2012.

[9]   N.C. Arjuman, and S. Manickam, "A review on ICMPv6 vulnerabilities and its mitigation techniques: classification and art", *International Conference on Computer, Communications, and Control Technology (I4CT),* pp. 323-327, 2015. [http://dx.doi.org/10.1109/I4CT.2015.7219590]

[10]   S.A. Abdulla, "Survey of security issues in IPv4 to IPv6 tunnel transition mechanisms", *International Journal of Security and Networks,* vol. 12, no. 2, pp. 83-102, 2017. [http://dx.doi.org/10.1504/IJSN.2017.083830]

[11]   F.A. Ghumman, "Effects of IPV4/IPv6 Transition Methods in IoT (Internet of Things): A survey", *SSRN,* 2019.https://ssrn.com/abstract=3402664 [http://dx.doi.org/10.2139/ssrn.3402664]

[12]   A. Rayes, and S. Salam, "The Internet in IoT—OSI, TCP/IP, IPv4, IPv6 and Internet Routing", In: *Internet of Things From Hype to Reality.* Springer: Cham, 2017, pp. 35-56.

[http://dx.doi.org/10.1007/978-3-319-44860-2_2]

[13]   J. Jang, I.Y. Jung, and J.H. Park, "An effective handling of secure data stream in IoT", *Appl. Soft Comput.,* vol. 68, pp. 811-820, 2018.
       [http://dx.doi.org/10.1016/j.asoc.2017.05.020]

[14]   D. Goyal, R. Singh, and N. Hemrajani, "Comparative study of IPv4 & IPv6 point to point architecture on various OS platforms", *IOSR J. Comput. Eng.,* vol. 13, no. 5, pp. 27-34, 2013.
       [http://dx.doi.org/10.9790/0661-1352734]

[15]   "The ABCs of IP Version 6, CISCO IOS Learning services", *CISCO Services,* 2011. Available: www.cu.ipv6tf.org

[16]   S. Dey, and N. Shilpa, "Issues in IPv4 to IPv6 migration", *International Journal of Computer Applications in Engineering Sciences,* vol. 1, no. 1, pp. 9-13, 2011.

[17]   E. Çalışkan, "IPv6 transition and security threat report", *NATO Cooperative Cyber Defence Centre of Excellence, Tallinn, Estonia.* Available: http:// www.ccdcoe.org

[18]   S.C. Virgeniya, and V. Palanisamy, "Attacks on IPv4 and IPv6 protocols and its performance parameters", *Int. J. Comput. Trends Tech.,* vol. 4, no. 8, pp. 2429-2434, 2013.

[19]   A.N.A. Ali, "Comparison study between IPv4 & IPv6", *International Journal of Computer Science Issues,* vol. 9, no. 3, pp. 314-317, 2012.

[20]   S. Hogg, and E. Vyncke, *IPv6 Security.* CISCO Press, 2008.

[21]   K. Cabaj, M. Gregorczyk, W. Mazurczyk, P. Nowakowski, and P. Żórawski, "Network threats mitigation using software-defined networking for the 5G internet of radio light system", *Secur. Commun. Netw.,* vol. 2019, pp. 1-22, 2019.
       [http://dx.doi.org/10.1155/2019/4930908]

[22]   M.A. Zant, and A. Yasin, "Avoiding and isolating flooding attack by enhancing AODV MANET protocol (AIF_AODV)", *Secur. Commun. Netw.,* vol. 2019, p. 8249108, 2019.

[23]   A. Mallik, "Man-in-the-middle-attack: Understanding in simple words", *Cyberspace: Jurnal Pendidikan Teknologi Informasi,* vol. 2, no. 2, pp. 109-134, 2019.

[24]   N. Community, *Six Benefits Of IPv6,* 2011.https://www.networkcomputing.com/networking/six-benefits-ipv6/1148014746

[25]   A. Ghosh, and A. Senthilrajan, "An approach for detecting Man-In-The-Middle attack using DPI and DFI", *International Conference on Computer Networks, Big Data and IoT,* Springer: Cham, pp. 563-574, 2020.
       [http://dx.doi.org/10.1007/978-3-030-43192-1_64]

[26]   M.I. Al-Saleh, "Network Reconnaissance Investigation: A memory forensics approach",
       [http://dx.doi.org/10.1109/IACS.2019.8809084]

[27]   V. Yadav, "A Survey paper on Wireless Access Protocol", *International Journal of Computer Science and Information Technologies (IJCSIT),* vol. 6, pp. 3527-3534, 2015.

[28]   J. Ullrich, K. Krombholz, H. Hobel, A. Dabrowski, and E. Weippl, "IPv6 security: Attacks and countermeasures in a nutshell", *Workshop on Offensive Technologies,* 2014.

[29]   A. Gupta, A. Srivastava, and R. Anand, "Cost-effective smart home automation using internet of things", *Journal of Communication Engineering & Systems,* vol. 9, no. 2, pp. 1-6, 2019.

[30]   R. Anand, A. Sinha, A. Bhardwaj, and A. Sreeraj, "Flawed security of social network of things", In: *Handbook of Research on Network Forensics and Analysis Techniques.* IGI Global, 2018, pp. 65-86.
       [http://dx.doi.org/10.4018/978-1-5225-4100-4.ch005]

[31]   A. Gupta, A. Srivastava, R. Anand, and T. Tomažič, "T., "Business application analytics and the internet of things: The connecting link", In: *New Age Analytics.* Apple Academic Press, 2020, pp. 249-273.

[http://dx.doi.org/10.1201/9781003007210-10]

[32]   *What is an IP address,* 2018.https://www.apnic.net/get-ip/faqs/what-is-an-ip-address/

[33]   *3 Reasons Why IPv6 Is Important For the Internet Of Things,* 2015.https://www.link-labs.com/blog/why-ipv6-is-important-for-internet-of-things

[34]   G. Mulligan, *"IPv6 for IoT and gateway,"* in *Internet of Things and Data Analytics Handbook.* John Wiley & Sons, 2017, pp. 187-196.

[35]   N. Kushalnagar, G. Montenegro, and C. Schumacher, "IPv6 Over Low-power Wireless Personal Area Networks (6LoWPANs): Overview, Assumptions, Problem Statement, and Goals", *RFC,* vol. 4919, pp. 1-12, 2007.
[http://dx.doi.org/10.17487/rfc4919]

[36]   S. Ziegler, A. Skarmeta, P. Kirstein, and L. Ladid, "Evaluation and recommendations on IPv6 for the Internet of Things", *IEEE 2nd World Forum on Internet of Things (WF-IoT),* pp. 548-552, 2015.
[http://dx.doi.org/10.1109/WF-IoT.2015.7389113]

CHAPTER 3

Recommender Systems and their Application in Recommending Research Papers

Sonam Gupta[1,*], **Lipika Goel**[2] and **Rohit Vashisht**[3]

[1] *Ajay Kumar Garg Engineering College, Ghaziabad, India*

[2] *Gokaraju Rangaraju Institute of Technology, Hyderabad, India*

[3] *ABES Engineering College, Ghaziabad, India*

Abstract: Recommendation systems are widely used today by online stores and various other leading sites, like Facebook, Instagram and LinkedIn, for providing suggestions to the users. The recommendation process helps the users to find the items that they may be interested in. Also, it is beneficial for the company to improve its overall profit. Recommendation engines use collaborative filtering technique or content-based approach to acquaint the users with such items. As these engines are so beneficial for users as well as for the trading websites, they have already been applied to a large number of fields, such as medical, education, tourism, finance, marketing and business; however, some areas are yet left unexplored. In this paper, we are presenting one such area where if recommendation engines are used, they can help a huge number of researchers around the globe. We propose a recommendation system that can help a number of scholars to get research papers based on the keyword entered by them, and the user will set a similarity index. This value of similarity will help in getting a limited number of papers from a huge pool.

Keywords: Collaborative filtering, Content-based, Recommender systems.

INTRODUCTION

In the past few years, we have moved from an era of scarcity to an era of profusion. Nowadays, a user interacts with a huge catalogue of items, ranging from movies at Netflix, music at Pandora, various products at Amazon to news and articles on Google News. There are two ways in which the user can discover items of his/her interest:

---

* **Corresponding author Sonam Gupta:** Ajay Kumar Garg Engineering College, Ghaziabad, India; E-mail: guptasonam6@gmail.com

Vikash Yadav, Parashuram Pal & Chuan-Ming Liu (Eds.)

a. The user knows exactly what he wants, and then simply he can go and search for that particular item of his choice from a vast list of the products. This approach is referred to as searching and provides accurate and reliable results.

b. The user is not clear about what he actually wants. This is where the recommender system comes into play. The system recommends to the user certain items that it assumes would attract the attention of the user, based on what the system knows about the user and the items. Various algorithms are used for making such recommendations.

Need for Recommendation System

Recommendation systems [1] help the users to find out items of similar taste in all fields ranging from movies and songs to books and outfits. They are used by the leading companies, like Amazon, Google and even Facebook. What has led to their rapid growth and popularity is the exponential increase in the number of internet users and the available products.

Imagine going to purchase some items to a nearby store 25 years ago; the products used to be arranged on shelves, however large the retailer may be (say, Walmart). Shelf space, as we all know, is a scarce commodity. It puts a check on the items that a retailer can carry as it involves real estate cost. With the advent of the Internet, now we can have as many products as we want because it involves near-zero-cost-dissemination of information about the products. This zero-cos--dissemination leads to a phenomenon, commonly known as the 'Long-Tail' phenomenon, as shown in Fig. (**1**).

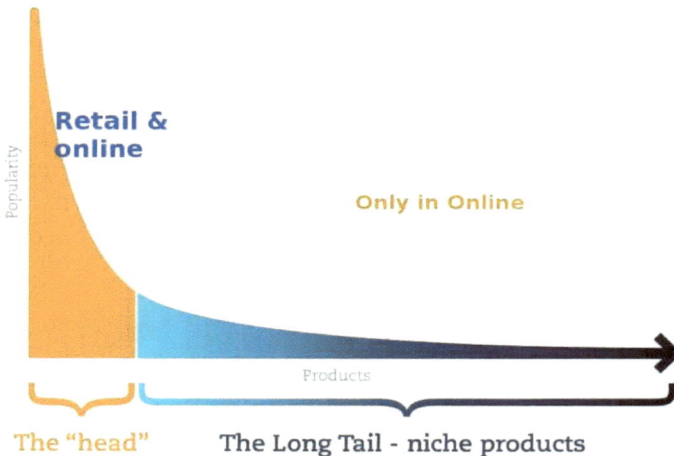

Fig. (1). A curve depicting the "Long-Tail" phenomenon; Isinkaye *et al.*, 2015.

Power of the Recommendation System

This could be explained through an example. 'Touching the void' was a book on mountaineering published in 1988. It was a pretty good book, liked by almost everyone who read it but not as famous as it should have been. About ten years later, in 1997, another book on the same topic, 'Into thin air' was published. It gained a lot of popularity and was sold in huge quantity on Amazon, as proposed by Gediminas *et al*. in 2005. The recommender engine of Amazon [2] gave recommendations of 'Touching the void' to the users who purchased 'Into thin air'; because of this, after ten years of its release, 'Touching the void' became the bestseller.

So, a good recommendation engine can acquaint people with such hidden gems that are either not known or are not very popular. This is the power of recommendation systems.

Prerequisite of Recommendation System

Natural Language Processing (NLP)

In today's era of big data, users often use the Recommendation System (RS) to make more informed decisions and selections. In general, content-based RS uses Natural Language Processing (NLP), which recommends an accurate opinion from a given text pool. In computer science, NLP is one of the hot research fields that automatically manipulates surplus content, such as speech or text written, in a natural language and produces inferred results. Sometimes, NLP is also referred to as Statistical NLP as the processing results are evaluated using various statistical techniques. With other elements of Artificial Intelligence (AI) that are machine learning and deep learning, NLP is a very important tool to eradicate the gap between human communication (in natural language) and computer understanding (in machine language). Today's computers, without exhaustion and in a clear, impartial manner, can analyse more language-based data than humans.

In today's era, Bidirectional Encoder Representations from Transformers can be used for multiple NLP tasks. The NLP tasks include questions, answers, and natural language inference. The innovation of BERT is in terms of technical purposes, *i.e.*, they apply to bi-directional training transformer, language model, *etc*. Text sequence appears in three ways, left to right, right to left, and combined left to right. BERT are useful to clear the difference between single direction trained model and bi-directional trained model. The bi-directional trained model contains a deeper sense of language and flow of language as compared to a single direction trained model. Researchers have also introduced Masked LM technique, which allows implementing a bidirectional training model, which was impossible in previous years.

The main goal of BERT is to generate a language model. Only the encoder mechanism is used for the language model. An encoder of the language model is used to read the text input, and also decoder is used to generate or produce the output to predict the task. BERT is used for multiple languages at the time of adding small layer to main model.

At the time of training language model, some challenges come in play, *i.e* ., defining the prediction goal and direct approach for limits context learning. For avoiding these two challenges, BERT technique follows two strategies, Masked LM and Next sentence LM. The BERT is used in machine learning for natural language processing to predict the text.

In view of the astounding amount of unstructured data generated every day, such as medical records, social media, *etc.*, NLP will be very crucial for effectively analyzing the text and speech data. The three structural components of NLP are Natural Language Understanding (NLU), processing techniques, and Natural Language Generation (NLG) as illustrated in Fig. (**2**).

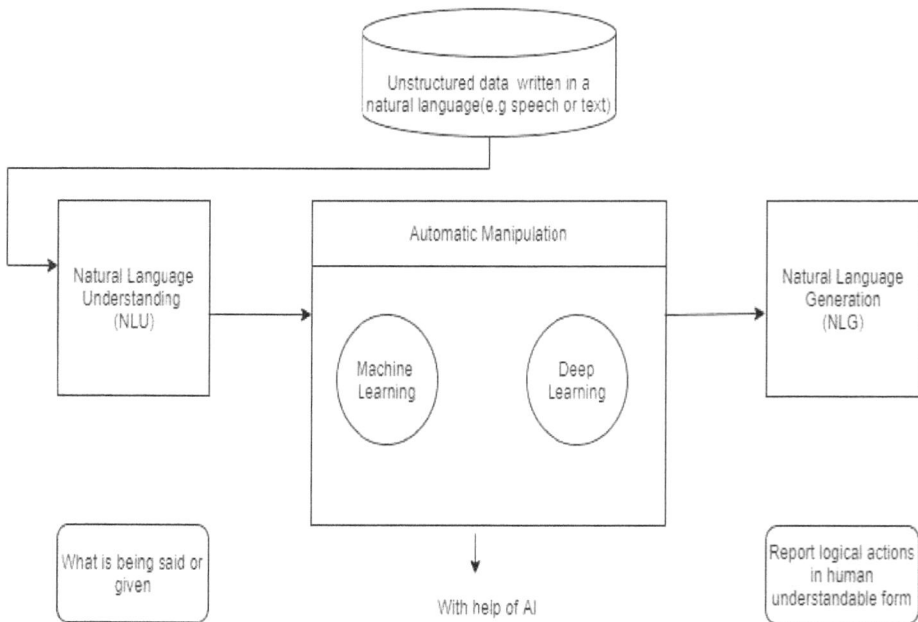

Fig. (2). Structural elements of NLP.

LSA Algorithm

The Latent Semantic Analysis (LSA) algorithm is a common algorithm that does text summarization and text classification based on cosine similarity. Schafer *et al.* [3] suggested that in LSA, a 2-D matrix termed Document-Term Matrix (DTM) is generated in which each row represents a unique word in each paragraph of the document and each column represents a paragraph number in the document. LSA deals with the three hierarchy levels of unstructured data, as shown in Fig. (**2**), which are document, paragraph and word/term. The basic assumption for the LSA algorithm is that in a similar extract of the text, words that are closer in their meaning would occur. To minimize the number of rows (number of unique words) in DTM, LSA uses the Singular Value Decomposition (SVD) method. At the same time, it always tries to retain a semantic similarity between paragraphs (columns of DTM). LSA has various applications, such as summarizing details of products, unstructured medical documents or even summarization of resumes. Topic modeling, dimension reduction and noise reduction are some other application areas of LSA. More detail about LSA is depicted in Fig. (**3**). The working of LSA is shown in Fig. (**4**).

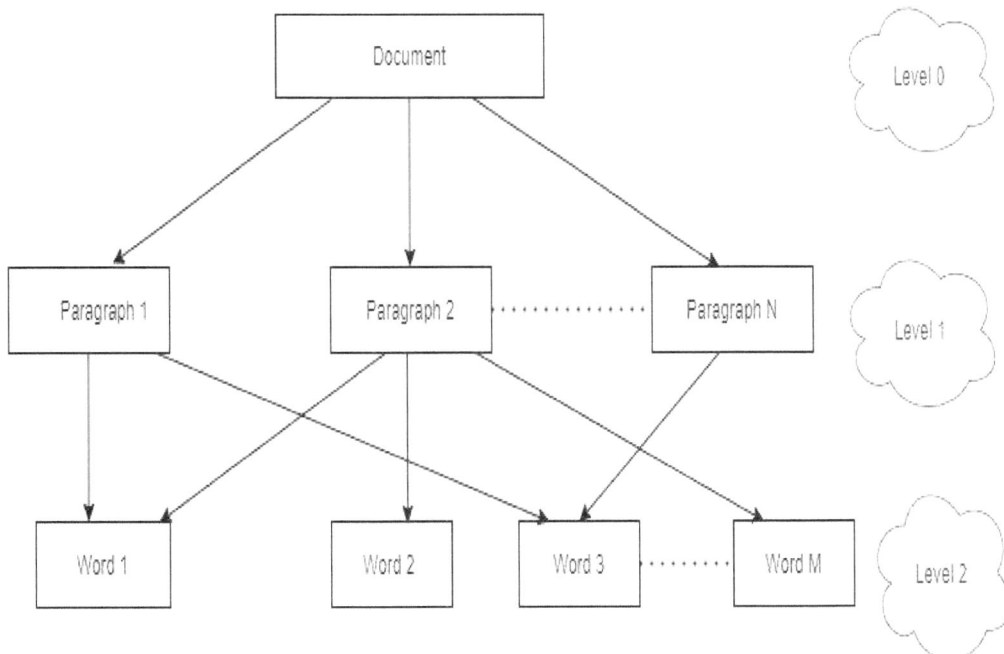

Fig. (3). Three level hierarchy of data in LSA.

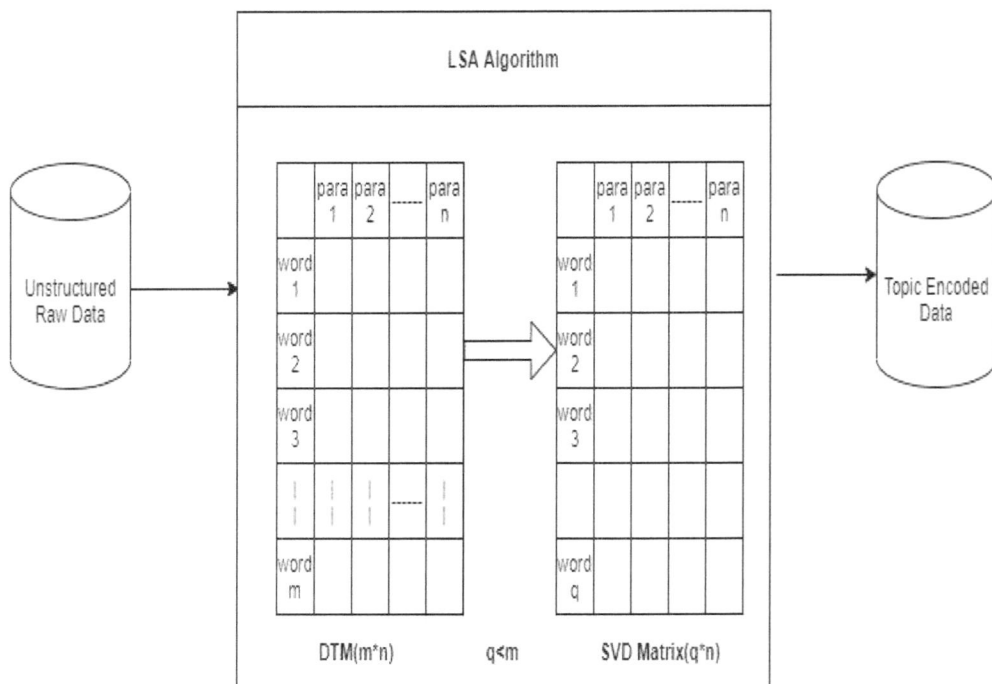

Fig. (4). Working of LSA.

Artificial Neural Network

The Artificial Neural Network (ANN) is a powerful processing system consisting of several interconnected computing components that generate dynamic output for each given input. It imitates the human brain in such a way that the functional unit of the brain, *i.e.*, neurons are represented by multiple activating nodes of ANN. *Via* connecting links, these nodes may communicate or pass data, and each connection is associated with a weight value. By altering these weight values, ANN can be made capable of learning. ANN can be divided into two categories: Feed-Forward Network (FFN) and Feed-Backward Network (FBN). A node in FFN can only transfer signals to the successive nodes. On the other hand, in FBN, a node can pass as well as receive signals from successive and preceding nodes. ANN has various applications, such as target tracking and facial recognition in military, speech recognition, medical reports analysis, traffic routing and vehicle scheduling in transportation, and many more.

LITERATURE SURVEY

A recommender system is defined as a decision-making strategy for users under complex information environments (http://www.longtail.com/about.html). Recommender system is also defined as a specific type of intelligent system, which exploits past user ratings of items and/or auxiliary information to make recommendations on items to the users, as presented by Ben *et al*. in 2007. The problem of recommending a user an item of his interest can be briefly described as estimating the ratings that the user would give to an item that he has not seen earlier. After knowing these ratings, we can recommend to a user the item that he may have given higher ratings; the same was proposed by Ben *et al*. in 1999. The works done by many authors in this area are presented in Table **1**.

Table 1. Working of LSA.

S. No.	Authors	Work
1.	J. Ben Schafer, Joseph Konstan, John Riedl	Showed how recommender systems help in increasing the sales of various e-commerce [4] sites. They also analyzed various leading websites that use one or more recommender systems.
2.	Pasquale Lops, Marco de Gemmis, Giovanni Semeraro	Discussed the concept, architecture, advantages and disadvantages of content-based recommender systems. They also described the traditional and advanced techniques for making item and user profiles.
3.	J. Ben Schafer, Dan Frankowski, Jon Herlocker, Shilad Sen	Introduced the concepts of collaborative filtering, its uses, and theory of CF algorithms. They also discussed methods of evaluation [5] of CF systems and concluded by leaving the further scope of research in that field.
4.	Sheng Zhang, Weihong Wang, James Ford, FilliaMakedon	Introduced two variations of Non-negative Matrix Factorization [6]: Expectation-Maximization (EM) and Weighted Non-negative Matrix Factorization (WNMF). They also proposed a hybrid algorithm by considering the advantages of both the algorithms.
5.	Robin Burke	Surveyed various hybrid recommenders and introduced a new hybrid system, called EntreeC, which combines collaborative filtering and knowledge-based recommendation to suggest restaurants.
6.	ZiedZaier, Robert Godin, Luc Faucher	Introduced the long-tail phenomenon and how it affects the recommender systems. Also presented a review of various datasets that were used to evaluate CF recommender algorithms and analysed which of those datasets provided the most relevant distribution that would follow power-law distribution.
7.	Paolo Cremonesi, Antonio Tripodu, Roberto Turrin	Focused on Cross-Domain collaborative recommender systems for recommending items belonging to multiple domains.

STEPS OF RECOMMENDATION PROCESS

Recommendation process involves the following 3 steps or phases, as shown in Fig. (**5**):

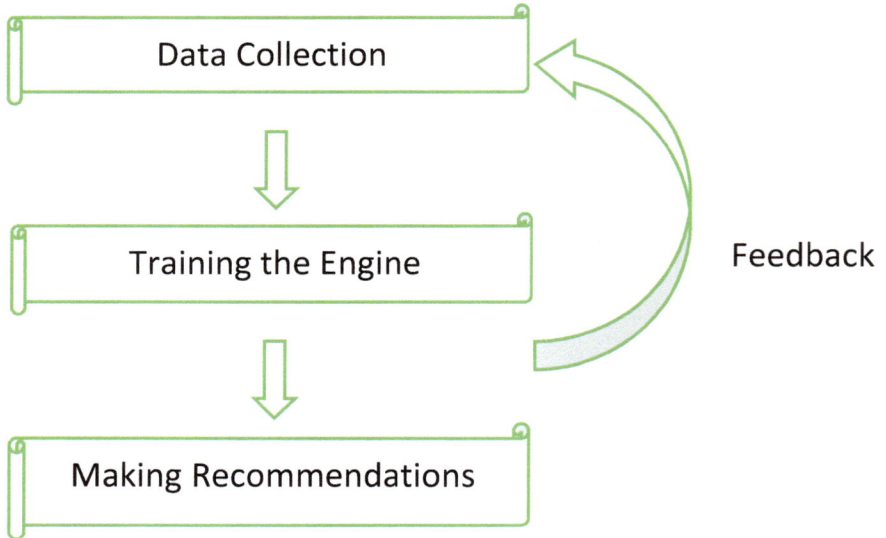

Fig. (5). Recommendation Process.

A. Data collection
B. Training the engine
C. Making recommendations

A. Data Collection

For making recommendations to a user, it is necessary to know about the user and his interests. The pertinent information about the user is collected, and a user profile is made based on the items previously purchased by the user. The information of the user for creating the user profile can be collected using the following methods:

1. Explicit Method

This method involves direct interaction with the users. The users are asked to rate the items on a certain scale, say 1 to 10 or star ratings from 0 to 5. The advantage of this method is its simplicity, and we get a direct response from the customers, who are our chief target. However, it has certain limitations, like some users may not give genuine feedback or ratings due to some or the other reason. On the other hand, most customers believe that giving feedback is merely a waste of time. Thus, it leads to data insufficiency as only a small fraction of users give a response.

2. Implicit Method

As the name suggests, this method infers the interests of the user by considering his actions and behavior. For *e.g.*, if a user purchases an item or downloads a movie, it may imply a high rating. It overcomes the limitation of data insufficiency in the explicit method, but the main problem with this method is that it is not easy to know about the low ratings.

3. Hybrid Method

To overcome the shortcomings of explicit and implicit method, most recommender systems generally use a combination of both, commonly known as the hybrid method [7].

A. Training Phase

The user profile that was built in the previous phase is utilized in this step. A learning algorithm is applied to filter and exploit the features of the user from his profile. The recommendation engine is trained to make further predictions.

B. Recommendation Phase

This is the last phase in which recommendations are made to the user based on his interests and preferences. It is done by considering the user matrix made in the data collection phase and then analyzing the taste of the user to predict what he may like.

FILTERING TECHNIQUES

Three filtering techniques are popularly used for recommender systems, as shown in Fig. (6).

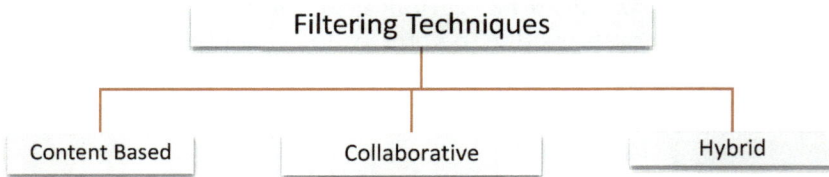

Fig. (6). Filtering techniques used in recommender system.

1. Content-based Filtering

It is a widely used technique for making recommendations. In this method [8], it is assumed that the items of a similar kind will be rated in a similar manner by the user, and hence, recommendations that are made to a person are based on his/her past choices and interests towards some particular item. The same has been illustrated in Fig (7). For example, if a user listens to a song on Pandora, the next songs would be suggested to him, considering that maybe he liked the singer, musician or the genre (say, romantic or classical) of the previous song. Friend suggestions on Facebook are given by viewing the similarity between two people, like they have many common friends or they belong to the same school or college. Its crucial component is the user modelling process in which user's interest can be determined by the items the user has interacted with. We take a user and look at all the items that he has previously rated highly (explicit) or purchased (implicit). Based on those items, an item profile that contains the description of the item is built, and from that, a user profile is derived.

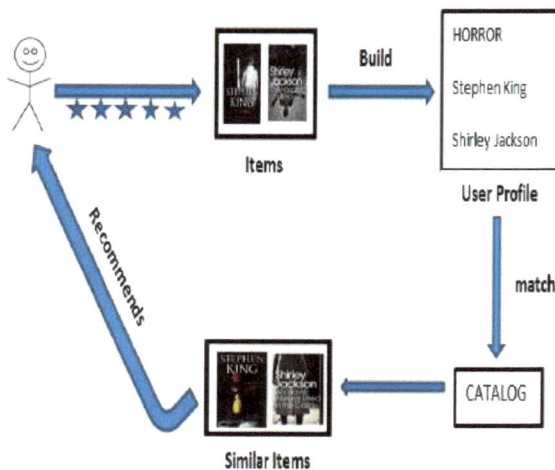

Fig. (7). How the content-based approach works.

Once we have the user profile, we can match it against the items that we have in the catalogue and correspondingly recommend the items to the user.

2. Collaborative Filtering

The collaborative filtering technique is used to generate recommendations to a user by utilizing the data of the similar neighbors of that user. The term collaborative filtering was coined by Doug Terry at Xerox PARC as part of the development of the Information Tapestry system for allowing the users to annotate the articles and documents that the user reads or the products that the system recommends. Its motivation for generating recommendations is the combination of ideas of a similar kind to users. For example, David and Billy both highly rated the movie Annabelle and The Conjuring (both belong to the horror genre). However, David also watched Don't Breathe (also horror), so now Don't Breathe would be recommended to Billy, who possesses a similar taste in movies like David. This is the main concept of Collaborative Filtering, which involves collecting, analyzing and processing a large amount of information. The working of this filtering is shown in Fig. (**8**).

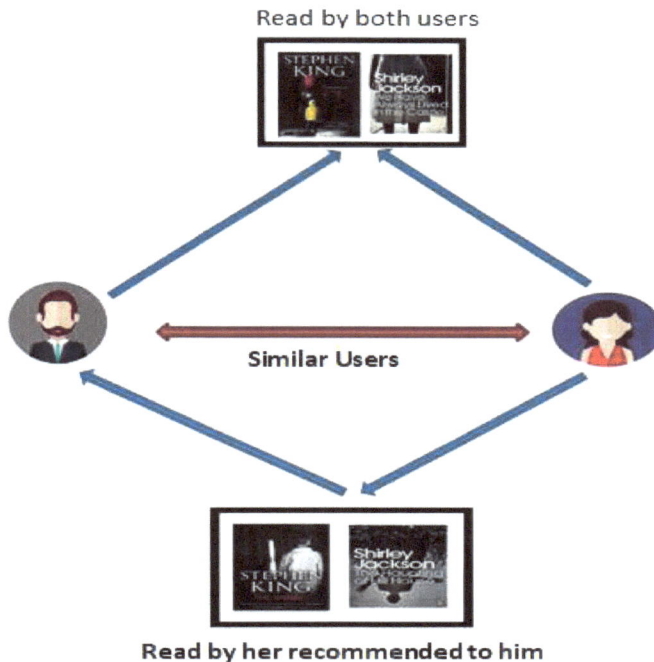

Fig. (**8**). How collaborative filtering works.

PROPOSED WORK

A. Problem Statement

Our goal is to design a Recommendation system that would assist the experienced as well as novice researchers to determine the topic in their domain of interest, in which they can perform their research work. It takes a lot of time to analyse all the previous papers from the huge pool of papers available online. Hence, we propose a platform where users can enter their field that they want to work in, and the system will generate a required response to help them in deciding what they can actually do, based on a similarity value.

However, there are certain issues that need to be tackled in this process which are as follows:

a. Proper dataset is not available that contains information from previous papers with required features that are needed in this project. So, we will have to create a database of our own, which is in itself a Herculean task.
b. The database needed for this approach would be large enough as it will contain all previous papers of all domains in all fields. It could not be handled by any normal computer. So, we require systems with high speed and high computational power for processing our algorithm.
c. Another limitation of our project is that the user needs to enter the generalized topic that he wants to work for, so that it could easily be matched with the keywords present in the previous papers.

B. Algorithm Used

The person, who wants to determine the work which he/she may do in a particular domain, would be required to enter some keywords related to his field of interest in which he wants to pursue his research. Then the entered keywords are analysed using the Artificial Neural Networks (ANN), and the research papers which come under the same domain of the same field are assembled together using the k-means clustering algorithm, the most widely used clustering algorithm. Example, a user wants to propose a paper related to the recommendation system. He would enter the keyword, *i.e.*, Recommendation systems. Now our algorithm would determine using ANN to which field this topic belongs, and the user will get the result that it comes under the Computer Science field. Next, the domain of the word will be determined, which will provide a response that it belongs to machine learning. The entered keyword is analysed using LSA (Latent Semantic Analysis) algorithm [9, 10]. This algorithm finds synonyms of the given keyword using the

WordNet database. The procedure of the algorithm is shown in Fig. (**9**). The results of the algorithm are compared against the database. The links of matched papers are displayed as output, and the user can download those papers from given links.

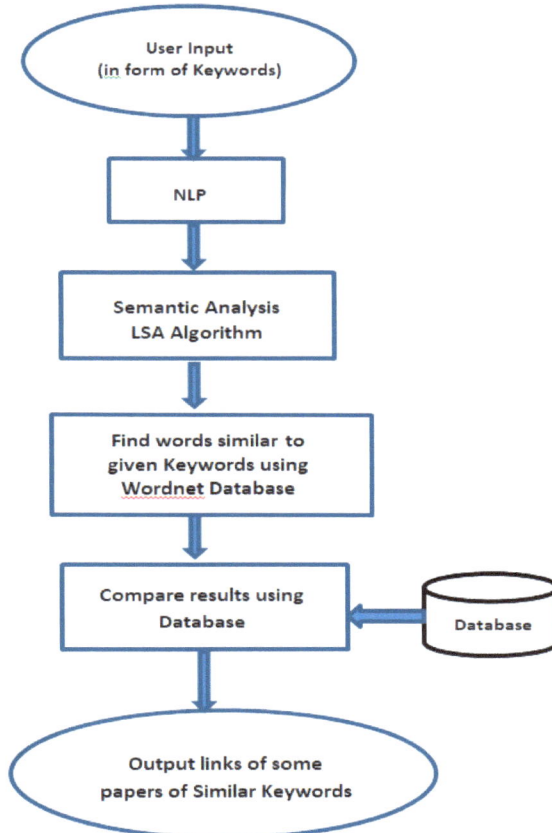

Fig. (9). Flowchart describing the working of our recommender system.

C. Result

Users can set the similarity index for a particular keyword and get corresponding similar papers to continue the research work.

Following screenshots have been taken for values of 2 similarity indexes (0.75 and 0.50) for the keyword fruit, and the respective links have been given as output in Figs. (**10** and **11**).

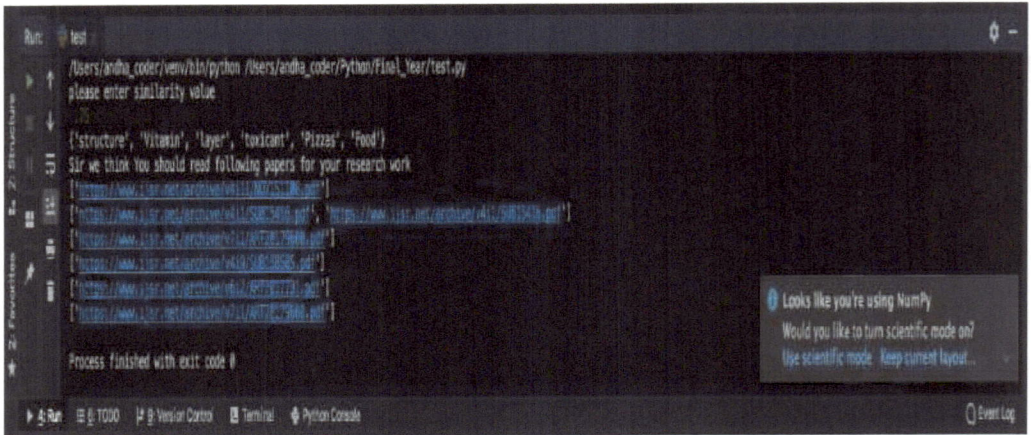

Fig. (10). Output of links corresponding to similarity index 0.75 and keyword.

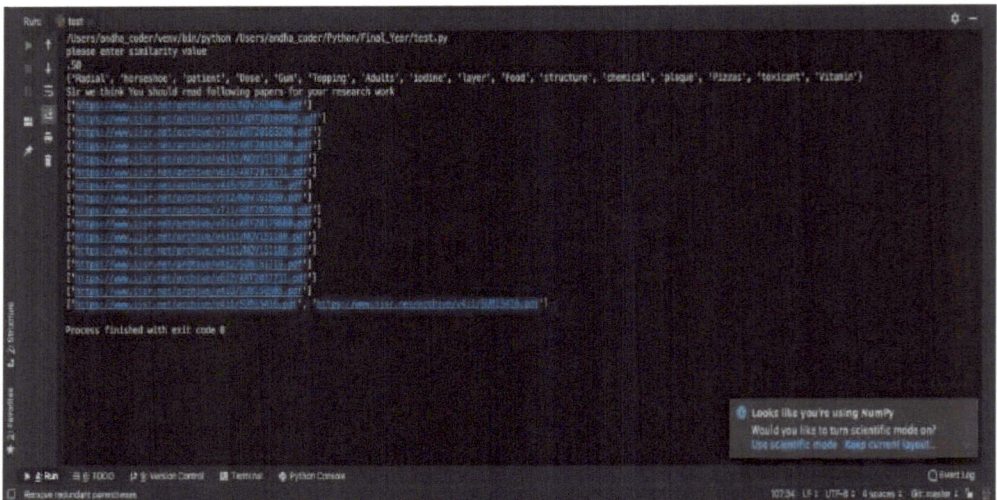

Fig. (11). Output of links corresponding to similarity index 0.50 and keyword 'Fruit'.

The proposed recommender system can also help in determining which is the currently trending topic for pursuing the research work. This could be done by taking the number of count of papers published in the past few years for some particular keywords and comparing those results can yield a trending topic.

This study is elaborated in the given line graphs, which show the comparison of a count of three keywords (Block Chain, Cloud Computing and Machine Learning) over the past 9 years (2010-2018), as shown in Figs. (**12 - 14**), respectively.

Year Vs Count for Block Chain

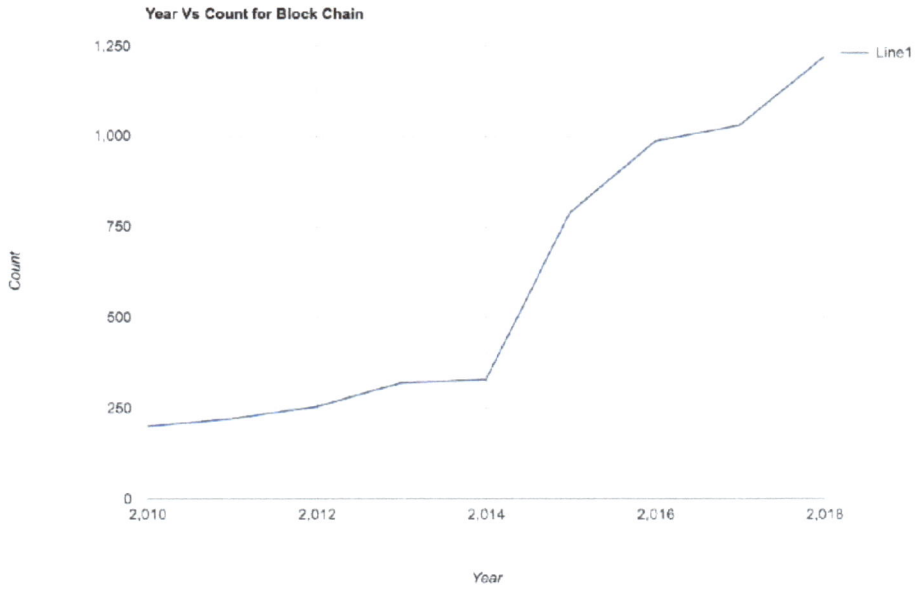

Fig. (12). Line graph representing statistics of the last 9 years against the count of published papers containing the keyword 'Blockchain'.

Year Vs Count for Cloud Computing

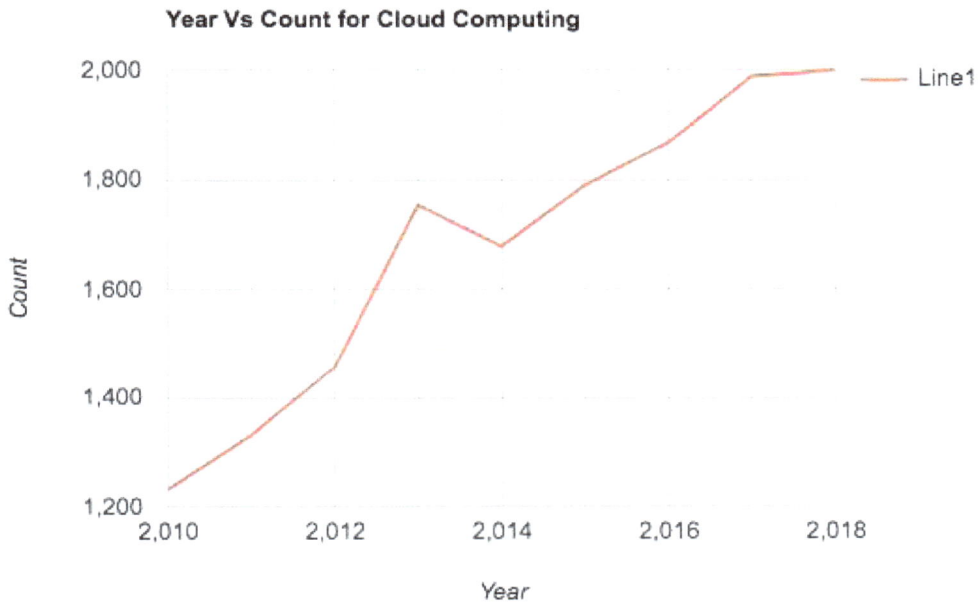

Fig. (13). Line graph representing statistics of the last 9 years against the count of published papers containing the keyword 'Cloud Computing'.

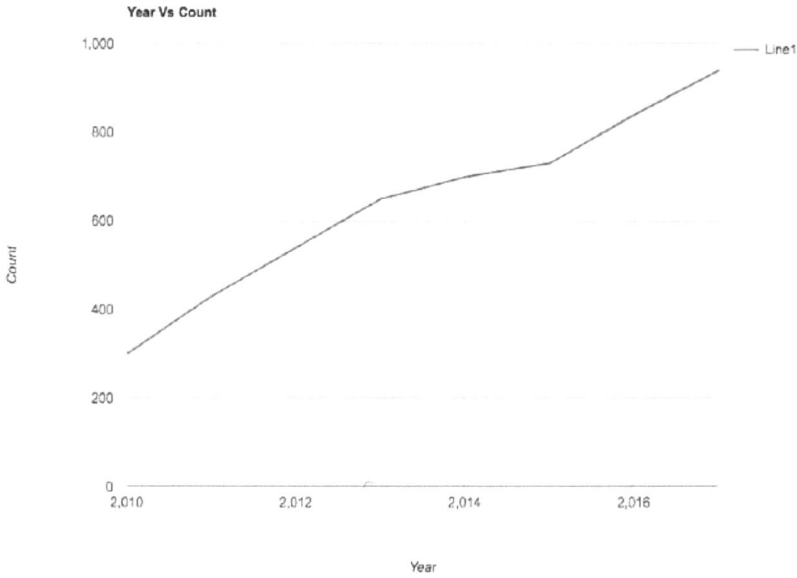

Fig. (14). Line graph representing statistics of the last 9 years against the count of published papers containing the keyword 'Machine Learning'.

CONCLUSION

Since the mid-90s, Recommendation systems have become an important area of research. Even though, in the past decade, a lot of work has been done in this field, it is astonishing that the passion of scholars still lies here because of its vast problem domain that is yet left untouched. In the paper, we have defined and discussed the recommendation system along with the steps of recommendation. We have briefed some of the works of different authors that they did in this field. We have also explained the types of filtering techniques (collaborative filtering, content-based and a hybrid of both) and examined their working and limitations. Finally, we have proposed a recommendation system that would enable the intellectual scholars around the world to choose the topic on which they can carry out their research. The result of the proposed solution would generate those points that have not been examined or explored yet, or if there is some drawback or limitation of an already done work, then researchers can suggest their improved technique, producing better results.

CONSENT FOR PUBLICATION

Not applicable.

CONFLICT OF INTEREST

The author declares no conflict of interest, financial or otherwise.

ACKNOWLEDGEMENTS

Declared none.

REFERENCES

[1]   F.O. Isinkaye, Y.O. Folajimi, and B.A. Ojokoh, "Recommendation systems: Principles, methods and evaluation", *Egyptian Informatics Journal,* vol. 16, no. 3, pp. 261-273, 2015.
[http://dx.doi.org/10.1016/j.eij.2015.06.005]

[2]   G. Adomavicius, and A. Tuzhilin, "Toward the next generation of recommender systems: a survey of the state-of-the-art and possible extensions", *IEEE Trans. Knowl. Data Eng.,* vol. 17, no. 6, pp. 734-749, 2005.
[http://dx.doi.org/10.1109/TKDE.2005.99]

[3]   Schafer J.B., Frankowski D., Herlocker J., and Sen S., "Collaborative Filtering Recommender Systems", In: *The Adaptive Web. Lecture Notes in Computer Science,* P. Brusilovsky, A. Kobsa, W. Nejdl, Eds., vol. 4321. Springer: Berlin, Heidelberg.

[4]   J. Ben Schafer, Konstan Joseph, and Riedl John, "Recommender Systems in E-Commerce", *Proceedings of the 1ˢᵗ ACM conference on Electronic commerce,* pp. 158-166, 1999.
[http://dx.doi.org/10.1145/336992.337035]

[5]   Z. Zaier, R. Godin, and L. Faucher, "Evaluating Recommender Systems", *2008 International Conference on Automated Solutions for Cross Media Content and Multi-Channel Distribution,* pp. 211-217, 2008.
[http://dx.doi.org/10.1109/AXMEDIS.2008.21]

[6]   S. Zhang, and W. Wang, "Learning from Incomplete Ratings Using Non-negative Matrix Factorization", *Proceedings of the 2016 SIAM International Conference on Data Mining,* pp. 549-553, 2016.

[7]   P. Lops, M. Degemmis, and G. Semeraro, ""Content-based Recommender Systems: State of the Art and Trends." ", In: *Recommender Systems Handbook*, 2011.

[8]   Rashid A.M., Albert I., Cosley D., Lam S.K., McNee S.M., Konstan J.A., and Riedl J., "Getting to know you: Learning new user preferences in recommender systems", *Proceedings of the 7ᵗʰ international conference on Intelligent user interfaces,* pp. 127-134, 2002.
[http://dx.doi.org/10.1145/502716.502737]

[9]   C. Graesser, X. Hu, B.A. Olde, M. Ventura, A. Olney, and M. Louwerse, "Implementing latent semantic analysis in learning environments with conversational agents and tutorial dialog", *24ᵗʰ Annual Meeting of the Cognitive Science Society,* Erlbaum: Mahwah, NJ, p. 37, 2002.

[10]   M. Rahul, and V. Yadav, "Movie Recommender System using Single Value Decomposition and K-means clustering", *1ˢᵗ International Conference on Computational Research and Data Analytics (ICCRDA-2020),* 2020.

CHAPTER 4

An Intelligent Surveillance System for Human Behavior Recognition: An Exhaustive Survey

Ruchi Jayaswal[1,*] and **Manish Dixit**[1]

[1] *Department of CSE & IT, Madhav Institute of Technology and Science, Gwalior, M.P., India*

Abstract: Understanding the behavior of humans is a very important concern for social communication. Especially in real-time, predicting human activity and behavior has become the most vigorous research area in digital image processing and computer vision. To enhance the security in public and private domains in the field of human-computer interaction and intelligent video surveillance, human behavior analysis is an important challenge in various applications. There are many basic approaches to analyze human activity, but recently, deep learning approaches have been shown that yield very interesting results in different domains. Human actions and behavior can be observed in the open as well as in sensitive areas, such as airports, banks, bus and train station, colleges, parking areas, *etc.*, and prevent terrorism, theft, accidents, fighting, as well as other abnormal and suspicious activities through visual surveillance. This chapter thus seeks to reflect on methods of human activity recognition. This chapter presents a brief overview on human behavior recognition along with its challenges or issues and applications. Also, we have discussed the framework of recognition of suspicious human activity and various datasets used to train the system. The objective of this chapter is to provide general information about human behavior analysis and recent methods used in this field.

Keywords: Activity recognition, Convolutional neural network, Deep learning, Feature extraction, Human behavior analysis, Object classification, Object segmentation.

INTRODUCTION

There is an increasing demand for intelligent methods to monitor the massive amount of surveillance video data formed continuously by video surveillance systems. In recent years, there is a growing interest of researchers in the human-computer interaction field in the real-time environment to develop an intelligent system in various domains. Among all applications, human behavior analysis or

---
[*] **Corresponding author Ruchi Jayaswal:** Department of CSE & IT, Madhav Institute of Technology and Science, Gwalior, M.P., India; E-mail: ruchi.jayaswal23@gmail.com

Vikash Yadav, Parashuram Pal & Chuan-Ming Liu (Eds.)
All rights reserved-© 2022 Bentham Science Publishers

human activity recognition is engraving in computer vision and the HCI field. Activity recognition in computer vision to attain detection, tracking, feature extraction, analysis and recognition method of human activities in real-time video image is an important factor in the fields of pattern recognition. Human activity analysis is necessary in public places, like shopping malls, airports, public roads, *etc.*, so that unusual activity could be prevented through camera-based surveillance. Previously, human behavior was unpredictable since there was no capacity for storing huge amounts of data and analyzing them that goes into the intelligent system and makes the decision. But, now at present, the sophisticated computer systems and cloud help to store massive collections of data that lead to the development of deep learning.

Activity identification tactics can be broadly categorized into two categories. The first tactic is focused on Model Matching, and the second tactic is the State Space-based behavior recognition process. The method of behavior recognition is based on a model matching state that first begins to find the exact template video image sequence to denote human's static target action, then it matches the target pattern image sequence in the models, and if the match succeeds, the behavior from the behavior characteristics of the pattern implies that the behavior is normal activity otherwise the behavior is unusual. State space-based behavior recognition refers to the particular posture state, and then the state is related in the similar way [1].

The automated classification of suspicious activity will be used in the video monitoring system to inform the associated authority of potential illegal or disruptive acts (*e.g.*, burglary in public areas, murder, bag loitering at airports terminals or stations). Action recognition is a very challenging task because of changes in viewpoint variations and cluttered backgrounds [1]. There are some typical issues with vision-based devices, such as occlusions, vision-dependent characteristics, lighting, *etc.*, so the systems are improved with other sensors to prevent these shortcomings (binary sensors and RFID). Also, many other approaches are used to extract substitute features from low-level appearance and movement signals, such as texture and optical flow, rather than object following.

Basically, two kinds of surveillance systems exist. First, a semi-autonomous surveillance system, in which videos are captured and submitted to human experts for examination. Traditional video surveillance systems require constant human observation, which is a very tedious job and also costly to watch by a guard and prevent unusual behavior. In order to cope with these systems, a second type of surveillance system is a Fully Autonomous system. This system implements low-level tasks, such as gesture detection, tracking, classification and recognition of unusual events [2].

The aim of this type of system is to create smart video surveillance despite conventional passive video surveillance so that abnormal or unusual actions implemented by people can be recorded by camera, further analyzing and generating an alert *via* alarms or by some other techniques to thwart abnormal actions [3].

Over the last few years, various approaches have been put forth to identify normal and unusual activity. Many approaches concentrate on motion directions to irregular activity categories [4], namely clustering, supervised techniques, deep learning techniques, and CNN techniques. Deep learning algorithms have recently been successfully applied to recognize unusual behaviors and produce efficient results.

Classification of Human Behavior

Generally, human behavior is broadly classified into two categories, as shown in Fig. (1), which are normal behavior and abnormal behavior. Depending on these categories, an intelligent system sets a template, and then the image sequence matches with the target and obtains the results according to user desire.

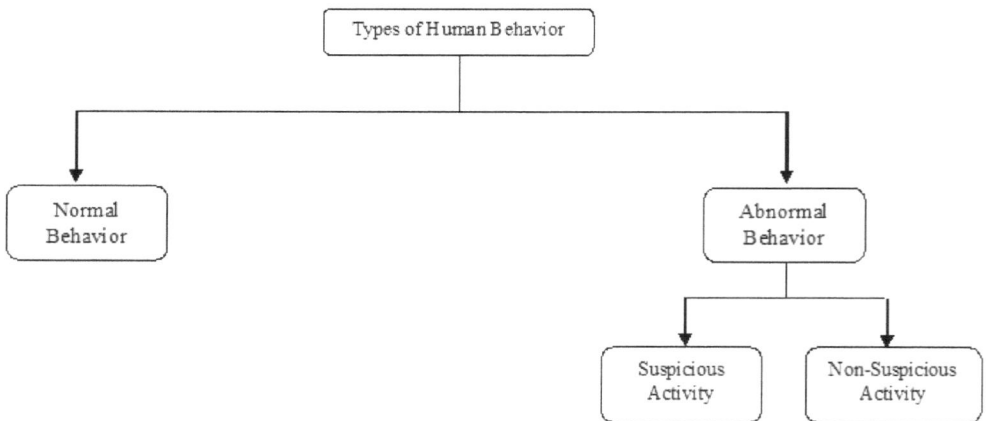

Fig. (1). Classification of human behavior.

Normal Behavior

A behavior is said to be normal if the individual human's activity is the same as the activity of others in society, or we can say any behavior that follows the social patterns, for example, running, walking, jogging, clapping, waving, driving, *etc*.

Abnormal Behavior

A behavior is said to be abnormal if the individual human's activity is different from one's neighbor activity in society or we can say any behavior that is against the social norms, for example, shooting, bag loitering, theft, slapping, punching, hitting, shooting, *etc.*

Suspicious Activity

Any activity arising from abnormal behavior might indicate malicious behavior, for example, shooting, bag loitering, running at a shopping mall which indicates suspicious activity, slapping, and violence.

Non-suspicious Activity

Any activity that does not arise from abnormal behavior does not indicate malicious behavior, for example, health monitoring of elders or patients, fall detection, illegal parking, illegal U-turns, *etc.*

Problems and Challenges

In order to design a smart video monitoring system for automated detection of irregular human behavior analysis, a range of concerns and challenges need to be addressed. The problems of human behavior analysis are still an open challenge for researchers. Massive amounts of data, such as video, cannot be directly processed as a classifier, which contains much redundant information and causes high computational complexity. The goal of any successful application is choosing the appropriate representation. However, it is extremely challenging because of the accompanying reasons:

- Action patterns diverge within the same class of actions [5]: The class of actions can belong to any category, like walking, jogging, clapping, or classification of the type of target event, like normal and abnormal. There exist a high-assorted variety of data in one class because of the varieties in style and appearance. The representation ought to be general to catch the varieties in human movement, human-human, and human-object interactions.
- Environmental challenge and noisy data [5]: Real-time video contains a lot of noise and varies in terms of illumination effect and background dynamics. There should be some good methods that can handle environmental challenges.

Sometimes motion object detection is very challenging to process reliably in a natural scene, and some waving tree branches make noise, which becomes difficult at the time of analysis of an object.

- Partial or whole occlusions of objects: Often objects are partially or fully obstructed in videos, which makes an issue for the object to be separated effectively.
- More crowds: Identification of the item from the rush field is very difficult. In such circumstances, unused object detection, bag loitering, theft detection, *etc.*, become very challenging tasks.
- Static object detection and real-time processing: Fixed object detection is a very challenging task for abandoned object detection by background subtraction since this method only detects movable objects as foreground detection. Designing an autonomous security system in real-time is also a more difficult task. Since images have complicated backgrounds, it takes more time to remove objects and trace moving objects.

Motivation and Recent Trends

The motivation is to design an intelligent human behavior recognition system, so that abnormal and suspicious actions can be detected in public areas, thus preventing explosive attacks, fall detection, theft cases, fighting, slapping, punching, personal attacks, *etc.*, in different extremely highly sensitive areas, such as shopping malls, banks, public roads, hospitals, home (for older people), borders, *etc.*

There are many application areas in this field as discussed below:

- Surveillance: In public places, security is a major concern for all human beings. Robbery cases, shoplifting, snatching, killing, theft, and terrorist attacks can happen in schools, colleges, banks, shopping malls, crowded places, airports, railways and bus stations, where the safety of people is a very important challenge for any nation. A real-time suspicious or non-suspicious human activities identification device from a smart video system offers a high degree of protection in highly delicate places. It helps monitoring the platforms, routes, parking lots, tunnels, and prime target places of attacks through CCTV cameras in public areas.

In the bank sector, video surveillance camera helps enhance the security. It prevents robbery from taking place. ATM and automated bank machine is the prime target for attackers. These cameras help to detect fraud, theft cases, and monitor all branches to detect suspicious behavior.

Similarly, in the retail trade, these surveillance cameras are used to monitor human activities, such as parking lots, or can be used to record video evidence of theft cases or any kind of adverse event.

- Sports: In the video surveillance field, the normal behavior of humans can be captured and differentiated from the abnormal behavior through an intelligent video processing system. Sports constitutes a major significant percentage of the entire public and commercial television transmissions. Increasing requests of purchasers/viewers require propelled video capturing and video processing abilities. A large pool of storing capabilities, *i.e.*, more TV channels, offers full coverage of large sports event, due to which, it becomes more attractive to consumers. Video abstract or summary of sports videos is a very fruitful tool, as several times some games may be boring to consumers, so watching a summary can spare a lot of time.
- Medical: Handling and semantically getting data from recordings has helped the health and care area of the general public as of late. From dosing problems to respiratory and care for older people, researchers are discovering novel techniques to make the general public well-being a superior area. Real-time video analysis may also be used to observe patients in clinics, at home or the behavior of elderly persons in the medical field, as well as domestic violence or check children's activity. The activity of patients, such as fall detection, and abnormal activities, such as vomiting and fainting, can also be monitored through video surveillance.

Framework for Abnormal Human Activity and Behavior Analysis

The general framework of abnormal or suspicious human behavior recognition is presented in Fig. (**2**). This block diagram shows the abnormal event in video sequences. A number of steps are followed to develop the intelligent surveillance system. In this section, we will talk about the basic approach to abnormal behavior recognition.

Preprocessing and Foreground Object Detection

Preprocessing is the primary stage during video frame processing. This technique is applied to remove illumination, occlusion and noisy data, thus enhancing the quality of the frames. To enhance the quality of blob detection of moving objects in video and to handle the different types of noise in frames, morphological operation, various filters like Gaussian, wiener, and average filters, may be applied using function. The basic method for stationary camera segmentation is background subtraction because it is easy to use and gives better efficiency. This background subtraction contains just the fixed background scene with no foreground scene, and any frame change is thought to be caused uniquely by movable objects [6].

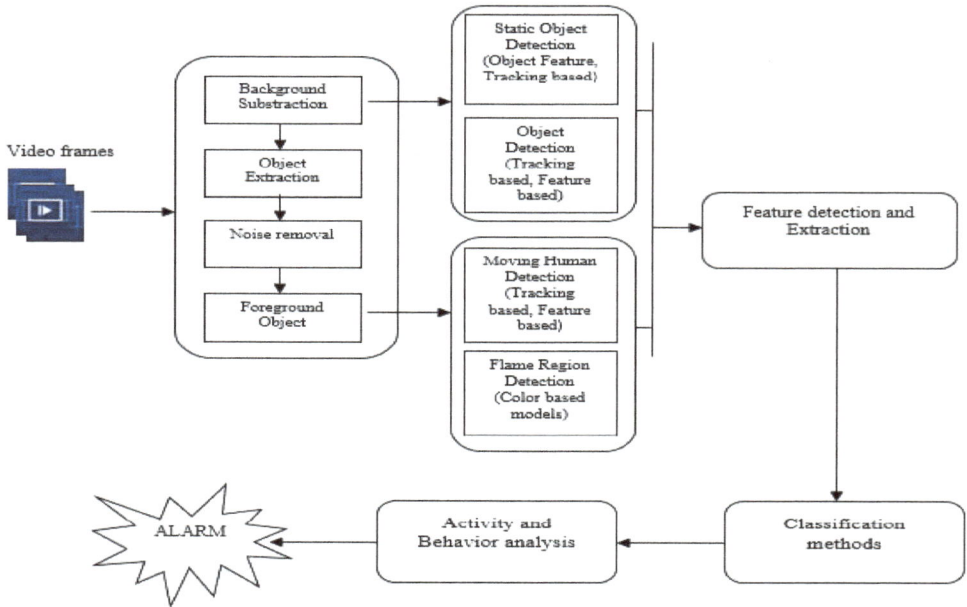

Fig. (2). Framework of human behavior recognition.

Foreground object detection is an important step for moving objects. It is a primary and crucial step of suspicious human activity recognition. Foreground objects comprise moving items and recently showed up objects in a video which get fixed after sometime, for example, left luggage. Motion object extraction can be accomplished through two methods; the first is Background Modeling, which attempts to produce the background model utilizing some spatial and transient prompt. The second method is a change detection-based approach. This method calculates the variance to boost motion among two consecutive frames and further uses post-processing techniques to recuperate the entire picture.

Object Tracking

It is a crucial and interesting task. It aids in creating the trajectory or the direction of an object over a period of time as it is placed in consecutive video monitoring frames to track human behavior. The representation of the object form is used to follow it, *i.e.*, points, contour, object outline, basic geometric shapes, enunciated shapes and skeletal models. Tracking an object is difficult since there is noise present in the image, partial or total occlusion of objects, and lighting changes are also present in the frames. Kalman filter is the well-known method for object tracking because of its simplicity and real-time operation capability. Basically, there are three types of tracking; kernel tracking is used for tracking, and point tracking and shape tracking for distance, color, and object size. Different forms of tracking are used by researchers for variations.

For the identification of abandoned objects, theft detection, fall detection, crime detection, fire detection, suspicious behavior on rush paths, and tracking-based methods and non-tracking tactics are used.

Feature Extraction and Motion Information

Extraction of features is basically a dimensionality reduction technique in which the most suitable features are selected and large feature sets are reduced. The selection of the best feature is a tedious chore in order to solve the critical problem. The aim of feature extraction is to catch the most valuable information in the recorded videos.

Extracting moving information from video frames is the primary stage of motion-based detection. These extracted features are the input arrangements for the statistical, syntactic and probabilistic models for behavior recognition. There are typically three techniques for features that derive the information of movable objects from image succession. Optical flow patterns are dependent on trajectory features and region or image characteristics.

Optical Flow Features

In this method, at each pixel, image motions are recuperate from spatial-temporal image based on splendor varieties. It is the field of velocity that wraps individual images into another image. A few strategies have been developed, but still a strong strategy needs to be discovered.

Trajectory-based Features

Trajectory-based features method is very popular because it is easy to extract features. These trajectories are acquired from the areas of the specific points on an arbitrary object in a fixed period of time. These trajectories of motions are generated from the order of images in which tokens (in each frame of a scene) are recognized, and correspondence of such tokens is transferred from one frame to another. Tokens can be a corner, region, or area of interest.

Region-based Features

Sometimes, for certain objects or motions, exact motion information is not required, rather an overall thought of the frame is useful. Features are produced from the utilization of data over a moderately enormous district or over the entire image, and are known as image- or region-based features.

Classification and Activity Recognition

Classification is the method of separating the actions into a number of classes. After finding stationary and moving foreground objects in a frame and extracting features of objects, the classification of object steps is used for the recognition of normal and unusual behavior. Object classification step is used to differentiate the static human from stationary-abandoned object, battling from boxing, face color from skin color object, daylight from artificial lights, falling human posture from laying human posture, and so forth. In general, there are 2 main types of approaches for categorizing moving objects, which are Shape-based classification and Motion-based classification. Most of the researchers have applied the variants features with variants classifiers, such as S.V.M., Neural Network, Multi S.V.M., Classification trees, Fuzzy classifier, Linear Discriminate Analysis (LDA), HAR, and many more that are used to examine people's behavior and recognition of usual and unusual actions.

Some Activity Recognition Methods and Techniques

There are some activity recognition methods and techniques that can be applied on the basis of applications and outcomes. After classification, depending upon the proportion of former information and human contribution to the learning, we may extensively divide the research techniques into action, activity and behavior finding, particularly anomalous behavior identification, as in Supervised, Unsupervised and Semi-supervised. We have discussed some of the major techniques as follows:

Artificial Neural Network (ANN)

"ANN is a computational structure that is propelled by the perceived process in natural networks of biological neurons in the brain". It comprises simple computational units known as neurons, which are profoundly interrelated. Neurons are received signals *via* synapses placed on the dendrites of the neurons. Once the strong signals are received, the neuron is triggered and emits the signal, and these signals might be sent to one another and then activate other neurons. In order to acquire the preferred output from the network, various algorithms are proposed. Both unsupervised and supervised learning is probable through the artificial neural network.

The most promising learning procedure in an ANN is the Back-propagation algorithm; it utilizes the data values to change the network's weights and thresholds value in order to limit the inaccuracy in its expectations of the training or learning set. There are numerous types of ANNs algorithms, like Radial Basis Function (RBF), Kohonen networks and Multilayer Perceptron, Fuzzy associative method (FAM). For example, FAM is used to find various actions, like walking, sidewalking, jumping and running, from the video.

Clustering

In clustering, the training or learning procedure for unusual action detection involves gathering analogous image or video clip features together and generate limited numeral clusters that have unique cluster structures and exist as a semantic structure. Extracted features are grouped using low-level abstraction to explain the activities. A statistical model is constructed and clustering-based anomaly detection is trained with the help of labeled or unlabeled data of either just usual or abnormal separately or together normal and abnormal event features. For clustering, mainly k-means algorithm is used. Some other improved algorithms are also available, such as k-medoids, radius-based and ant-based clustering [7].

The statistical clustering properties of Dynamic Bayesian Networks (DBNs) and Hidden Markov Model (HMMs) are suggested in clustering behavior. Among two of them, HMMs have gained more popularity in behavior recognition.

Hidden Markov Model (HMM)

Hidden Markov Model (HMM) is good for obtaining high accuracy classification method. It is a type of stochastic state machine. This model uses hidden states that relate to various stages in the performance of the action. Training and classification are two stages of HMM. The states of the HMM must be at the training stage, and their subsequent state transformation and outcome probabilities must be improved so that the symbols produced can contribute to the perceived examples of image characteristics within the explicit movement class. In the second stage, the probability that the test symbol sequence corresponding to the perceived image descriptors will be generated by a unique HMM is estimated. This technique is used to solve three problems- i) to compute the chance of a sequence of observed events given in a particular model. ii) to find the most probable development of an unusual movement that is represented by the HMM. ii) to evaluate HMM parameters and produce a good representation of the most probable state sequence.

Through HMMs, American Sign Language (ASL) has been identified. Generally, HMMs do best DTW with undivided time series data and are therefore extensively applied to behavioral comprehension. Several machine vision applications can be solved by HMMs.

Deep Learning Models

In last few years, many deep learning algorithms have been developed in the field of image recognition, speech recognition, and eventually extended to research on action analysis with time series [8].

Deep neural framework for unusual activity recognition in a smart monitoring system contains 3 sections.

• Human recognition and discrimination module

• Module on pose classification

• An unusual action analysis module

For the above three modules, the models used correspondingly are as follows:

• You Only Look Once (YOLO) network

• A VGG-16 network

• Long Short-Term Memory (LSTM) and Recurrent Neural Network (RNN)

Based on object discrimination, Kalman filter is applied. "Posture classification" study recognizes ten kinds of poses.

In order to detect abnormal events in videos, an in-depth explanation of looks and gestures proposes a novel model called AMDN. It learns the representation of the function automatically. The proposed model uses layered de-noising auto-encoders for learning, looks and motion features individually and together. After learning, the multiple one-class Support Vector Machine is trained. Now these

SVMs calculate the abnormality score of each input. Further, these scores are pooled and an unusual event is recognized. Double fusion architecture is used in the model [9].

Convolutional Neural Network

Convolutional is a powerful network for deep learning methods. This is useful for images as inputs; however, it is also used for other applications, such as text, signals, *etc*. This framework is inspired by the biological structure of a visual cortex that includes the arrangements of simple and complicated cells. Visual field is based on the sub-regions and then activates these cells. Sub-areas are known as Receptive fields. The neurons in a CNN layer interface with sub-districts of the layers before that layer instead of being totally associated with various types of neural organization. Instead of being completely aligned with different kinds of neural structure, the neurons in a CNN layer interface with sub-districts of the layers before that layer. The neurons in the picture are latent in the regions beyond these sub-districts. A CNN diminishes the number of parameters relative to a less number of connections, mutual weights and down sampling. This architecture contains several layers, such as convolutional layers, maximum or average pooling layers, softmax functions or grouping layers, and fully connected layer [10].

A CNN-based approach for suspicious activity identification was proposed in a paper [2]. Automatically, this CNN-based approach discovers the characteristics of unusual behaviors. This methodology is applied to various topics, including different background effects, such as a person, two people, and crowd interactions, and tests the system's efficiency.

Recurrent Neural Network

RNN is best suitable for abnormal behavior recognition in real-time video. It is the most promising method of DNN. There are some variations of RNNs, known as LSTMs, VRNNs and GRU [11]. The sequence of activities and their spatial and temporal information with time series is crucial to scramble activities like an elderly person's daily routines. This type of information can provide crucial cues to recognize the daily patterns, and thus detect any abnormalities in those patterns. HMMs and RNNs approaches are used to capture the temporal and spatial association between activities that do not work in SVMs methods. Training sets and their corresponding labels of the datasets are fed as input into the RNNs. The learned model allots labels to each behavior case of that sequence when a new test sequence is added. In addition, the confidence value of the allocated mark for the new sequence is created by each trained model. At that point, the mean of certainty esteems is figured. Subsequently, when the model doles out it to a class label with a confidence score more noteworthy than the mean worth, another measure is added; at that point, the arrangement is known as usual activity, else it is treated as an unusual activity. RNN structures are utilized with regard to regular action and unusual event identification.

Vanilla Recurrent Neural Network (VRNN)

It is presumed that entire inputs and outputs are not dependent on one another in feed-forward network, whereas hidden states exist in RNNs whose activation at each point is dependent on the old times at each stage. It can also be said that RNN is well known for storing memory, which records the information that has been computed so far. Although, Vanilla RNNs have some drawbacks. They are not equipped for catching long-term dependencies on sequences due to the dying gradient problem. In theory, Recurrent Neural Network can utilize data in randomly long sequences; however, in practice, they are restricted to looking back on only some steps. Therefore, two other RNNs frameworks (LSTM, GRU) are proposed to overcome these drawbacks.

Long Short-Term Memory (LSTM)

LSTM's primary goal is to explain the question of long-term dependence on short-term memory. For temporal characteristics for successive frames, long short-term memory (LSTM) approach based on CNN is not sufficient for temporal variation in the facial components. The LSTM cells are designed to counter the effect of decreasing the gradients as error derivatives are backpropagated across several layers through time in repeating networks. An internal state representing the memory is monitored by each LSTM unit. After some time, the cells learn to output, and overwrite their internal memory, depending on their present input and previous internal states. This requires three gates (input, forget and output) that control the flow of information in and out of their memory.

Gated Recurrent Unit (GRU)

The GRU [11] is similar to LSTM, but includes fewer parameters than LSTM (except the output gate). Each hidden unit has two gates in the GRU architecture, known as an update gate and a reset gate. The Gated Recurrent Unit also controls the movement of information without using a memory unit to inhibit the vanishing gradient problem.

Datasets

A training and evaluation dataset has to be carefully curated in order to design a new recognition system or improve an existing system. To test the precision and efficiency of the proposed method, a dataset is a critical module. Various standard datasets are accessible in the diverse fields of human activity recognition.

Datasets of Abandoned Object Detection

• PETS dataset: This dataset is proposed to test the accuracy of the abandoned object detection system in the year 2006. There are numerous video scenes featuring various baggage and people involved in the case and the spatial relationship between the people and baggage. This database contains real-time video sequences of Multiview videos with occlusion, lightning effect, luggage drops, or left and crowd captures. Seven different situations are taken from different points of view by 4 cameras.
• CAVIAR dataset: This dataset covers two separate scenarios: a lobby entrance and a shopping center. Real-life activities include captured walking, engaging with other individuals, window shopping, visiting and exiting shops, fighting, passing and leaving luggage or bundle in a public area. 384 * 288 pixels are the resolution of these images.
• I-LIDS dataset: The I dataset is an intelligent detection system imagery library. Unattended bags of pictures of an underground station on the platforms are present in this dataset.
• CVSG dataset: There are various sequences in this dataset, and chrome-based methods for the simple removal of foreground masks have been documented. These masks are then compiled for various backgrounds. This sequence now has differing degrees of complexity with respect to the difficulty of segmentation of the foreground. Relinquished objects and objects that have been eliminated from the scene image are available in sequences.

Theft Detection Datasets

• Bank dataset: This database consists of video sequences. Out of 6 videos, four video sequences are composed of distinct instances of bank robberies, and two videos are of normal activities in the bank. Only one static camera is used to record the bank scenario in this dataset.

Falling Detection Dataset

● Multiple cameras fall dataset: This dataset involves standing, walking, dropping, laying on the floor and couch, crouching, and jumping up and down. So, with 8 cameras, there are 24 possibilities.
● Video sequences: This dataset was recorded in MJPEG format from an uncalibrated IP camera with a 320*240-pixel resolution. The assessment video consists of thirty normal daily exercises, such as leaning down, walking, sitting down and squatting down, as well as twenty-one replicated falls due to human imbalance, such as forward as well as backward falls, sideway falls and more falls.
● CAVIAR dataset: This dataset incorporates the fall of a person from various camera perspectives.

Violence Detection Datasets

● UCF101 dataset: This dataset is the largest and most challenging human action dataset. It includes varieties of actions with different camera viewpoints and cluttered background. It consists of 101 human acts, categorized into 5 forms of contact between human objects, person-person interaction, musical instruments, body-motion only, and games or sports. There are 50 actions from sports.
● Fight CIVAR dataset: It includes 4 video categorizations of battle scenes. The first and second video categories are composed of two persons meeting, battling and fleeing, while in the third video category, two persons meet, then battle among them, and one down and another person flees. Last in the fourth video category, two persons meet, and then battle, and subsequently chase each other.

Fire Detection Datasets

● Dynamic texture dataset from DynTex: It has a distinct array of dynamic surface videos of high quality. Processes, such as waves, flames, a banner flying in the wind, fire, a running elevator and a crowd, normally make up a dynamic floor. Most of the actual textures present in video sequences are dynamic, and both their set and dynamic characteristics must depend on them.
● MESH dataset: Many news videos are included. Videos relating to fire are eligible for efficiency assessment of the fire detection system.
● Sample dataset for fire and smoke video clips: This dataset includes smoke and fire video clips for estimating system performance.
● Fire sense dataset: In this dataset, there are 10 non-fire videos and 11 fire videos to validate the reliability of the system.

Miscellaneous Dataset

- KTH Dataset: Another dataset for human motion is KTH. In four different scenarios, this dataset contains 6 forms of human behavior (walking, jogging, running, boxing, hand-waving and hand clapping) conducted by 25 subjects. This dataset's resolution is 160*120 pixels. It has a homogeneous and chaos-free history. The frame number used for video classification in this dataset is about 1000 frames per video.
- BEHAVE dataset: This dataset contains both types of actions (normal and abnormal). It captures 25 frames per second, and the resolution of this dataset is 640*480 pixels. This dataset contains normal behaviors, such as walking together, splitting, running together, following and the meeting, and abnormal actions include ignoring, chasing, loitering and fighting. It has various actions; each video clip is manually split into some video sequences, and each sequence involves only one behavior. As a result, the dataset is divided into 1200 different behaviors that include 250 unusual behaviors and 950 usual behaviors.
- BOSS dataset: This dataset is recorded by 9 cameras at 25 frames per second at the training time and a resolution of 720*76 pixels. It contains three normal and eleven abnormal behavior videos. Abnormal behavior videos include grabbing mobile, fighting, harassing, fainting, grabbing the newspaper, and panicking. Segmentation of video sequences follows the same approach as in BEHAVE dataset. A total of 600 normal and 400 abnormal behaviors are split in this dataset.
- UT1 dataset: In this dataset, a total of six classes of human motion videos are included. It involves 976 pictures of handshaking, 983 pictures of pointing, 904 pictures of hugging, 1027 pictures of pushing, 872 pictures of kicking, and 847 images of punching. It also contains outdoor lawn images. A total of 24 videos of normal and 30 videos of abnormal behaviors are split.
- Hollywood human actions (HOHA): This dataset contains numerous video sequences from 32 films with 8 styles of acts, including Answering Phone, GetOutCar, Handshake, Hug Human, Kiss, Sit-Down, Sit-Up and Stand-Up. In addition, 1200 minutes of video is also available in which four new acts, Drive Vehicle, Feed, Fight and Run, are named. In this dataset, individuals in the photographs are mostly focused, and there is also cluttering in the background. Thus, this dataset is very interesting and challenging.
- CMU dataset: This dataset has eleven videos of which 6 are normal activity videos and 5 are abnormal activity videos. Normal behavior in this dataset comprises walking, shaking hands, and jogging, while uncommon behavior requires resistant acts and offensive movements. There are a total of 2477 images, of which 1209 are positive training images and 1268 are negative for research purposes. These images have a resolution of 32*240 pixels, and are then resized to 32*32 smaller pixels to reduce the training time.

Evaluation Metrics

To validate the exactness and the robustness of the smart video surveillance system for falling detection, violence detection, *etc.*, the evaluation metrics [12, 13] are one of the main tasks to check the performance of the system. There are two approaches for evaluating the different behaviors- Quantitatively and Qualitatively. In the Qualitative approach, the evaluation is based on pictorial interpretation by taking a gander at the processed image produced by the algorithm (for example, noise handling, illumination handling, shadow elimination *etc.*). While on the other hand, in the quantitative approach, facts and figures of calculated results are compared with factual data, and it is very challenging.

Here, we discuss several metrics that evaluate the performance of an IVS.

Accuracy

The accuracy metrics can be reported as a *True Positive* (TP) signifying the suspect behavior for the detection of an irregular activity, and a *False Negative* (FN) that applies to the unusual action classification as usual; *a False Positive* (FP) represents the classification of an usual activity as unusual, and a *True Negative* (TN) represents that the non-suspicious action is classified correctly. Several researchers use this metric by finding the TP, FP, FP, and FN from their research.

$$Accuracy = \frac{TP + TN}{TP + TN + FP + FN} \tag{1}$$

Precision (P_R), Recall (R_P) and F-measure (F_M)

The percentage of true alarms is calculated by P_R, whereas R_P is used to measure the percentage of detected events. F_M represents the model's accuracy on a dataset. Researchers have used precision and recall metrics together and evaluated the performance of the system.

$$Precision = \frac{TP}{TP + FP} \tag{2}$$

$$Recall = \frac{TP}{TP + FP} \tag{3}$$

$$F - measure = \frac{2 * Precision * Recall}{Precision + Recall} * 100 \qquad (4)$$

Sensitivity and Specificity

The authors use these metrics to check the performance of the person falling detection system. High in sensitivity applies to the maximum falls observed and the high specificity means that the usual actions are not known.

$$Sensitivity = \frac{TP}{TP + FN} \qquad (5)$$

$$Specificity = \frac{TN}{TN + FP} \qquad (6)$$

Percent Events Detected (P.E.D.) and Percent Alarms True (P.A.T.)

The PED score is the proportion of true alerts from factual data that are positively detected by the module to the number of actual data alarms. PAT score defines the proportion of alarms that correspond to the real alarm of factual data to the whole fractional alarms identified by the module. If the PED score is high, then it means that most items that can activate an alert are detected by the module, and if the PAT score is high, the module rarely triggers false alarms.

$$PED(\%) = \left(\frac{Number\ of\ real\ alarms\ detected}{Number\ of\ alarms} detected\right) * 100 \qquad (7)$$

$$PAT(\%) = \left(\frac{Number\ of\ real\ alarms\ detected}{Total\ number\ of\ alarms} detected\right) * 100 \qquad (8)$$

Confusion Metrics

A confusion matrix is often known as an error matrix or contingency table. This confusion matrix is used to evaluate the average and complete accuracy of the system and easily interprets the classification of wrong results. It is basically used to check the performance of a supervised system. The matrix of each column corresponds to the expected class, though each row signifies an actual class. It is very clear to understand, by the confusion matrix, where the method is perplexing or ambiguous between the classes.

ROC Curve

A ROC curve is a graphic representation that shows a binary classifier's output. By plotting the True Positive Rate at distinct threshold settings in the False Positive Rate proposal, the efficiency of the distinct parameters is measured using the ROC curve.

CONCLUSION

This chapter has discussed the framework and activity methods and techniques of an intelligent video surveillance system. We have discussed thoroughly the human behavior techniques, especially for normal and abnormal actions, such as abandoned or object detection, theft detection, violence activity, robbery, walking, running, *etc*. We have studied the techniques of preprocessing, foreground object identification, features extraction techniques, and classification, and also addressed some of the key techniques used in the identification of human actions. There are three common strategies to extract the features, optical flow, trajectory-based and region-based features. Various researchers have used different techniques to analyze the behavior of humans, such as ANN, HMM, Clustering, Deep learning models, CNN, LSTM, RNN, and GRU. Several researchers have utilized deep models to understand human behavior due to their better results. Many researchers have proposed their novel work with noise reduction and methods of handling occlusion to minimize the identification of false objects. Apart from these techniques, there are various standard datasets available for different purposes that have also been reviewed in this chapter. To check the performance of the system, there is a need for evaluation metrics. We have thus discussed accuracy, precision, recall, f-measure, sensitivity, specificity, PED, PAT, and confusion metrics in this chapter.

FUTURE SCOPE

As far as the future scope is concerned, a more vigorous detection and recognition algorithm must also be developed that can provide considerable performance at the time of occlusion, illumination effect, lightening state, shadow effect, and noisy data. In the future, at the time of the creation process, scholars can concentrate more on the speed and efficiency of the algorithm in the real-time environment. Earlier algorithms must be tested in real-time videos for better accuracy and consistency. However, still, some abnormal activities may not be recognized fairly because of their background effect. Apart from these suggestions, researchers may use deep learning techniques to resolve the background and other issues because of their different applications in various domains (for example, action recognition, language recognition, rehabilitation engineering, bio-medical, surveillance, *etc.*).

CONSENT FOR PUBLICATION

Not applicable.

CONFLICT OF INTEREST

The author declares no conflict of interest, financial or otherwise.

ACKNOWLEDGEMENTS

Declared none.

REFERENCES

[1]   R.K. Tripathi, A.S. Jalal, and S.C. Agrawal, "Suspicious human activity recognition: a review", *Artif. Intell. Rev.,* vol. 50, no. 2, pp. 283-339, 2018.
        [http://dx.doi.org/10.1007/s10462-017-9545-7]

[2]   N.C. Tay, T. Connie, T.S. Ong, K.O.M. Goh, and P.S. Teh, "A Robust Abnormal Behavior Detection Method Using Convolutional Neural Network", In: *Computational Science and Technology, Lecture Notes in Electrical Engineering.,* R. Alfred, Y. Lim, A. Ibrahim, P. Anthony, Eds., vol. 481. Springer: Singapore.
        [http://dx.doi.org/10.1007/978-981-13-2622-6_4]

[3]   K.K. Verma, B.M. Singh, and A. Dixit, "A review of supervised and unsupervised machine learning techniques for suspicious behavior recognition in intelligent surveillance system", *Int. J. Inf. Technol,* 2019.

[4]   J. Wang, and L. Xia, "Abnormal behavior detection in videos using deep learning", *Cluster Comput.,* vol. 22, no. S4, pp. 9229-9239, 2019.
        [http://dx.doi.org/10.1007/s10586-018-2114-2]

[5]   Y.S. Chong, and Y.H. Tay, "Modeling Representation of Videos for Anomaly Detection using Deep Learning: A Review", *Asian Control Conference (ASCC),* pp. 1-8, 2015.

[6]   Amrit Sarkar, *Human Activity and Behavior Recognition in Videos: A Brief Review.* GRIN Verlag GmbH Publication, 2014.https://www.grin.com/document/276054

[7]   O.P. Popoola, and Kejun Wang, "Video-based abnormal human behavior recognitiona review", *IEEE Trans. Syst. Man Cybern. C,* vol. 42, no. 6, pp. 865-878, 2012.
        [http://dx.doi.org/10.1109/TSMCC.2011.2178594]

[8]   B. Yu, "Design and Implementation of Behavior Recognition System Based on Convolutional Neural Network", *ITM Web Conf.,* vol. 12, p. 01025, 2017.
        [http://dx.doi.org/10.1051/itmconf/20171201025]

[9]   G. Sreenu, and M.A. Saleem Durai, "Intelligent video surveillance: a review through deep learning techniques for crowd analysis", *J. Big Data,* vol. 6, no. 1, p. 48, 2019.
        [http://dx.doi.org/10.1186/s40537-019-0212-5]

[10]   V. Yadav, and R. Shukla, "Human Behavioral Analyzer using Machine Learning Technique", *Int. J. Eng. Adv. Technol.,* vol. 8, no. 6, pp. 5150-5154, 2019. [IJEAT].
        [http://dx.doi.org/10.35940/ijeat.F8531.088619]

[11]   D. Arifoglu, and A. Bouchachia, "Activity Recognition and Abnormal Behaviour Detection with Recurrent Neural Networks", *Procedia Comput. Sci.,* vol. 110, pp. 86-93, 2017.
        [http://dx.doi.org/10.1016/j.procs.2017.06.121]

[12]   R. Jayaswal, and J. Jha, "A hybrid approach for image retrieval using visual descriptors", *Proceeding - IEEE International Conference on Computing, Communication and Automation, ICCCA 2017,* vol. 2, 2017.
[http://dx.doi.org/10.1109/CCAA.2017.8229965]

[13]   R. Jayaswal, and M. Dixit, "Comparative Analysis of Human Face Recognition by Traditional Methods and Deep Learning in Real-Time Environment", *IEEE 9th International Conference on Communication Systems and Network Technologies,* pp. 66-71, 2020.
[http://dx.doi.org/10.1109/CSNT48778.2020.9115779]

CHAPTER 5

Load Balanced Clustering in WSN using MADM Approaches

Lekhraj[1,*], **Alok Kumar**[1], **Avjeet Singh**[1] and **Anoj Kumar**[1]

[1] *Motilal Nehru National Institute of Technology Allahabad, Prayagraj Uttar Pradesh, India*

Abstract: Over the last several decades, wireless sensor networks have grabbed a lot of attention because of their wide range of applications in scientific communities as well as industrial aspects. In WSN, sensor nodes are created with very limited resources, imposing energy constraints. Therefore, it is important to design a less energy-consuming, ascendible and power-efficient approach by selecting the optimal cluster heads (CHs) to enhance the life of these networks. Clustered sensor network is a method to optimize the power consumption in the network, which greatly affects the performance of the networks. In this article, we looked at clustering and routing issues by employing intelligent optimization techniques by considering the maximum attribute of the wireless sensor networks (WSN), which are conflicting in nature. The efficiency of WSN mainly depends upon the conflicting attributes, like residual energy, CH to base station distance, normal node to CH distance, *etc*. In this paper, multi-attribute decision making (MADM) technique is considered for choosing the optimal CHs, so that energy consumption of the nodes is minimized and lifetime of the network can be maximized. The proposed approach is compared with other approaches like LEACH, HEED, *etc*. Results verified that the proposed algorithm is outmatched in comparison to existing algorithms.

Keywords: Clustering, EECS, HEED, LEACH, LEACH-C, Multi-attribute decision making, Multi-objective decision making.

INTRODUCTION

VLSI, MEMS, and other technologies have led to the growth of tiny, cheap, and low-energy wireless sensor nodes equipped with three main units: a radio frequency (RF) transceiver, a processor, and a sensor unit that can sense, calculate, and communicate wirelessly. Battery-powered sensor nodes are often located at remote geographic locations, and their energy source cannot be replenished. New applications for monitoring, environmental control and protection are possible due to the deployment of a large number of sensor nodes

*[*] **Corresponding author Lekhraj Chaudhary:** Motilal Nehru National Institute of Technology Allahabad, Prayagraj Uttar Pradesh, India; E-mail: lekhraj@mnnit.ac.in

Vikash Yadav, Parashuram Pal & Chuan-Ming Liu (Eds.)

in the target area and the processing of information received from them. The wireless sensor node network (WSN) is capable of sensing environmental information, such as temperature, pressure, humidity, lighting, *etc.* The network is also capable of compressing, filtering, and analyzing data to some extent. The information collected and processed is usually transmitted to one or more base stations. Nodes forward data through intermediate nodes designed for the base station. A base station (BS) serves as a gateway between a wired network and a wireless network. Thus, nodes act as routers in addition to recognition. Nodes can communicate directly with nodes within their maximum transmission range. Unit Disk Graphs (UDGs) are node intersection graphs with equal transmission ranges and provide a theoretical graph model for developing algorithms for WSNs.

While conventional networks strive to achieve high-quality services or high bandwidth, sensor network protocols should focus primarily on communication efficiency, focusing on energy saving. For the development of WSN protocols, this trade-off offers the possibility of extending the service life due to lower throughput or higher node deployment density. The lifetime of a network in sensor networks is called the time elapsed until the first node (or last node) in the network completely depletes its energy. In applications where all nodes are critical, the lifetime refers to the time when the first node dies.

Recently, wireless sensor networks (WSNs) have received a lot of attention as no existing communication infrastructure is required to deploy sensor nodes. They are widely used in health monitoring [1], video and audio search [2], forest fire detection, surveillance purposes [3], *etc.* Such networks consist of nodes with various sensor sensors, a battery source, processor, and storage components [4] to collect data from hard-to-reach areas, called remote areas. The main thing to use effectively is battery power in the sensor nodes because once the sensor assembly is deployed, recharging or replacing the battery is not an easy task. The many algorithms designed to provide energy savings for WSN clustering arethose based on statistics.

Clustering is a method by which a cluster head (CH) is selected to conserve power in the WSN, as shown in Fig. (**1**). The CH channel collects data from its member nodes by using a technique called time division multiple access (TDMA), and after receiving the data from all the member nodes, CH applies an aggregation technique to that data for removing the redundancy. After applying aggregation and compression, CH sends the resultant data to the base station [5].

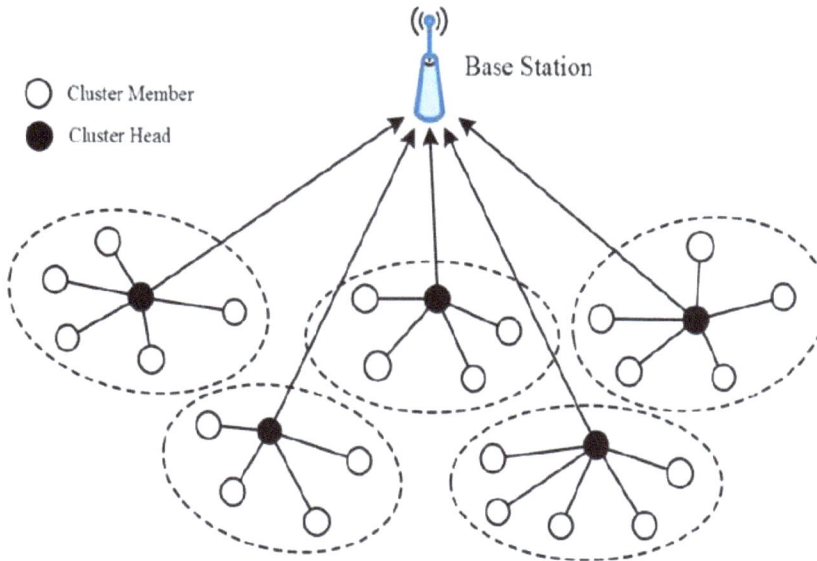

Fig. (1). Clustering in WSNs [5].

Clustering gives many fruitful benefits, like bandwidth management and allowing nodes to remain idle for a period of time, scalability to the network, and reducing the communication between nodes within a cluster, which leads to energy savings. Network performance of the clustering-based approaches is directly affected by the performance of the CHs, so the selection of CH is a very important step in every clustering technique. Choosing CH based on one criterion (for example, residual energy) can lead to poor performance, because the chosen CH cannot be a good selection. Besides the residual energy, other parameters also need to be considered, such as the distance from other nodes and distance from the member nodes to respective CHs, the centroid cluster, *etc.*

In the current work, we have expanded the criteria for selecting a cluster head to eight different parameters so that the most efficient node can be selected as a cluster head using the TOPSIS and PROMETHEE approaches. The parameters are shown in Table **1**.

Table 1. Criterion values supposed for our experimental purpose.

Criterion Description	Symbol	Parameter Value
Number of nodes	N	100
Deployment area	M*M	100*100, 200*200
BS position	-	Variable

(Table 1) cont.....

Criterion Description	Symbol	Parameter Value
Data packet size	-	4000 bit
Control packet size	-	100 bit
Energy consumed by the amplifier at free space model	ε_{fs}	10 pj/bit/m^2
Energy consumed by amplifier at multipath model	ε_{mp}	0.0013 pj/bit/m^4
Initial sensor nodes' energy	-	0.2 j
Initial energy of the gateways	-	1 j
Energy consumed in the circuit	E_{elec}	50 nj/bit
Gateways chosen as CHs	-	Calculated

LITERATURE SURVEY

To provide power businesslike approach towards a WSN is a difficult task in the current environment. So there is a need for such an approach that gives long duration to the WSN network in the data collection or communication. Because in a traditional network, data communication is done directly, which is not efficient.

Direct communication limits the lifetime of the WSN because it consumes more energy to transmit the data to the Base Station (BS). To overcome this limitation, clustering approaches are employed. Various clustering approaches have been suggested by many researchers [6, 7].

Several works have been done to aggregate data on a wireless sensor network, which reduces power consumption. Clustering in WSN is an efficient procedure for reducing the power consumption of sensor nodes. In cluster routing algorithms for wireless networks, LEACH is known for its simplicity and efficiency. In LEACH, CHs are randomly selected, and all non-CHs are generated based on the received signal strength from the CHs. In LEACH, every node can become a channel, there is no channel selection scheme, and all nodes have the same chance of becoming a communication channel, so LEACH is ineffective. The channels are chosen at random, and the energy is distributed equally among all the nodes. Channels collect all sensed information from their cluster.

LEACH protocol uses clustering for exchanging the information from one sensor to another. It makes a cluster by considering the signal strength of the sensors. In LEACH, every cluster sends the data to BS after performing aggregation over the data. CH is selected periodically among the cluster nodes. It forms a cluster based on individual perception of the nodes, and this type of clustering belongs to distributed category. In this approach, every channel has a direct link to the sink, whether it is nearer to the sink or not [8, 9].

All existing approaches require either knowledge of network density or uniform dispersion of nodes in the field. Eunice and Fahmy [10] proposed hybrid energy-efficient distributed clustering (HEED). HEED makes no assumptions about the network, such as density and size. Each node operates individually in the HEED protocol. At the end of the process, each node becomes either a cluster head or a child with respect to the cluster head. The residual energy of the node is the first parameter when choosing the cluster header, and the proximity to its neighbors or the degree of the node is the second. HEED generates a single-level hierarchical clustering structure for intra-cluster communication. HEED also does not guarantee that the selected number of elected CHs would be optimum. In a study [11], a hybrid approach to aggregation based on clusters has been presented, which adaptively selects the appropriate data aggregation function. This document shows the improvement in power consumption versus target speed. Dynamic clustering shows the best performance at high target speeds.

The Energy Efficient Distributed Unequal Clustering (EEDUC) algorithm provides a new way to create distributed clusters. Here, each sensory node sets a waiting time. This waiting time is considered as a function of the residual energy of the number of nodes in the neighborhood. It uses latency to distribute cluster headers, and Fast Local Clustering (FLOC) creates non-overlapping clusters of roughly the same size. Clustering is performed in such a way that all nodes within a unit distance from the cluster head belong to its cluster, and a node located at a distance of m units from the cluster head can belong to its cluster.

The Energy Efficient Clustering Scheme (EECS) is an improved clustering algorithm over LEACH and is suitable for periodic data collection applications. Here, the network is divided into several clusters, and communication is carried out between the CH channel and the base station. In the EECS, CH candidates compete to advance to CH in a given round. In this competition, candidates broadcast their residual energy to neighboring candidates. If a given node does not find a node with higher residual energy, it becomes CH. Differing from leaching in terms of forming clusters, EECS extends LEACH by dynamically sizing clusters based on the distance of the cluster from the base station.

In Threshold Sensitive Energy Efficient Sensor Network (TEEN) [12], the CH channel sends hard and soft thresholds to its members. Due to the increased power consumption, a lower soft threshold value generates more accurate network information, so users can control the trade-off between energy efficiency and data accuracy by adjusting the parameters. Moreover, the soft threshold can be changed, and users can change the new parameters as needed each time the cluster changes.

In recent studies, optimization approaches have shown good performance in clustering [13, 14]. Particle Swarm Optimization (PSO) is a way to increase the lifetime of the network. The algorithm proposes to construct paths and distribute routing data through clusters near base stations or the heads of gateway nodes to maximize the network time axis.

Genetic Algorithm (GA) belongs to optimization [15], which can be used for clustering to provide efficient solution in CHs selection. The algorithm can be changed by selecting many other attributes in the function [16], such as selecting one of the two signal ranges from normal sensors, the state of the sensor node, and selecting the appropriate channel. GA [17] can select the best topology management to obtain less power consumption and achieve balance.

In addition to these approaches for selecting nodes as CH, there are some other approaches [18 - 21]. In these approaches, gateways play a role like CHs, responsible for collecting and transmitting data. The power of the gateways is higher than ordinary nodes. As presented in an article [22], receivers can acts as gateways to collect information from sensors. AHP [23] is widely used in various fields of technology [24 - 29]. AHP is also used to select CH based on power, movement and distance to the centroid of the cluster. TOPSIS [30] is used to select CH channels [31] based on three parameters distance from the node to BS, total neighbors of the CH and remaining energy of the node. However, we cannot conclude that these are sufficient to achieve an optimal approach, since power loss can depend on other parameters; for example, the CHs closest to the BSs having higher residual energy can be chosen, but it is possible that some sensors have a longer communication distance to transmit detected information, which degrades network life and detection capabilities. Thus, MADM is a new application method in WSN, but some more important factors must be taken into account.

RADIO MODEL AND UNDERTAKING

The network model selected by the algorithm in this article is as follows:

Undertaking

1. Nodes are distributed randomly in a 2-dimensional space.

2. Sensor nodes sense the data from their surrounding and communicate the sensed information to the respective CHs.

3. Few gateways work as CHs, which accept the sensed data from the nodes.

4. Gateways' energy is five times more than the nodes.

5. BS knows the location of the gateways and nodes.

6. BS has infinite energy for communication.

7. Sensor nodes can change their mode from active to sleep and sleep to active.

Radio Model

In the WSN, the sensor senses information from its vicinity and sends data to corresponding CHs, and the CHs send the aggregated information to the sink after collecting the information. In this kind of process, we need representation to adjust the power exhaustion. We adopted an ordinal model of hardware energy consumption, as shown in Fig. (**2**).

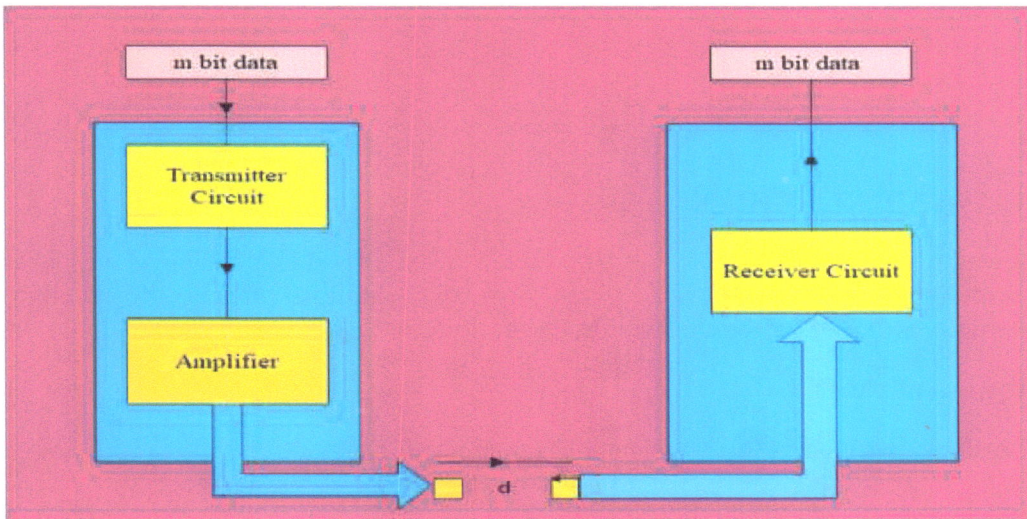

Fig. (2). Energy model.

For experimental purposes, we believe that fading in multipath and space-free channel depends on the distance between the transmitter and the receiver. The energy amplifier can limit the power exhaust and control it; for example, if the transmission distance is smaller than the threshold 1 d0', only the free space model is used, and if its value is larger than the threshold, then multipath model is used to transmit the data. For transmitting m bit message data to d distance, the required energy is:

$$X_{2ij} = X_{1ij} * W_j \, i = 1, 2 \ldots p \text{ and } j = 1, 2 \ldots k \ldots$$

Transmitter end's power consumption to transmit the message is represented as follows:

$$E_{TX} = \frac{m * E_{elec} + m * \varepsilon_{fs} * d^2 \quad if\ d \leq d0}{m * E_{elec} + m * \varepsilon_{mp} * d^4 \quad if\ d \geq d0} \cdots$$ (1)

Receiver end's energy consumption to receive the message is presented as follows:

$$E_{RX} = m * E_{elec} \quad \cdots$$ (2)

The optimal number of CHs is calculated for the simulation [3], as shown in equation 3.

$$k_{opt} = \sqrt{\frac{n}{2\pi}} * \sqrt{\frac{\varepsilon_{fs}}{\varepsilon_{mp}}} * \frac{M}{d^2_{to\ BS}} \cdots$$ (3)

MADM APPROACHES

Nowadays, MADM approaches are widely used to solve problems, which are uncertain in nature. MADM gives the best solution among the available alternatives based on certain attributes or criteria.

Topsis Approach

The steps involved in the Topsis approach are as follows:

Step 1: Evaluate an initial matrix of p populations and k attributes, matrix $(X_{ij})_{p*k}$

Step 2: Calculate normalized matrix $(X_{1ij})_{p*k}$:

$$X_{1ij} = \frac{X_{ij}}{\sqrt{\sum_{i=1}^{p} X_{ij}^2}} i = 1, 2 \ldots p \text{ and } j = 1, 2 \ldots k \ldots$$ (4)

Step 3: Compute weighted normalized matrix $(X_{2ij})_{p*k}$

$$X_{2ij} = X_{1ij} * W_j i = 1, 2 \ldots p \text{ and } j = 1, 2 \ldots k \ldots$$ (5)

Where, W_j represents j^{th} attribute weight and $\sum W_j = 1$.

Step 4: Best V_j^+ and worst V_j^- for each attribute is selected.

Step 5: Calculate Euclidean distance from best and worst conditions:

$$F_y{}^+ = \sqrt{\Sigma_{j=1}^{p}(X_{2ij} - V_j{}^+)^2}\,i = 1,2\dots p\dots \tag{6}$$

$$F_y{}^- = \sqrt{\Sigma_{j=1}^{p}(X_{2ij} - V_j{}^-)^2}\,i = 1,2\dots p\dots \tag{7}$$

Step 6: Calculate the similarity of the alternative to the ideal solution (P_i):

$$P_i = \frac{S_i{}^-}{S_i{}^+ + S_i{}^-}\dots \tag{8}$$

Step 7: Available solutions are promoted on the basis of Pi value, the larger value of Pi takes the highest rank.

Promethee Approach

The steps included in the Promethee approach are as follows:

Step 1: Generate matrices of size p*p, called domination matrices for every attribute.

Step 2: Calculate the final matrix D_{p*p} by adding all weighted metrics-

$$\left(M_j\right)_{p*p} = \left(D_j\right)_{p*p} * W_j\dots \tag{9}$$

Where, W_j represents j^{th} attribute weight and $\Sigma W_j = 1$.

$$D_{p*p} = \Sigma_{j=1}^{k}\left(M_j\right)_{p*p}\,i = 1,2\dots p\dots \tag{10}$$

Step 3: Compute μ^+ by performing summation to all rows and μ^- by performing summation to all columns of domination matrices-

$$\mu_i{}^+ = \Sigma_{j=1}^{k} D_{i*j}\,i = 1,2\dots p^{th}\,\text{row}\dots \tag{11}$$

$$\mu_i{}^- = \Sigma_{i=1}^{k} D_{j*i}\,j = 1,2\dots p^{th}\,\text{column}\dots \tag{12}$$

Step 4: Compute net flow μ_i

$$\mu_i{}^- = \mu_i{}^+ - \mu_i{}^-\dots \tag{13}$$

Step 5: Available solutions are promoted on the basis of μ_i value, the larger value of μ_i takes the highest rank.

ATTRIBUTES USED IN SIMULATED WORK

There are various attributes that affect data collection in WSN. We consider 8 attributes. Among these, few are beneficiary in nature, and few are non-beneficiary. Beneficiary criteria require a larger value for efficient energy consumption, but for non-beneficiary criteria, a smaller value is good for providing the best solution. The description of attributes is presented in Table **2**.

Table 2. Attributes' nature distribution.

S.no.	Attributes	Nature of Attributes
1	Coverage_of_CHs	Beneficial
2	CHs_Avg_Distance	Non-Beneficial
3	BS_Avg_Distance	Non-Beneficial
4	Avg_Eresidual	Beneficial
5	CHs_Avg_lifetime	Beneficial
6	BS_CH_Bearing	Beneficial
7	BS_Max_Distance	Non-Beneficial
8	Eres_Con_CHS	Beneficial

Coverage_of_CHs

In this case, the number of sensor nodes is calculated, whose respective CHs are equal to or less than "d_0". The higher value confirms lower power consumption, because in this case, a larger number of nodes will be closer to the corresponding CH. This is a beneficial attribute, so this attribute requires a higher value.

$$\text{Coverage\_of\_CHs} = \frac{\left(Count_{Nodes_t}\left(Min\left(Dist_{(Node_t} - CHs\right)\right) \leq d_0\right)\right)}{n} * 100 \qquad (14)$$

Where, $d_0 = \sqrt{\frac{\varepsilon_{fs}}{\varepsilon_{mp}}}$; $Dist_{(Nodes_t - CH_s)}$ denotes the distance of nodes to the CHs &$Count\_Nodes_t$count number of nodes t.

CHs_Avg_Distance

It calculates the mean distance from all nodes to the corresponding CH. This is a non-beneficial attribute, so this attribute requires a lower value. The lower value stipulates that to transmit the data from nodes to corresponding CHs, smaller distance is needed.

$$\text{CHs\_Avg\_Distance} = \frac{\sum_{t=1}^{n} Dist(Node_t - Near_{CH})}{n} \tag{15}$$

BS_AVG_DISTANCE

It presents all distances' average from the selected CH to the BS. A smaller value stipulates that CHs are closer to the BS. The suggested value is computed:

$$\text{BS\_Avg\_Distance} = \frac{\sum_{t=1}^{Tot\_Opt\_CHS} Dist_{(CH_t - BS)}}{Tot\_Opt\_CHs} \tag{16}$$

Where, $Dist_{(CH_t - BS)}$ indicates CH 't' to BS distance and Tot_Opt_CHs shows total optimal CHs.

Avg_Eresidual

It presents the mean of the CHs unfinished power. The larger value indicates that selected gateways as CHs have higher remaining power and that they can accept more data and communicate it to BS. The calculation formula is as follows:

$$\text{Avg\_Eresidual} = \frac{\sum_{t=1}^{Tot\_Opt\_CHS} Eresidual\_CH_t}{Tot\_Opt\_CHs} \tag{17}$$

Where, $Eresidual\_CH_t$ shows selected CHs remaining energy.

CHs_Avg_lifetime

It presents the average lifespan of CH. A larger value indicates that the CH can transmit further information, which means that the life of the CH is longer. The calculation formula is as follows:

$$\text{CHs\_Avg\_lifetime} = \frac{\sum_{t=1}^{Tot\_Opt\_CHS} (Eres_{CH_t} / Avg\_Transmission\_Energy\_required)}{Tot\_Opt\_CHs} \tag{18}$$

Where $Avg\_Transmission\_Energy_{required}$ indicates the average of the transmission energy required to transfer the data.

BS_CH_Bearing

It presents that the CHs are in a total distance less than d0 from the BS. A higher value indicates that the distance from the selected CH to the BS is shorter, which means that less power of the CH will be consumed in the data transmitted to the BS. The calculation formula is as follows:

$$\text{BS\_CH\_Bearing} = \frac{\left(Count\_CHs_t\left(\left(Dist_{(CH_t}-BS)\leq d_0\right)\right)\right)}{Tot\_Opt\_CHs} \tag{19}$$

Where, $(Dist_{(CH_t} - BS)$ indicates CH 't' to BS distance; $Count_{CHs_t}$ shows CH count.

BS_Max_Distance

It represents the farthest distance between any selected CH and BS. A lower value of that shows that the selected CHs need a shorter distance to this value for the information transmission. This suggests that the total energy consumption is very less. The calculation formula is:

$$\text{BS\_Max\_Distance} = Max\left(Distance_{CH_t} - BS\right) \tag{20}$$

Eres_Con_CHS

The CHs with the smaller distance to the BS are called the "connected CH". It computes the average remaining energy of CHs with a smaller distance to BS. Its higher value indicates that the distance of CH is less than "d_0" and it has higher residual power. The calculation formula is:

$$\text{Eres\_Con\_CHS} = \frac{\sum_{t=1}^{Tot\_Opt\_CHs} Dist(CH_t-BS)\leq d_0}{Tot\_Opt\_CHs} \tag{21}$$

DATA SET AND EVOLUTION METHOD

MATLAB is used to model the WSN. Twenty random populations are created to preserve greater differences between the alternatives. The difference gives good direction for the proposed technique. Data set has been computed using equations 14-21 for each population. Abbreviations of the attributes are presented in Table 3. Table **4** shows generated data set. Table **6** contains attribute weights for this simulation.

Table 3. Abbreviation table of attributes.

Abbreviation	Attributes
β1	Coverage_of_CHs
β 2	CHs_Avg_Distance
β 3	BS_Avg_Distance
β 4	Avg_Eresidual
β 5	CHs_Avg_lifetime
β 6	BS_CH_Bearing
β 7	BS_Max_Distance
β 8	Eres_Con_CHS

Table 4. Generated dataset.

Pop	Attributes							
	β 1	β 2	β 3	β 4	β 5	β 6	β 7	β 8
1	99.5124	38.5431	65.9821	0.5972	2286.9306	0.5926	435.862	1.7962
2	94.1703	42.9621	75.3921	0.6895	2385.8605	0.5875	550.8952	2.587
3	95.128	46.8075	77.891	0.6975	1506.9382	0.489	432.379	3.9705
4	96.2753	32.9705	58.002	0.7529	1475.9309	0.7985	485.8592	0.7935
5	96.5803	78.8073	61.8705	0.7786	1008.7542	0.786	570.7029	1.8971
6	100	50.8703	69.9325	0.7297	1276.8452	0.827	525.8502	1.9602
7	92.5803	41.7306	71.8971	0.513	1487.9305	0.6297	467.897	2.0928
8	93.7853	52.738	75.9073	0.4359	2210.8509	0.7542	490.7305	2.5276
9	94.1897	65.9302	56.5185	0.5078	985.8675	0.7689	515.7802	1.0902
10	100	58.7009	59.9075	0.6975	1210.8675	0.5439	456.7834	1.097
11	98.7362	56.8905	81.7036	0.3174	1225.9375	0.587	634.8972	3.8706
12	97.1935	55.7306	86.7952	0.3256	1376.8795	0.554	520.7396	3.879
13	97.1837	98.7306	62.739	0.3876	1465.8709	0.5966	614.8972	3.0502
14	99.6392	86.7958	66.587	0.4895	1585.9306	0.7552	602.7392	1.0972
15	96.8932	68.9001	68.9372	0.469	1175.2436	0.7992	610.8705	1.9972
16	93.5871	38.5496	70.0025	0.4952	2020.9265	0.8229	594.8762	1.8765
17	98.73	72.5306	70.2926	0.5875	2010.8534	0.6242	484.8702	2.0502
18	99.8409	69.8971	80.9305	0.593	2520.5211	0.5999	472.5971	0.9972
19	100	63.509	85.9372	0.5525	2227.5647	0.7999	532.876	1.8609
20	92.185	66.5397	81.9076	0.254	2068.9752	0.7142	542.8769	1.9872

Table 5. Normalized matrix.

Pop	Attributes							
	$\beta\,1$	$\beta\,2$	$\beta\,3$	$\beta\,4$	$\beta\,5$	$\beta\,6$	$\beta\,7$	$\beta\,8$
1	0.22976	0.13964	0.20488	0.23699	0.19347	0.19208	0.18365	0.17318
2	0.21743	0.15565	0.2341	0.27362	0.30616	0.19043	0.23211	0.24943
3	0.21964	0.16958	0.24186	0.27679	0.19338	0.1585	0.18218	0.38282
4	0.22229	0.11945	0.1801	0.29878	0.1894	0.25882	0.20471	0.076507
5	0.22299	0.28551	0.19211	0.30898	0.12945	0.25477	0.24046	0.18291
6	0.23089	0.1843	0.21715	0.28957	0.16385	0.26806	0.22156	0.189
7	0.21376	0.15119	0.22325	0.20358	0.19094	0.20353	0.19714	0.20178
8	0.21654	0.19107	0.2357	0.17298	0.28371	0.24446	0.20676	0.2437
9	0.21747	0.23886	0.17549	0.20151	0.12651	0.24923	0.21732	0.10511
10	0.12389	0.21267	0.18602	0.27679	0.15538	0.1763	0.19246	0.10577
11	0.22797	0.20611	0.2537	0.12596	0.15732	0.19027	0.26751	0.37319
12	0.22441	0.20191	0.26951	0.12921	0.17669	0.17957	0.21941	0.374
13	0.22439	0.35769	0.19481	0.15381	0.18811	0.19338	0.25908	0.29409
14	0.23006	0.31445	0.20676	0.19425	0.20351	0.24479	0.25396	0.10579
15	0.22372	0.24962	0.21406	0.18612	0.15081	0.25905	0.25738	0.19256
16	0.21608	0.13966	0.21736	0.19651	0.25933	0.26673	0.25065	0.18093
17	0.22796	0.26277	0.21826	0.23314	0.25804	0.20233	0.2043	0.19767
18	0.23052	0.25323	0.2513	0.23532	0.32344	0.19445	0.19912	0.096147
19	0.23089	0.23009	0.26684	0.21925	0.28585	0.25928	0.22452	0.17942
20	0.21284	0.24107	0.25433	0.1008	0.2655	0.2315	0.22874	0.1916

Table 6. Weights used in computation.

Attributes	$\beta\,1$	$\beta\,2$	$\beta\,3$	$\beta\,4$	$\beta\,5$	$\beta\,6$	$\beta\,7$	$\beta\,8$
Weights	0.125	0.125	0.125	0.125	0.125	0.125	0.125	0.125

CHs Selection using TOPSIS

TOPSIS approach follows the following steps for computation:

Step 1: Initial generated data set is shown in Table **4**.

Step 2: Table **5** contains normalized data; normalized matrix is calculated by using equation 4 after applying to Table **4**.

Step 3: Table **7** shows the weighted normalization matrix, calculated by using equation 5 after applying to Table **5**.

Table 7. Weighted normalized matrix.

Pop	Attributes							
	β 1	**β 2**	**β 3**	**β 4**	**β 5**	**β 6**	**β 7**	**β 8**
1	0.028720	0.017455	0.025610	0.029624	0.036684	0.024010	0.022956	0.0216480
2	0.027179	0.019456	0.029262	0.034202	0.038271	0.023804	0.029014	0.0311790
3	0.027455	0.021197	0.030232	0.034599	0.024172	0.019813	0.022772	0.0478530
4	0.027786	0.014931	0.022513	0.037347	0.023675	0.032353	0.025589	0.0095633
5	0.027874	0.035689	0.024014	0.038622	0.016181	0.031846	0.030057	0.0228640
6	0.028861	0.023037	0.027143	0.036197	0.020481	0.033508	0.027695	0.0236250
7	0.026720	0.018898	0.027906	0.025447	0.023867	0.025441	0.024643	0.0252230
8	0.027067	0.023883	0.029462	0.021623	0.035463	0.030558	0.025846	0.0304630
9	0.027184	0.029857	0.021937	0.025189	0.015814	0.031154	0.027165	0.0131390
10	0.028861	0.026584	0.023252	0.034599	0.019423	0.022037	0.024058	0.0132210
11	0.028496	0.025764	0.031712	0.015745	0.019665	0.023784	0.033438	0.0466490
12	0.028051	0.025238	0.033688	0.016151	0.022086	0.022446	0.027426	0.0467500
13	0.028048	0.044712	0.024351	0.019227	0.023513	0.024173	0.032385	0.0367610
14	0.028757	0.039307	0.025845	0.024281	0.025439	0.030599	0.031745	0.0132240
15	0.027964	0.031202	0.026757	0.023265	0.018852	0.032381	0.032173	0.0240700
16	0.027010	0.017458	0.027170	0.024564	0.032417	0.033342	0.031331	0.0226160
17	0.028495	0.032847	0.027283	0.029143	0.032255	0.025291	0.025537	0.0247090
18	0.028815	0.031654	0.031412	0.029416	0.040431	0.024306	0.024891	0.0120180
19	0.028861	0.028761	0.033355	0.027407	0.035731	0.032410	0.028065	0.0224280
20	0.028720	0.017455	0.025610	0.029624	0.036684	0.024010	0.022956	0.0216480

Step 4: Table **8** shows Top and Bottom values of each attribute.

Table 8. Chosen attributes' Top and Bottom values.

Attributes	V^+_j	V^-_j
β1	0.028861	0.026606
β2	0.014931	0.044712
β 3	0.021937	0.033688
β 4	0.038622	0.0126

(Table 8) cont.....

Attributes	V^+_j	V^-_j
β 5	0.040431	0.015814
β 6	0.033508	0.019813
β 7	0.022772	0.033438
β 8	0.047853	0.0095633

Step 5: Table **9** shows Euclidean distance for every population, calculated by using equations 6-7.

Table 9. F^+_y and F^-_y values.

Pop	F^+_y	F^-_y
1	0.029049015	0.042562515
2	0.021519545	0.046168008
3	0.022471521	0.051954757
4	0.04196805	0.043660608
5	0.041274166	0.034453166
6	0.033420424	0.038917778
7	0.032329378	0.035832331
8	0.027667553	0.039106362
9	0.047295005	0.026425905
10	0.043218391	0.032340528
11	0.036442379	0.042217799
12	0.034268548	0.043118439
13	0.042560023	0.030859098
14	0.048162098	0.021378602
15	0.040592994	0.026932766
16	0.031894231	0.039523047
17	0.032816188	0.03242182
18	0.042205321	0.034184932
19	0.033875801	0.035051655
20	0.033875801	0.028838877

Step 6: Table **10** shows the performance score for each alternative, calculated by using equation 8.

Table 10. Calculated values of all populations.

Pop	P_w
1	0.58767
2	0.67102
3	0.68362
4	0.51003
5	0.4549
6	0.539
7	0.52108
8	0.58428
9	0.3582
10	0.42417
11	0.53217
12	0.55129
13	0.4172
14	0.30705
15	0.39902
16	0.55439
17	0.49239
18	0.44434
19	0.50879
20	0.41236

Step 7: Table **11** shows the ranking of alternatives based on their performance score.

Table 11. TOPSIS ranking.

Pop	1	2	3	4	5	6	7	8	9	10	11	12	13	14	15	16	17	18	19	20
Rank	18	19	20	11	8	14	12	17	2	6	13	15	5	1	3	16	9	7	10	4

CHs Selection using PROMETHEE

PROMETHEE approach follows the following steps for computation:

Step 1: Compute matrices of p*p size for criteria shown in Tables **12 - 19**.

Table 12. Coverage_of_CH domination matrix.

Pop	1	2	3	4	5	6	7	8	9	10	11	12	13	14	15	16	17	18	19	20
1	-	0	0	0	1	0	0	1	0	0	0	1	0	1	1	0	0	0	0	0
2	1	-	0	0	1	0	1	1	1	1	1	1	1	1	1	1	0	0	1	1
3	1	1	-	1	1	1	1	1	1	1	1	1	1	1	1	1	0	1	1	1
4	1	1	0	-	1	1	1	1	1	1	1	1	1	1	1	0	0	1	1	1
5	0	0	0	0	-	0	0	1	0	0	0	1	0	1	0	0	0	0	0	0
6	1	1	0	0	1	-	1	1	1	1	1	1	1	1	1	0	0	1	1	1
7	1	0	0	0	1	0	-	1	0	0	1	1	1	1	1	0	0	1	0	0
8	0	0	0	0	0	0	0	-	0	0	0	0	0	0	0	0	0	0	0	0
9	1	0	0	0	1	0	1	1	-	1	1	1	1	1	1	0	0	1	1	1
10	1	0	0	0	1	0	1	1	0	-	1	1	1	1	1	0	0	1	0	1
11	1	0	0	0	1	0	0	1	0	0	-	1	1	1	1	0	0	1	0	0
12	0	0	0	0	0	0	0	1	0	0	0	-	0	0	0	0	0	0	0	0
13	1	0	0	0	1	0	0	1	0	0	0	1	-	1	1	0	0	1	0	0
14	0	0	0	0	0	0	0	1	0	0	0	1	0	-	0	0	0	0	0	0
15	0	0	0	0	1	0	0	1	0	0	0	1	0	1	-	0	0	0	0	0
16	1	1	0	1	1	1	1	1	1	1	1	1	1	1	1	-	1	1	1	1
17	1	1	0	1	1	1	1	1	1	1	1	1	1	1	1	0	-	1	1	1
18	1	0	0	0	1	0	0	1	0	0	0	1	0	1	1	0	0	-	0	0
19	1	0	0	0	1	0	1	1	0	1	1	1	1	1	1	0	0	1	-	1
20	1	0	0	0	1	0	1	1	0	0	1	1	1	1	1	0	0	1	0	-

Table 13. CHs_Avg_Distance domination matrix.

Pop	1	2	3	4	5	6	7	8	9	10	11	12	13	14	15	16	17	18	19	20
1	-	1	1	1	1	1	1	1	1	1	1	1	1	1	1	1	1	1	1	1
2	0	-	1	1	0	1	1	1	1	1	1	0	1	1	1	1	1	1	1	0
3	0	0	-	1	0	1	1	1	0	1	1	0	0	1	1	1	1	1	1	0
4	0	0	0	-	0	1	0	1	0	0	0	0	0	0	1	0	1	1	1	0
5	0	1	1	1	-	1	1	1	1	1	1	1	1	1	1	1	1	1	1	1
6	0	0	0	0	0	-	0	1	0	0	0	0	0	0	1	0	0	1	1	0
7	0	0	0	1	0	1	-	1	0	0	1	0	0	1	1	1	1	1	1	0
8	0	0	0	0	0	0	0	-	0	0	0	0	0	0	0	0	0	0	0	0
9	0	0	1	1	0	1	1	1	-	1	1	0	0	1	1	1	1	1	1	0

(Table 13) cont.....

Pop	1	2	3	4	5	6	7	8	9	10	11	12	13	14	15	16	17	18	19	20
10	0	0	0	1	0	1	1	1	0	-	1	0	0	1	1	1	1	1	1	0
11	0	0	0	1	0	1	0	1	0	0	-	0	0	0	1	1	1	1	1	0
12	0	1	1	1	0	1	1	1	1	1	1	-	1	1	1	1	1	1	1	0
13	0	0	1	1	0	1	1	1	1	1	1	1	-	1	1	1	1	1	1	0
14	0	0	0	1	0	1	0	1	0	0	1	0	0	-	1	1	1	1	1	0
15	0	0	0	0	0	0	0	1	0	0	0	0	0	0	-	0	0	1	0	0
16	0	0	0	1	0	1	0	1	0	0	0	0	0	0	1	-	1	1	1	0
17	0	0	0	0	0	1	0	1	0	0	0	0	0	0	1	0	-	1	1	0
18	0	0	0	0	0	0	0	1	0	0	0	0	0	0	0	0	0	-	0	0
19	0	0	0	0	0	0	0	1	0	0	0	0	0	0	1	0	0	1	-	0
20	0	1	1	1	0	1	1	1	1	1	1	1	1	1	1	1	1	1	1	-

Table 14. BS_Avg_Distance domination matrix.

Pop	1	2	3	4	5	6	7	8	9	10	11	12	13	14	15	16	17	18	19	20
1	-	0	1	1	1	0	0	0	0	0	1	1	0	0	0	1	0	1	0	0	0
2	1	-	1	1	1	1	0	1	0	1	1	1	0	0	1	1	1	0	0	0
3	0	0	-	1	0	0	0	0	0	0	0	0	0	0	0	0	0	1	0	0
4	0	0	0	-	0	0	0	0	0	0	0	0	0	0	0	0	0	1	0	0
5	0	0	1	1	-	0	0	0	0	0	1	0	0	0	0	0	0	1	0	0
6	1	0	1	1	1	-	0	0	0	0	1	1	0	0	0	1	0	1	0	0
7	1	1	1	1	1	1	-	1	0	1	1	1	0	0	1	1	1	0	0	0
8	1	0	1	1	1	1	0	-	0	1	1	1	0	0	1	1	1	0	0	0
9	1	1	1	1	1	1	1	1	-	1	1	1	1	0	1	1	1	1	1	0
10	0	0	1	1	0	0	0	0	0	-	0	0	0	0	0	0	0	1	0	0
11	0	0	1	1	1	0	0	0	0	0	1	-	0	0	0	0	0	1	0	0
12	1	0	1	1	1	1	0	0	0	0	1	1	-	0	0	1	0	1	0	0
13	1	1	1	1	1	1	1	0	1	0	1	1	1	-	0	1	1	1	0	0
14	1	1	1	1	1	1	1	1	1	1	1	1	1	1	-	1	1	1	1	0
15	0	0	1	1	1	0	0	0	0	0	1	1	0	0	0	-	0	1	0	0
16	1	0	1	1	1	1	0	0	0	1	1	1	0	0	1	-	1	0	0	0
17	0	0	0	0	0	0	0	0	0	0	0	0	0	0	0	0	-	0	0	0
18	0	1	0	1	0	1	0	0	0	0	0	0	0	1	1	0	0	-	0	1
19	0	1	1	1	0	1	1	0	1	1	1	1	0	1	1	0	0	1	-	1

(Table 14) cont.....

Pop	1	2	3	4	5	6	7	8	9	10	11	12	13	14	15	16	17	18	19	20
20	0	1	0	1	0	0	0	0	0	0	0	0	0	1	0	0	1	0	0	-

Table 15. Avg_Eresidual domination matrix.

Pop	1	2	3	4	5	6	7	8	9	10	11	12	13	14	15	16	17	18	19	20
1	-	1	1	1	0	1	1	1	1	1	1	0	1	1	1	1	1	1	1	1
2	0	-	0	1	0	0	0	0	0	0	0	0	0	0	0	0	1	0	0	0
3	0	1	-	1	0	1	1	0	1	1	1	0	1	1	0	0	1	1	0	1
4	0	0	0	-	0	0	0	0	0	0	0	0	0	0	0	0	0	0	0	0
5	1	1	1	1	-	1	1	1	1	1	1	0	1	1	1	1	1	1	1	1
6	0	1	0	1	0	-	0	0	0	0	0	0	0	1	0	0	1	0	0	1
7	0	1	0	1	0	1	-	0	0	0	0	0	1	1	0	0	1	1	0	1
8	0	1	1	1	0	1	1	-	1	1	1	0	1	1	1	1	1	1	1	1
9	0	1	0	1	0	1	1	0	-	1	1	0	1	0	0	0	1	1	0	1
10	0	1	0	1	0	1	1	0	0	-	0	0	1	1	0	0	1	1	0	1
11	0	1	0	1	0	1	1	0	0	1	-	0	1	1	0	0	1	1	0	1
12	1	1	1	1	1	1	1	1	1	1	1	-	1	1	1	1	1	1	1	1
13	0	1	0	1	0	1	0	0	0	0	0	0	-	1	0	0	1	0	0	1
14	0	0	0	1	0	0	0	0	0	0	0	0	0	-	0	0	0	0	0	0
15	0	1	1	1	0	1	1	0	1	1	1	0	1	1	-	0	1	1	1	1
16	0	1	1	1	0	1	1	0	1	1	1	0	1	1	1	-	1	1	1	1
17	0	0	0	1	0	0	0	0	0	0	0	0	0	0	1	0	-	0	0	0
18	0	1	0	1	0	1	0	0	0	0	0	0	1	1	0	0	1	-	0	1
19	0	1	1	1	0	1	1	0	1	1	1	0	1	1	0	0	1	1	-	1
20	0	1	0	1	0	0	0	0	0	0	0	0	0	0	1	0	0	1	0	-

Table 16. CHs_Avg_lifetime domination matrix.

Pop	1	2	3	4	5	6	7	8	9	10	11	12	13	14	15	16	17	18	19	20
1	-	1	1	1	0	1	1	1	1	1	1	0	1	1	1	0	1	1	1	1
2	0	-	0	1	0	0	0	0	0	0	0	0	0	1	0	0	1	0	0	1
3	0	1	-	1	0	1	1	0	1	1	1	1	1	1	0	0	1	1	0	1
4	0	0	0	-	0	0	0	0	0	0	0	0	0	0	0	0	0	0	0	0
5	1	1	1	1	-	1	1	1	1	1	1	1	1	1	1	1	1	1	1	1
6	0	1	0	1	0	-	0	0	0	0	0	0	1	1	0	0	1	1	0	1

(Table 16) cont.....

Pop	1	2	3	4	5	6	7	8	9	10	11	12	13	14	15	16	17	18	19	20
7	0	1	0	1	0	1	-	0	0	1	0	0	1	1	0	0	1	1	0	1
8	0	1	1	1	0	1	1	-	1	1	1	1	1	1	0	0	1	1	0	1
9	0	1	0	1	0	1	1	0	-	1	1	0	1	1	0	0	1	1	0	1
10	0	1	0	1	0	1	0	0	0	-	0	0	1	1	0	0	1	1	0	1
11	0	1	0	1	0	1	1	0	0	1	-	0	1	1	0	0	1	1	0	1
12	0	1	0	1	0	1	1	0	1	1	1	-	1	1	0	0	1	1	0	1
13	0	1	0	1	0	0	0	0	0	0	0	0	-	1	0	0	1	1	0	1
14	0	0	0	1	0	0	0	0	0	0	0	0	0	-	0	0	0	0	0	0
15	1	1	1	1	0	1	1	1	1	1	1	1	1	1	-	0	1	1	1	1
16	1	1	1	1	0	1	1	1	1	1	1	1	1	1	1	-	1	1	1	1
17	0	0	0	1	0	0	0	0	0	0	0	0	0	1	0	0	-	0	0	0
18	0	1	0	1	0	0	0	0	0	0	0	0	0	1	0	0	1	-	0	1
19	0	1	1	1	0	1	1	1	1	1	1	1	1	1	0	0	1	1	-	1
20	0	0	0	1	0	0	0	0	0	0	0	0	0	1	0	0	1	0	0	-

Table 17. BS_CH_Bearing domination matrix.

Pop	1	2	3	4	5	6	7	8	9	10	11	12	13	14	15	16	17	18	19	20
1	-	0	0	1	0	0	0	0	0	0	0	0	0	0	0	0	1	0	0	0
2	0	-	0	1	0	0	0	0	0	0	0	0	0	0	0	0	1	0	0	0
3	0	0	-	1	0	0	0	0	0	0	0	0	0	0	0	0	1	0	0	0
4	0	0	0	-	0	0	0	0	0	0	0	0	0	0	0	0	0	0	0	0
5	1	1	1	1	-	1	1	1	0	1	1	1	1	0	1	1	1	1	1	1
6	1	1	1	1	0	-	0	1	0	1	0	0	1	0	0	1	1	1	0	0
7	1	1	1	1	0	0	-	1	0	1	0	0	1	0	0	1	1	1	0	0
8	0	0	0	1	0	0	0	-	0	0	0	0	0	0	0	0	1	0	0	0
9	1	1	1	1	0	1	1	1	-	1	1	1	1	0	1	1	1	1	1	1
10	0	0	0	1	0	0	0	0	0	-	0	0	0	0	0	0	1	0	0	0
11	1	1	1	1	0	0	0	1	0	1	-	0	1	0	0	1	1	1	0	0
12	1	1	1	1	0	1	1	1	0	1	1	-	1	0	1	1	1	1	1	1
13	0	0	0	1	0	0	0	0	0	0	0	0	-	0	0	0	1	0	0	0
14	1	1	1	1	0	1	1	1	0	1	1	1	1	-	1	1	1	1	1	1
15	1	1	1	1	0	0	0	1	0	1	0	0	1	0	-	1	1	1	0	0
16	0	0	0	1	0	0	0	0	0	0	0	0	0	0	0	-	1	0	0	0

(Table 17) cont.....

Pop	1	2	3	4	5	6	7	8	9	10	11	12	13	14	15	16	17	18	19	20
17	0	0	0	0	0	0	0	0	0	0	0	0	0	0	0	0	-	0	0	0
18	0	0	0	1	0	0	0	0	0	0	0	0	0	0	0	0	1	-	0	0
19	1	1	1	1	0	0	0	1	0	1	0	0	1	0	0	1	1	1	-	0
20	1	1	1	1	0	0	0	1	0	1	0	0	1	0	0	1	1	1	0	-

Table 18. BS_Max_Distance domination matrix.

Pop	1	2	3	4	5	6	7	8	9	10	11	12	13	14	15	16	17	18	19	20
1	-	0	1	1	1	0	0	0	0	1	1	0	0	0	1	0	1	0	0	0
2	1	-	1	1	1	1	0	1	0	1	1	1	0	0	1	1	1	0	0	0
3	0	0	-	1	0	0	0	0	0	0	0	0	0	0	0	0	1	0	0	0
4	0	0	0	-	0	0	0	0	0	0	0	0	0	0	0	0	1	0	0	0
5	0	0	1	1	-	0	0	0	0	1	0	0	0	0	0	0	1	0	0	0
6	1	0	1	1	1	-	0	0	0	1	1	0	0	0	1	0	1	0	0	0
7	1	1	1	1	1	1	-	1	0	1	1	1	0	0	1	1	1	0	0	0
8	1	0	1	1	1	1	0	-	0	1	1	1	0	0	1	1	1	0	0	0
9	1	1	1	1	1	1	1	1	-	1	1	1	1	0	1	1	1	1	1	0
10	0	0	1	1	0	0	0	0	0	-	0	0	0	0	0	0	1	0	0	0
11	0	0	1	1	1	0	0	0	0	1	-	0	0	0	0	0	1	0	0	0
12	1	0	1	1	1	1	0	0	0	1	1	-	0	0	1	0	1	0	0	0
13	1	1	1	1	1	1	1	1	0	1	1	1	-	0	1	1	1	1	0	0
14	1	1	1	1	1	1	1	1	1	1	1	1	1	-	1	1	1	1	1	0
15	0	0	1	1	1	0	0	0	0	1	1	0	0	0	-	0	1	0	0	0
16	1	0	1	1	1	1	0	0	0	1	1	1	0	0	1	-	1	0	0	0
17	0	0	0	0	0	0	0	0	0	0	0	0	0	0	0	0	-	0	0	0
18	1	1	1	1	1	1	1	1	0	1	1	1	0	0	1	1	1	-	0	0
19	1	1	1	1	1	1	1	1	0	1	1	1	1	0	1	1	1	1	-	0
20	1	1	1	1	1	1	1	1	1	1	1	1	1	1	1	1	1	1	1	-

Table 19. Eres_Con_CHs domination matrix.

Pop	1	2	3	4	5	6	7	8	9	10	11	12	13	14	15	16	17	18	19	20
1	-	1	1	1	0	1	1	1	0	1	0	0	1	1	1	1	1	1	0	1
2	0	-	0	1	0	0	0	0	0	0	0	0	1	1	0	0	1	0	0	1
3	0	1	-	1	0	0	0	0	0	0	0	0	1	1	0	0	1	1	0	1

(Table 19) cont.....

Pop	1	2	3	4	5	6	7	8	9	10	11	12	13	14	15	16	17	18	19	20
4	0	0	0	-	0	0	0	0	0	0	0	0	0	0	0	0	0	0	0	0
5	1	1	1	1	-	1	1	1	1	1	1	1	1	1	1	1	1	1	1	1
6	0	1	1	1	0	-	1	0	0	1	0	0	1	1	1	1	1	1	0	1
7	0	1	1	1	0	0	-	0	0	1	0	0	1	1	0	1	1	1	0	1
8	0	1	1	1	0	1	1	-	0	1	0	0	1	1	1	1	1	1	0	1
9	1	1	1	1	0	1	1	1	-	1	1	0	1	1	1	1	1	1	1	1
10	0	1	1	1	0	0	0	0	0	-	0	0	1	1	0	1	1	1	0	1
11	1	1	1	1	0	1	1	1	0	1	-	0	1	1	1	1	1	1	0	1
12	1	1	1	1	0	1	1	1	1	1	1	-	1	1	1	1	1	1	1	1
13	0	0	0	1	0	0	0	0	0	0	0	0	0	-	0	0	0	1	0	0	0
14	0	0	0	1	0	0	0	0	0	0	0	0	0	1	-	0	0	1	0	0	0
15	0	1	1	1	0	0	1	0	0	1	0	0	1	1	-	1	1	1	0	1
16	0	1	1	1	0	0	0	0	0	0	0	0	1	1	0	-	1	1	0	1
17	0	0	0	1	0	0	0	0	0	0	0	0	0	0	0	0	-	0	0	0
18	0	1	0	1	0	0	0	0	0	0	0	0	1	1	0	0	1	-	0	1
19	1	1	1	1	0	1	1	1	0	1	1	0	1	1	1	1	1	1	-	1
20	0	0	0	1	0	0	0	0	0	0	0	0	1	1	0	0	1	0	0	-

Step 2: Final domination matrix is calculated by using equations 9 and 10, and Table **20** containing the data.

Table 20. Final domination matrix.

Pop	1	2	3	4	5	6	7	8	9	10
1	-	0.5	0.75	0.875	0.5	0.5	0.5	0.625	0.375	0.75
2	0.375	-	0.375	0.875	0.375	0.375	0.25	0.5	0.25	0.5
3	0.125	0.5	-	1	0.125	0.5	0.5	0.25	0.375	0.25
4	0.125	0.125	0	-	0.125	0.25	0.125	0.25	0.125	0.125
5	0.5	0.625	0.875	0.75	-	0.75	0.625	0.75	0.5	0.875
6	0.5	0.625	0.5	0.75	0.375	-	0.25	0.375	0.125	0.75
7	0.5	0.75	0.5	0.875	0.375	0.625	-	0.5	0	0.625
8	0.25	0.25	0.5	0.75	0.375	0.875	0	-	0.5	0.625
9	0.625	0.25	0.25	0.5	0.5	0.5	0.25	0.25	-	0.375
10	0.125	0.625	0.5	0.75	0.625	0.5	0.75	0.375	0.5	-
11	0.375	0.75	0.5	0.875	0.75	0.5	0.875	0.375	0.625	0.5

(Table 20) cont.....

Pop	1	2	3	4	5	6	7	8	9	10
12	0.625	0.25	0.5	0.75	0.25	0.5	0.75	0.375	0.75	0.5
13	0.375	0.25	0.25	0.5	0.25	0.25	0.5	0.5	0.25	0.5
14	0.375	0.625	0.5	0.75	0.625	0.5	0.75	0.375	0.25	0.25
15	0.125	0.25	1	0.125	0.75	0.5	0.875	0.375	0.625	0.5
16	0.5	0.625	0.5	0.75	0.625	0.5	0.75	0.375	0.75	0.5
17	0.125	0.75	0.5	0.875	0.75	0.5	0.875	0.375	0.625	0.5
18	0.375	0.25	0.5	0.75	0.25	0.5	0.75	0.375	0.75	0.5
19	0.625	0.375	0.375	0	0.25	0.25	0.5	0.5	0.25	0.5
20	0.5	0.25	0.375	0.625	0.875	0.125	0.75	0.5	0.25	0.25

Table 20. Final domination matrix (continued).

Pop	11	12	13	14	15	16	17	18	19	20
1	0.375	0.375	0.5	0.625	0.875	0.375	0.875	0.5	0.375	0.5
2	0.375	0.375	0.375	0.625	0.5	0.375	0.875	0.25	0.25	0.375
3	0.25	0.25	0.5	0.625	0.25	0.125	1	0.625	0.25	0.5
4	0.125	0.125	0.125	0.125	0.25	0	0.375	0.25	0.25	0.125
5	0.5	0.5	0.625	0.625	0.625	0.625	0.875	0.625	0.625	0.625
6	0.125	0.125	0.5	0.5	0.625	0.25	0.875	0.625	0.25	0.5
7	0.375	0.375	0.625	0.625	0.625	0.625	0.375	0.625	0.375	0.5
8	0.25	0.25	0.375	0.375	0.625	0.875	0.625	0.625	0.5	0.375
9	0.25	0.25	0.25	0.5	0.5	0.5	0.25	0.25	0.375	0.375
10	0.625	0.625	0.5	0.75	0.625	0.5	0.75	0.375	0.5	0.625
11	-	0.75	0.5	0.875	0.75	0.5	0.875	0.375	0.625	0.5
12	0.875	-	0.5	0.75	0.25	0.5	0.75	0.375	0.75	0.5
13	0.5	0.25	-	0.5	0.25	0.25	0.5	0.5	0.25	0.5
14	0.25	0.625	0.5	-	0.625	0.5	0.75	0.375	0.25	0.25
15	0.25	0.25	1	0.125	-	0.5	0.875	0.375	0.625	0.5
16	0.625	0.625	0.5	0.75	0.625	-	0.75	0.375	0.75	0.5
17	0.625	0.75	0.5	0.875	0.75	0.5	-	0.375	0.625	0.5
18	0.625	0.25	0.5	0.75	0.25	0.5	0.75	-	0.75	0.5
19	0.625	0.375	0.375	0	0.25	0.25	0.5	0.5	-	0.5
20	0.875	0.25	0.375	0.625	0.875	0.125	0.75	0.5	0.25	-

Step 3: Compute μ^+ by performing summation over rows and μ^- by performing summation over columns of matrices by using equations 11 and 12 and Table **21** containing the data.

Table 21. Evaluated values of μ^+ and μ^-

μ^+	μ^-
10.75	7.125
8.25	8.625
8	9.25
3	13.125
12.5	8.75
8.625	9
9.875	10.625
9	8
7	7.875
10.625	9.375
11.875	8.5
10.5	7.375
7.125	9.125
9.125	10.625
9.625	10.125
11.375	7.875
11.375	13.375
9.875	8.5
7	8.625
9.125	8.75

Step 4: Perform net flow by using equation 13 and data shown in Table **22**.

Table 22. Net flow (μ).

Pop	μ
1	3.625
2	-0.375
3	-1.25
4	-10.125
5	3.75

(*Table 22*) cont.....

Pop	μ
6	-0.385
7	-0.75
8	1
9	-0.875
10	1.25
11	3.375
12	3.125
13	-1.95
14	-1.5
15	-0.5
16	3.5
17	-2
18	1.375
19	-1.625
20	0.375

Step 5: Rank the solution based on the value of net flow shown in Table **23**.

Table 23. PROMETHEE ranking.

Pop	1	2	3	4	5	6	7	8	9	10	11	12	13	14	15	16	17	18	19	20
Rank	2	10	15	20	1	11	13	8	14	7	4	5	18	16	12	3	19	6	17	9

SIMULATION RESULTS

Simulation is performed using MATLAB, which can provide pragmatic and effective modeling of WSN. There are 40 possible CHs to choose from. Half of them are selected randomly, and half are selected as CH through k-means clustering. The operation model is the same as reported earlier [3], and uses a round operation process. Each round includes two phases, one is the clustering phase and the second is the data transmission phase.

In the clustering phase, the MADM method is used to select the CH from the active gateway. In the data transmission phase, each working sensor will send an amount of information to appropriate CH. After performing some quantification, CH will send that data to BS. Such modeling gives a direction to find the life of the network through multiple rounds. Here, a network crash means a round in which 75% of sensors or 75% of gateways die. When one of the two described conditions is met, it means that WSN eventually runs out of data collection operations.

In this work, three comparison parameters have been used to compare the proposed results with the predefined methods. The comparison is done of first_N_dead, first_G_dead and Net_dead values of suggested methods. This means that the rounded value of first_N_dead indicates the death of the first round using a different algorithm, while the rounded value of first_G_dead and Net_dead indicates that when the gateways get die the first time, the fully network dies appropriately.

For the comparison purpose, 6 algorithms are considered for case study 1 and 2. Table **24** shows the abbreviations used for the algorithms, and the results are shown in Figs. (**3** and **4**).

Table 24. Abbreviation used for approaches.

Abbreviation	Name of Algorithms
X1	Proposed using PROMETHEE
X2	Proposed using TOPSIS
X3	Algorithm used [30] using TOPSIS
X4	LEACH [3]
X5	LEACH-C [3]
X6	EECS [32]

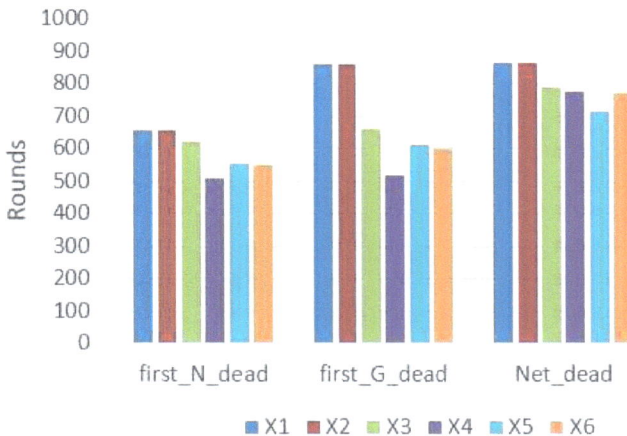

Fig. (3). Presentation graph for scenario 1.

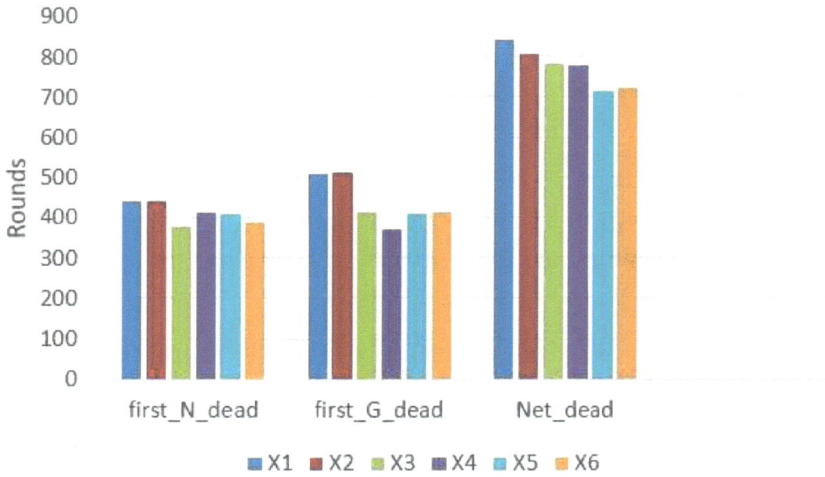

Fig. (4). Presentation graph for scenario 2.

Scenario 1: Total nodes: 100; Coverage 100*100; BS Coordinate: (0, 0)

Scenario 2: Total nodes: 100; Coverage 200*200; BS Coordinate: (0, 0)

Evaluated results show the comparison of the proposed algorithm to existing approaches. For simulation, we considered 8 attributes for better CHs selection. In Fig. **(3)**, both the proposed TOPSIS and PROMETHEE approaches give equal results and better result compared to the existing approaches. In Fig. **(4)**, PROMETHEE gives a better result than the proposed TOPSIS, and both proposed approaches give better result thans the existing approaches. For comparison purpose, here, we have selected three criteria as first_N_dead, first_G_dead and Net_dead. The conclusion reached suggests that the approach provided a better result as compared to existing approaches.

CONCLUSION

In this article, we have proposed a method for selecting and sorting cluster heads using PROMETHEE and TOPSIS in WSN. In addition, in terms of network lifetime, it has been compared with LEACH, LEACH-C and EECS approaches. The best number of cluster heads has been selected by using TOPSIS and PROMETHEE, and clusters have been formed. The simulation results show that, compared to existing approaches, TOPSIS and PROMETHEE can save a lot of energy and extend the network life. In the proposed method, we considered eight attributes for plotting the results. In the future, we can consider more attributes that affect the energy of the WSNs for cluster head selection.

CONSENT FOR PUBLICATION

Not applicable.

CONFLICT OF INTEREST

The author declares no conflict of interest, financial or otherwise.

ACKNOWLEDGEMENTS

Declared none.

REFERENCES

[1]   Y. Yao, Q. Cao, and A.V. Vasilakos, "EDAL: An Energy-Efficient, Delay-Aware, and Lifetime-Balancing Data Collection Protocol for Heterogeneous Wireless Sensor Networks", *IEEE/ACM Transactions on Networking,* vol. 23, pp. 810-823, 2013.
[http://dx.doi.org/10.1109/TNET.2014.2306592]

[2]   I.F. Akyildiz, and I.H. Kasimoglu, "Wireless sensor and actor networks: research challenges", *Ad Hoc Netw.,* vol. 2, no. 4, pp. 351-367, 2004.
[http://dx.doi.org/10.1016/j.adhoc.2004.04.003]

[3]   C.S. Raghavendra, K.M. Sivalingam, T. Znati, Ed., *Wireless sensor networks.* Springer, 2006.
[http://dx.doi.org/10.1007/b117506]

[4]   Z. Sheng, S. Yang, Y. Yu, A. Vasilakos, J. Mccann, and K. Leung, "A survey on the ietf protocol suite for the internet of things: standards, challenges, and opportunities", *IEEE Wirel. Commun.,* vol. 20, no. 6, pp. 91-98, 2013.
[http://dx.doi.org/10.1109/MWC.2013.6704479]

[5]   W.B. Heinzelman, A.P. Chandrakasan, and H. Balakrishnan, "An application-specific protocol architecture for wireless microsensor networks", *IEEE Trans. Wirel. Commun.,* vol. 1, no. 4, pp. 660-670, 2002.
[http://dx.doi.org/10.1109/TWC.2002.804190]

[6]   O. Younis, and S. Fahmy, "HEED: a hybrid, energy-efficient, distributed clustering approach for ad hoc sensor networks", *IEEE Trans. Mobile Comput.,* vol. 3, no. 4, pp. 366-379, 2004.
[http://dx.doi.org/10.1109/TMC.2004.41]

[7]   D. Baker, A. Ephremides, and J. Flynn, "The Design and Simulation of a Mobile Radio Network with Distributed Control", *IEEE J. Sel. Areas Comm.,* vol. 2, no. 1, pp. 226-237, 1984.
[http://dx.doi.org/10.1109/JSAC.1984.1146043]

[8]   R. Wairagu, "Extending leach routing algorithm for wireless sensor network", In: *Data Communications Engineering, Makerere University,* 2009.

[9]   N. Batra, A. Jain, and Dhiman Surender, "An optimized energy efficient routing algorithm for wireless sensor network", *International Journal of Innovative Technology and Creative Engineering,* vol. 1, no. 5, 2011.

[10]   O. Younis, and S. Fahmy, "Distributed clustering in ad-hoc sensor networks: A hybrid, energy-efficient approach", In: *IEEE INFOCOM 2004,* vol. 1. IEEE, 2004.

[11]   V. Yadav, and M. Verma, "A Survey Paper on Wireless Access Protocol", *Int. J. Comput. Sci. Inf. Technol.,* vol. 6, no. 4, pp. 3527-3534, 2015. [IJCSIT].

[12]   Y. Ge, S. Wang, and J. Ma, "Optimization on TEEN routing protocol in cognitive wireless sensor network", *EURASIP J. Wirel. Commun. Netw.,* vol. 2018, no. 1, p. 27, 2018.

[http://dx.doi.org/10.1186/s13638-018-1039-z]

[13]   T. Camilo, C. Carreto, J. Sá Silva, and F. Boavida, "An Energy-Efficient Ant-Based Routing Algorithm for Wireless Sensor Networks", In: *Ant Colony Optimization and Swarm Intelligence, ANTS 2006, Lecture Notes in Computer Science,* M. Dorigo, L.M. Gambardella, M. Birattari, A. Martinoli, R. Poli, T. Stützle, Eds., vol. 4150. Springer: Berlin, Heidelberg, 2006.
[http://dx.doi.org/10.1007/11839088_5]

[14]   B. Zeng, and Y. Dong, "An improved harmony search based energy-efficient routing algorithm for wireless sensor networks", *Appl. Soft Comput.,* vol. 41, pp. 135-147, 2016.
[http://dx.doi.org/10.1016/j.asoc.2015.12.028]

[15]   S. Jin, M. Zhou, and A. Wu, "Sensor network optimization using a genetic algorithm", *Proceedings of the 7th world multiconference on systemics, cybernetics and informatics,* 2003.

[16]   K.P. Ferentinos, T.A. Tsiligiridis, and K.G. Arvanitis, "Energy optimization of wireless sensor networks for environmental measurements", *2005 IEEE International Conference on Computational Intelligence for Measurement Systems and Applications,* pp. 250-255, 2005.
[http://dx.doi.org/10.1109/CIMSA.2005.1522872]

[17]   D. Lee, W. Lee, and J. Kim, "Genetic algorithmic topology control for two-tiered wireless sensor networks", *International Conference on Computational Science,* Springer: Berlin, Heidelberg, 2007.
[http://dx.doi.org/10.1007/978-3-540-72590-9_53]

[18]   P. Kuila, and P.K. Jana, "Energy efficient clustering and routing algorithms for wireless sensor networks: Particle swarm optimization approach", *Eng. Appl. Artif. Intell.,* vol. 33, pp. 127-140, 2014.
[http://dx.doi.org/10.1016/j.engappai.2014.04.009]

[19]   N. Kumar, Azharuddin Md, and Jana P.K, "Energy efficient fault-tolerant clustering algorithm for wireless sensor networks", *2015 International Conference on Green Computing and Internet of Things (ICGCIoT),* IEEE, 2015.

[20]   P. Kuila, S.K. Gupta, and P.K. Jana, "A novel evolutionary approach for load balanced clustering problem for wireless sensor networks", *Swarm Evol. Comput.,* vol. 12, pp. 48-56, 2013.
[http://dx.doi.org/10.1016/j.swevo.2013.04.002]

[21]   P. Kuila, and P.K. Jana, "A novel differential evolution based clustering algorithm for wireless sensor networks", *Appl. Soft Comput.,* vol. 25, pp. 414-425, 2014.
[http://dx.doi.org/10.1016/j.asoc.2014.08.064]

[22]   S. Li, L. Li, and Y. Yang, "A local-world heterogeneous model of wireless sensor networks with node and link diversity", *Physica A,* vol. 390, no. 6, pp. 1182-1191, 2011.
[http://dx.doi.org/10.1016/j.physa.2010.11.034]

[23]   T.L. Saaty, *Decision Making for Leaders: The Analytic Hierarchy Process for Decisions in a Complex World.* RWS publications, 1990.

[24]   T.L. Saaty, *Analytic hierarchy process. Encyclopedia of Operations Research and Management Science.* Springer US: Boston, MA, 2013, pp. 52-64.
[http://dx.doi.org/10.1007/978-1-4419-1153-7_31]

[25]   Y. Yin, J. Shi, Y. Li, and P. Zhang, "Cluster Head Selection Using Analytical Hierarchy Process for Wireless Sensor Networks", *2006 IEEE 17th International Symposium on Personal, Indoor and Mobile Radio Communications,* 2006.
[http://dx.doi.org/10.1109/PIMRC.2006.254181]

[26]   O. Durán, and J. Aguilo, "Computer-aided machine-tool selection based on a Fuzzy-AHP approach", *Expert Syst. Appl.,* vol. 34, no. 3, pp. 1787-1794, 2008.
[http://dx.doi.org/10.1016/j.eswa.2007.01.046]

[27]   A. Azadeh, S.F. Ghaderi, and H. Izadbakhsh, "Integration of DEA and AHP with computer simulation for railway system improvement and optimization", *Appl. Math. Comput.,* vol. 195, no. 2, pp. 775-785, 2008.

[http://dx.doi.org/10.1016/j.amc.2007.05.023]

[28]   C.C. Wei, C.F. Chien, and M.J.J. Wang, "An AHP-based approach to ERP system selection", *Int. J. Prod. Econ.,* vol. 96, no. 1, pp. 47-62, 2005.
[http://dx.doi.org/10.1016/j.ijpe.2004.03.004]

[29]   C-L. Hwang, Y.J. Lai, and T.Y. Liu, "A new approach for multiple objective decision making", *Comput. Oper. Res.,* vol. 20, no. 8, pp. 889-899, 1993.
[http://dx.doi.org/10.1016/0305-0548(93)90109-V]

[30]   F. Hamzeloei, and M.K. Dermany, "A TOPSIS based cluster head selection for wireless sensor network", *Procedia Comput. Sci.,* vol. 98, pp. 8-15, 2016.
[http://dx.doi.org/10.1016/j.procs.2016.09.005]

[31]   P. Azad, and V. Sharma, "Clusterhead selection using multiple attribute decision making (MADM) approach in wireless sensor networks", In: *International Conference on Heterogeneous Networking for Quality, Reliability, Security and Robustness* Springer: Berlin, Heidelberg, 2013.
[http://dx.doi.org/10.1007/978-3-642-37949-9_12]

[32]   M. Ye, C. Li, G. Chen, and J. Wu, "EECS: an energy efficient clustering scheme in wireless sensor networks", *PCCC 2005. 24th IEEE International Performance, Computing, and Communications Conference,* 2005.

CHAPTER 6

An Overview of Energy Efficient and Data Accuracy Target Tracking Methods in WSN

Urvashi Saraswat[1,*] and **Anita Yadav[2]**

[1] *Research Scholar, Department of Computer Science and Engineering, Harcourt Butler Technical University, Kanpur, Uttar Pradesh, India*

[2] *Associate Professor, Department of Computer Science and Engineering, Harcourt Butler Technical University, Kanpur, Uttar Pradesh, India*

Abstract: Target tracking plays an important role in an application of WSN (Wireless Sensor Networks) with its growing popularity for various industrial as well commercial purposes. Many researches have been done for laying the framework of a target tracking algorithm to achieve accuracy while tracking down the target. Although the basic structure of a target tracking algorithm focuses on accuracy but the cooperation of both data accuracy and efficient energy utilization is quite distinct goal in the designing of target tracking algorithms. Through this survey, we present some recent target-based tracking algorithms that focus on dual goal, *i.e.*, efficient power consumption along with the data accuracy. In this paper, we present a comparative structure that showcases that all surveyed algorithms are still on the verge of improved tracking accuracy with energy efficiency and there is still a need of optimization in terms of energy-efficient usage. The primary focus of the paper is to survey the level of energy efficiency in different categories of target tracking algorithms laid down in Wireless Sensor Networks.

Keywords: Classification, Data accuracy, Energy, Monitoring, Network lifetime, Target tracking, WSNs.

INTRODUCTION

Wireless based sensor network is an attractive research area where energy saving techniques are worked upon. It is formed from a set of small-sized mobile sensors. The wide range of type of sensors enables the sensing of various environmental entities, like gas, humidity, temperature, *etc*. These sensors play a vital role for identification and monitoring purposes.

---

[*] **Corresponding author Urvashi Saraswat:** Harcourt Butler Technical University, Kanpur, Uttar Pradesh, India; E-mail: urvashi.saraswat28@gmail.com

Target tracking is an influential application of WSNs that is used for detection and discovery of specific target(s) depending on the application used. Target tracking has contributed major applications in the areas of battlefield surveillance [1], healthcare [2, 3], wildlife monitoring [4, 5], oil spills [6], *etc.* One of the major concerns in order to keep a track of a certain target in this application is the energy consumption. There have been developments and advancements in this field of application because of its major role in the military and industrial sector. 'Mote' is another name of sensor node, which is accomplished to collect as well process sensor-based statistics and establish communication with remaining involved sensor nodes from the network structure. These tiny sensor nodes possess low cost as well have limited energy, where most of them have irreplaceable batteries or cannot be charged again. This is a major drawback where network lifetime becomes a challenge in most of the target tracking applications [7]. Thus, enhancing the quality of tracking and overall energy is a major goal to achieve for target tracking application. Although, both of the aforementioned parameters are contrary.

Generally, the target tracking performs two operations, where in the first step, target identification and distance calculation are performed, followed by continuous monitoring of the target. Because the senor nodes are dependent on the battery, thus limited lifetime becomes a challenge. Here, we have discussed different target tracking methods that focus on enhancing the energy consumption and how they contribute overall towards the performance of these methods. We have also analyzed these methods to draw the current research challenges and future directions.

Overview of Recent Target Tracking Methods in WSN

In this section, we discuss the state of art of some recent target tracking methods that focus on energy efficiency. The sensor nodes involved in the mechanism of tracking need to be optimized with some energy efficient strategies with the operations of activation and deactivation of specific sensor nodes. The classification of target tracking approach is majorly classified under tree structure-based, cluster structure-based, and prediction-based mechanisms.

The *tree structure approach* forms the entire network of sensor nodes in a tree topology for smooth data collection. Here, one node is the root node and is responsible for information collection as well as communication. This node is mobile in nature and causes a drift in position as per the frequent changes in the target position, according to which node insertion and deletion in the tree take place. Even in case if the battery dies or the target alters its position, there is a change in the topological structure of tree [8, 9]. If the sink node becomes the root node, the shortest path is calculated for each node resulting in network flooding. The tree approach can also form a distributed database framework using a message-pruning tree mechanism. Here, a query point is used as the root for establishing connection using the update and query phase [10].

The *cluster-based mechanism* in target tracking provides the collaborative approach wherein the goal of the method is to save the energy while achieving target tracking. The mechanism of clustering provides high scalability to the entire network as well as diminishes the overhead caused in communication. Clustering mechanism can be either static cluster [11, 12], or dynamic cluster [13], and even hybrid approach [14]. The static approach forms the clusters during the deployment of network and remains unchanged [15]. The drawback of boundary problem exists in this type of approach wherein the different existing clusters are unable to collaborate among themselves for any information exchange, especially in case of mobile targets. Although static clustering has a simple structure, here the cluster head loses its energy because of power depletion, which leaves the entire cluster unfunctional.

In *dynamic clustering* approach, the cluster generation depends on the mobility of the target making this mechanism more flexible as compared to the static clustering technique. Therefore, here cluster can be easily generated as per the requirement and a sensor node is not constrained within a single cluster. When the sensor nodes exchange information, specific nodes detecting the presence of target decide the selection of cluster head, thus reducing the localization error. But, due to the uncertain situation while localizing the target, the tracking is unreliable [16].

DELTA [17] is a dynamic clustering-based algorithm that tracks the target moving in a constant speed, whereas varying speed is still unexplored. To reduce the overall energy consumption, RARE [11] (node and area) method uses dynamic clustering for target tracking, wherein it prunes the involvement of sensor nodes during the process of tracking. The two sub-algorithms of RARE are formed for achieving energy efficiency, RARE-Node algorithm, which minimizes the participation of nodes, and RARE-Area algorithm, which assures the involvement of specific nodes (satisfying the data quality) in tracking.

Both static and dynamic clustering approaches depend on the cluster head, thus there can be security breaches wherein the intruder can obstruct the communication through cluster head or even falsify the entire tracking by undermining the cluster head. Thus, to address the issues of static and dynamic clustering simultaneously while maintaining the energy efficiency, hybrid clustering mechanism distributes the role of tracking in between the two strategies. Here, the characteristic of static clustering (simple and energy efficient) and dynamic clustering (quality of tracking and flexibility) is maintained by the hybrid approach. The cluster formed is static in nature during time of network deployment, which is the initial phase. During occurrence of an event (or activity), the cluster is able to form self-fusion of the data, which is generated from the event. In case of the event involving more than one cluster, the dynamic cluster is formed. Therefore, this is neither pure static nor pure dynamic form of clustering, resulting in cost-efficient as well as more efficient in terms of energy consumption [14].

In DCAT [18], a hybrid clustering algorithm was formed to overcome the boundary problem, which exists in the static clustering, and in another work [19], the algorithm has been proposed with respect to efficient energy utilization using a CHEW (Cluster Head Election Window) mechanism, which is responsible for utilizing the residue energy as well as stretch from target, wherein the selected sensor node that has a small CHEW (nearest to the target) and possesses high energy will form a cluster for the detected target. In a study [20], the dynamic clustering is used to form a target tracking that focuses on efficient energy consumption as well reduces the tracking errors by layering technique. Here the sensor nodes are divided into concentric tube-shaped layers to perform dynamic clustering separately for each layer.

The prediction-based tracking mechanism uses the prediction strategy to generate estimation about the future target site [21]. Using prediction strategy in target tracking can result in saving energy by utilizing specific sensor nodes at specific time around the vicinity of the target. The different methods to forecast the future target site are implemented under Kalman Filter [22, 23] and the Particle Filter [24, 25].

Kalman proposed this estimation method for noisy framework [23]. In the Kalman filter method, fusion of redundant data is done where the inaccurate observed values are used at specific time to evaluate more accurate values. For the control of the system, KF uses noise as the information and a linear operator (also using noise) to release the observed values from the real state. The two main recursive phases used by KF approach are the predict phase and the correct phase. Here, initially the next step is estimated in the predict phase for a specific time following The EECGKFT [23] algorithm that uses the CGKF [26] for estimating the position of the target and minimizes the computational complexity. It is in need for transmission of data during the condition where accuracy in terms of predicted values is higher than the threshold. This algorithm predicted future target location as well as overcame the existing boundary problem in case of static clusters by the measurement update for enhancing by incorporating the updated values [27].

In the Particle Filter (PF) approach, Monte Carlo method is the idea behind where the recursion of this sequential approach occurs [24]. This approach is an alternate method to the KF in the applications to overcome the complex issue of posterior administration of the non-Gaussian methods. The aim of PF is to create posterior density function so as to generate random samples. Prediction is the first phase in PF, where each particle is altered to match the model and random noise is added. In the second phase of correction, revaluation of the particle weight is done with respect to the updated values by removing less weighted particles.

An extended PF was used by the DLSTA-a tree structure-based target tracking approach [9] to enhance the accuracy of estimation. Here the sensor node to nearest vicinity of target node was finalized to become the root of the structure. An energy efficient method was proposed based on the prediction mechanism that used the Gaussian distribution over two-dimensional network framework [28]. For energy management, a wakeup strategy is implemented for triggering the specific nodes (nearest to estimated target site) in prior.

Characteristics Maintaining Energy Efficiency in Target Tracking Algorithms

A quintessential mechanism of target tracking approach comprises three primary sub-operative systems, as shown in Fig. (1).

Fig. (1). Components in target tracking.

The link between sensing and the communication is the estimation scheme which digs out the information from the data transmitted by the active nodes within the framework.

The cluster or tree structure is maintained by the communication component, which uses self-organization in order to reduce the message exchange.

The prediction subsystem is used to forecast the actual target site so as to create next sampling state. It is assumed in this paper that in target tracking algorithms to achieve energy efficiency, all nodes are initially kept at sleep state. The sensor nodes deployed at the border are only kept in active state. Therefore, the target identification is initially performed by the nodes at the border, and using the external activation message passing mechanism gradually, other nodes become active when needed. This message transmission is done using a less power consuming paging channel.

In a fundamental target tracking algorithm, the following parameters play a major role for energy management.

1. Quality of target detection: The quality of detection depends on the coverage formed by the deployed network. This involves the sensing range as well as the density of the network and the quality depends on node selection for performing tracking operation. Here the focus should be more on as to which node should be selected, or how many nodes to be involved, *etc.*

2. The type of prediction strategy: The use of right estimation or prediction strategy is important while keeping the check on the target tracking algorithm. The distributive or light-weight prediction strategy should be selected depending on the condition model, target model, and noise model. Approaches, like KF [23], are the most appropriate method for prediction strategy for efficient tracking because of their smooth implementation. Different variations of KF have been implemented so far, like PF, Extended Kalman Filter [29], Unscented Kalman Filter [30 - 32].

3. Data reporting: The data reporting is performed for connectivity after the estimation has been done. The selection of accurate data reporter is another issue here, where the nearest nodes (to the target) possessing high energy have to be selected. The reconfiguration of network can also occur where the selected node is at a larger distance from the target. Hybrid clustering approaches serve as solution to such problems.

4. Activation range: This depends on the velocity of the target node. Here, to overcome the problem of target loss, the activation mechanism is considered under multiple steps. Depending on the tracking measurement error, static or dynamic activation range can be used.

5. Logic-based network structure: Flat network structure is not the key to optimizing communication. Thus, provisional construction of clusters and trees (depending on structure needed) helps in localization. Problems, such as leader selection, tree reconfiguration, cluster reorganization, and boundary determination should be overcome by the target tracking algorithms.

Self-Organizing Network Approaches in Target Tracking

The self-organization strategy is the primary goal that contributes to increasing the network lifetime. There are many target tracking applications where many nodes do not participate in communication. In such situation, these nodes can be turned off to a sleep state in order to conserve the energy. Thus, for selecting right sensor nodes for this operation, prediction information can be used. This is done by removing the weak nodes from selection by observing their state and reforming the topology to be dynamic in nature.

There are different approaches, like sleep scheduling [33, 34], coverage-based [35 - 37] and geometric-based [38 - 40] that possess network self-organization approach for extending the network lifetime. The target tracking approaches proposed earlier [12, 41, 42] utilize a paging channel to operate the radio of the nodes for switching on them using an awake message. The future location prediction and awake method enables specific selected sensor nodes to become active for tracking operation.

Discussion and Comparison

The above discussed target tracking schemes focus on two main goals, *i.e.*, enhancing the accuracy of target tracking as well as reducing the overall energy consumption so as to achieve quality target tracking. The sensing and communication sub-systems contribute to an indispensable task of maintaining energy efficiency as well as accuracy in terms of quality of data extraction and precision in estimation of target position.

As shown in Table **1**, we have summarized achievement of both goals proposed in discussed target tracking methods. The primary intent of accuracy is contradictory to that of energy consumption as accuracy depends on the network coverage and observed values. Thus, for an efficient topology construction, coverage constraints have to be considered where communication cost is the issue. On the other hand, self- organization of network is an important technique for enhancing the network lifetime, thus maintaining energy efficiency.

Table 1. A relative analysis of target tracking methods with dual objective.

Algorithm/Author, Year	Mechanism	Accuracy in Tracking	Energy Consumption
RARE [11], 2007	Clustering	Less	Medium
Deldar and Yaghmaee [12], 2011	Clustering + prediction	Medium	Medium
DELTA [17], 2007	Clustering	Less	Medium
DCAT [18], 2004	Clustering	Medium	Medium
DLSTA [9], 2014	Clustering + prediction	Medium	Medium
Chunming [25], 2019	Clustering + prediction	Medium	Medium
GRNN+UKF [30], 2019	Prediction	Medium	Less
Rahman [40], 2011	Prediction	Less	Medium
EECGKFT [23], 2017	Clustering+ Prediction	Medium	Medium

CONCLUSION AND FUTURE WORK

For balancing the energy consumption in target tracking algorithms, the involvement of count of sensor nodes has to be optimized time to time. The selection of active sensor nodes is another important constraint, which involves the estimation strategies as well. Along with such different strategies, an important characteristic for an algorithm should be self-network re-organization. The energy management is still an active research sector where target tracking algorithms are proposed. As surveyed in this paper, we have come across the discussed approaches that can maintain moderate accuracy and energy consumed. The major two goals, to preserve the network energy and maintain data accuracy, are not fully achieved simultaneously. Due to the limitation of the resources of energy for the nodes, increasing network lifespan has become an active challenge while designing a target tracking algorithm. Through this survey, we have summarized the recent implementations of target tracking focusing together on optimizing data accuracy and energy consumption, where energy consumption is an active research issue that needs to be addressed.

CONSENT FOR PUBLICATION

Not applicable.

CONFLICT OF INTEREST

The author declares no conflict of interest, financial or otherwise.

ACKNOWLEDGEMENTS

Declared none.

REFERENCES

[1]   M.P. Đurišić, Z. Tafa, G. Dimić, and V. Milutinović, "A survey of military applications of wireless sensor networks", *Mediterranean Conference on Embedded Computing (MECO)*, pp. 196-199, 2012.

[2]   M. Al Ameen, J. Liu, and K. Kwak, "Security and privacy issues in wireless sensor networks for healthcare applications", *J. Med. Syst.*, vol. 36, no. 1, pp. 93-101, 2012.
[http://dx.doi.org/10.1007/s10916-010-9449-4] [PMID: 20703745]

[3]   H. Alemdar, and C. Ersoy, "Wireless sensor networks for healthcare: A survey", *Comput. Netw.*, vol. 54, no. 15, pp. 2688-2710, 2010.
[http://dx.doi.org/10.1016/j.comnet.2010.05.003]

[4]   M.F. Othman, and K. Shazali, "Wireless sensor network applications: A study in environment monitoring system", *Procedia Eng.*, vol. 41, pp. 1204-1210, 2012.
[http://dx.doi.org/10.1016/j.proeng.2012.07.302]

[5]   P. Wamuyu, "A conceptual framework for implementing a wsn based cattle recovery system in case of cattle rustling in Kenya", *Technologies (Basel)*, vol. 5, no. 3, p. 54, 2017.
[http://dx.doi.org/10.3390/technologies5030054]

[6]   H. Hong, S. Oh, J. Lee, and S. Kim, "A Chaining Selective Wakeup Strategy for a Robust Continuous Object Tracking in Practical Wireless Sensor Networks", *International Conference on Advanced Information Networking and Applications (AINA)*, pp. 333-339, 2013.

[7]   Y.A. Ur Rehman, M. Tariq, and T. Sato, "A Novel Energy Efficient Object Detection and Image Transmission Approach for Wireless Multimedia Sensor Networks", *IEEE Sens. J.*, vol. 16, no. 15, pp. 5942-5949, 2016.
[http://dx.doi.org/10.1109/JSEN.2016.2574989]

[8]   E.L. Souza, A. Campos, and E.F. Nakamura, "Tracking targets in quantized areas with wireless sensor networks", *36th Conference on Local Computer Networks*, pp. 235-238, 2011.
[http://dx.doi.org/10.1109/LCN.2011.6115197]

[9]   A. Alaybeyoglu, A. Kantarci, and K. Erciyes, "A dynamic lookahead tree based tracking algorithm for wireless sensor networks using particle filtering technique", *Comput. Electr. Eng.*, vol. 40, no. 2, pp. 374-383, 2014.
[http://dx.doi.org/10.1016/j.compeleceng.2013.06.014]

[10]   B. Liu, "Effective Reconstruction of the Message-Pruning Trees in Wireless Sensor Networks", *Fourth International Conference on Genetic and Evolutionary Computing*, pp. 695-698, 2010.

[11]   E. Olule, G. Wang, M. Guo, and M. Dong, "RARE: An Energy-Efficient Target Tracking Protocol for Wireless Sensor Networks", *International Conference on Parallel Processing Workshops (ICPPW 2007)*, pp. 76-76, 2007.
[http://dx.doi.org/10.1109/ICPPW.2007.71]

[12]   F. Deldar, and M.H. Yaghmaee, "Designing an energy efficient prediction-based algorithm for target tracking in wireless sensor networks", *International Conference on Wireless Communications and Signal Processing (WCSP)*, pp. 1-6, 2011.
[http://dx.doi.org/10.1109/WCSP.2011.6096835]

[13]   J. Zhang, C. Wu, P. Ji, and Y. Huang, "Collaborative Target Tracking Based on Energy Consideration in WSNs", *International Conference on Wireless Communications, Networking and Mobile Computing*, pp. 1-4, 2011.
[http://dx.doi.org/10.1109/wicom.2011.6040370]

[14]   J. Feng, B. Lian, and H. Zhao, "Coordinated and Adaptive Information Collecting in Target Tracking Wireless Sensor Networks", *IEEE Sens. J.,* vol. 15, no. 6, pp. 3436-3445, 2015.
[http://dx.doi.org/10.1109/JSEN.2014.2388234]

[15]   X. Zhu, L. Shen, and T.S.P. Yum, "Hausdorff Clustering and Minimum Energy Routing for Wireless Sensor Networks", *IEEE Trans. Vehicular Technol.,* vol. 58, no. 2, pp. 990-997, 2009.
[http://dx.doi.org/10.1109/TVT.2008.926073]

[16]   Z. Wang, W. Lou, Z. Wang, J. Ma, and H. Chen, "A novel mobility management scheme for target tracking in cluster-based sensor networks", *International Conference on Distributed Computing in Sensor Systems,* Springer: Berlin, Heidelberg, pp. 172-186, 2010.
[http://dx.doi.org/10.1007/978-3-642-13651-1_13]

[17]   M. Wälchli, P. Skoczylas, M. Meer, and T. Braun, "Distributed event localization and tracking with wireless sensors", *International Conference on Wired/Wireless Internet Communications,* Springer: Berlin, Heidelberg, pp. 247-258, 2007.
[http://dx.doi.org/10.1007/978-3-540-72697-5_21]

[18]   Wei-Peng Chen, and J. C. Hou, *IEEE Trans. Mobile Comput.,* vol. 3, no. 3, pp. 258-271, 2004.
[http://dx.doi.org/10.1109/TMC.2004.22]

[19]   K. Huang, H. Wang, W. Wang, and Y. Wang, "A dynamic tracking mechanism for mobile target in wireless sensor networks", *International Symposium on Intelligent Signal Processing and Communications Systems,* pp. 822-826, 2012.
[http://dx.doi.org/10.1109/ISPACS.2012.6473605]

[20]   V. Yadav, "A Survey paper on Wireless Access Protocol", *Int. J. Comput. Sci. Inf. Technol.,* vol. 6, no. 4, pp. 3527-3534, 2015. [IJCSIT].

[21]   A.A. Kumar, and K.M. Sivalingam, "Target tracking in a WSN with directional sensors using electronic beam steering", *Fourth International Conference on Communication Systems and Networks (COMSNETS 2012),* pp. 1-10, 2012.
[http://dx.doi.org/10.1109/COMSNETS.2012.6151338]

[22]   X. Wang, X. Wang, and H. Zhang, "Target tracking in wireless sensor networks using sequential implementation of the extended Kalman filter", *Chinese Automation Congress,* pp. 132-137, 2013.
[http://dx.doi.org/10.1109/CAC.2013.6775715]

[23]   K. Hirpara, and K. Rana, "Energy-efficient constant gain Kalman filter based tracking in wireless sensor network", *Wirel. Commun. Mob. Comput.,* vol. 2017, pp. 1-7, 2017.
[http://dx.doi.org/10.1155/2017/1390847]

[24]   B. Kalpana, and R. Sangeetha, "A collaborative target tracking framework using particle filter", *Joint IFIP Wireless and Mobile Networking Conference (WMNC),* pp. 1-4, 2013.
[http://dx.doi.org/10.1109/WMNC.2013.6548992]

[25]   Chunming Wu, Chen Zhao, and Haoquan Gong, "A constant gain Kalman filter approach to track maneuvering targets, IEEE", *International Conference on Control Applications (CCA),* pp. 562-567, 2019.
[http://dx.doi.org/10.1007/s13319-018-0210-y]

[26]   A. Yadav, P. Awasthi, N. Naik, and M.R. Ananthasayanam, "A constant gain Kalman filter approach to track maneuvering targets", *International Conference on Control Applications (CCA),* pp. 562-567, 2013.
[http://dx.doi.org/10.1109/CCA.2013.6662809]

[27]   J. Xu, J. Li, and S. Xu, "Data fusion for target tracking in wireless sensor networks using quantized innovations and Kalman filtering", *Sci. China Inf. Sci.,* vol. 55, no. 3, pp. 530-544, 2012.
[http://dx.doi.org/10.1007/s11432-011-4533-z]

[28]   M.Z.A. Bhuiyan, G. Wang, L. Zhang, and Y. Peng, "Prediction-based energy-efficient target tracking protocol in wireless sensor networks", *J. Cent. South Univ. Technol.,* vol. 17, no. 2, pp. 340-348, 2010.

[http://dx.doi.org/10.1007/s11771-010-0051-1]

[29]   Y. Wang, and X. Feng, "Maneuvering Target Tracking in Wireless Sensor Network with Range Only Measurement", In: *Journal of Physics: Conference Series* vol. 1325. no. 1, p. 012171.
[http://dx.doi.org/10.1088/1742-6596/1325/1/012171]

[30]   S.R. Jondhale, and R.S. Deshpande, "GRNN and KF framework based real time target tracking using PSOC BLE and smartphone", *Ad Hoc Netw.,* vol. 84, no. 1, pp. 19-28, 2019.
[http://dx.doi.org/10.1016/j.adhoc.2018.09.017]

[31]   S. Jafarzadeh, C. Lascu, and M.S. Fadali, "State Estimation of Induction Motor Drives Using the Unscented Kalman Filter", *IEEE Trans. Ind. Electron.,* vol. 59, no. 11, pp. 4207-4216, 2012.
[http://dx.doi.org/10.1109/TIE.2011.2174533]

[32]   H.M.T. Menegaz, J.Y. Ishihara, G.A. Borges, and A.N. Vargas, "A Systematization of the Unscented Kalman Filter Theory", *IEEE Trans. Automat. Contr.,* vol. 60, no. 10, pp. 2583-2598, 2015.
[http://dx.doi.org/10.1109/TAC.2015.2404511]

[33]   Y.E.M. Hamouda, and C. Phillips, "Metadata-Based Adaptive Sampling for Energy-Efficient Collaborative Target Tracking in Wireless Sensor Networks", *IEEE International Conference on Computer and Information Technology,* pp. 313-320, 2010.
[http://dx.doi.org/10.1109/CIT.2010.84]

[34]   S. Dai, C. Tang, S. Qiao, Y. Wang, H. Li, and C. Li, "An Energy-Efficient Tracking Algorithm Based on Gene Expression Programming in Wireless Sensor Networks", *First International Conference on Information Science and Engineering,* pp. 774-777, 2009.
[http://dx.doi.org/10.1109/ICISE.2009.259]

[35]   G. Simon, M. Molnar, L. Gonczy, and B. Cousin, "Dependable k-coverage algorithms for sensor networks", *IEEE Instrumentation & Measurement Technology Conference IMTC,* vol. 2007, pp. 1-6, 2007.

[36]   G. Bergmann, M. Molnár, L. Gönczy, and B. Cousin, "Optimal Period Length for the CGS Sensor Network Scheduling Algorithm", *Sixth International Conference on Networking and Services,* pp. 192-199, 2010.
[http://dx.doi.org/10.1109/ICNS.2010.33]

[37]   X.R. Li, and V.P. Jilkov, "Survey of Maneuvering Target Tracking. Part II: Motion Models of Ballistic and Space Targets", *IEEE Trans. Aerosp. Electron. Syst.,* vol. 46, no. 1, pp. 96-119, 2010.
[http://dx.doi.org/10.1109/TAES.2010.5417150]

[38]   X. Ji, Y. Zhang, S. Hussain, D. Jin, E. Lee, and M. Park, "FOTP: Face-Based Object Tracking Protocol in Wireless Sensor Network", *Fourth International Conference on Computer Sciences and Convergence Information Technology,* pp. 128-133, 2009.
[http://dx.doi.org/10.1109/ICCIT.2009.246]

[39]   M.Z.A. Bhuiyan, G. Wang, and J. Wu, "Polygon-Based Tracking Framework in Surveillance Wireless Sensor Networks", *15th International Conference on Parallel and Distributed Systems,* pp. 174-181, 2009.
[http://dx.doi.org/10.1109/ICPADS.2009.54]

[40]   A.A.U. Rahman, M. Naznin, and M.A.I. Mollah, "Energy-Efficient Multiple Targets Tracking Using Target Kinematics in Wireless Sensor Networks", *Fourth International Conference on Sensor Technologies and Applications,* pp. 275-280, 2010.
[http://dx.doi.org/10.1109/SENSORCOMM.2010.101]

[41]   Y. Xu, and J. Winter, "Dual prediction-based reporting for object tracking sensor networks", *The First Annual International Conference on Mobile and Ubiquitous Systems: Networking and Services,* pp. 154-163, 2004.

[42]   J.M. Hsu, C.C. Chen, and C.C. Li, "POOT: An efficient object tracking strategy based on short-term optimistic predictions for face-structured sensor networks", *Comput. Math. Appl.,* vol. 63, no. 2, pp. 391-406, 2012.
[http://dx.doi.org/10.1016/j.camwa.2011.07.034]

CHAPTER 7

A Survey of Current Mobile Learning Technology in India

Pooja Gupta[1,*] and **Vimal Kumar**[1]

[1] *Meerut Institute of Engineering and Technology, Meerut, Uttar Pradesh, India*

Abstract: Mobile learning technology is playing a vital role in today's education due to COVID-19. The ongoing pandemic has increased its demand and usage everywhere in the world. It is a technology that enables students to learn, interact, collaborate, and access education from any place and at any time by using internet-enabled mobile devices. These mobile devices include laptops, tablets, and mobile phones for distance learning. In the current scenario, this distance learning has proved as a boon, especially in the education and corporate sector widely. However, M-learning can also be applied in other fields, such as financial sectors, including banking, and non-financial sectors, including healthcare, industrial sector, *etc*. Mobile learning acceptance is a requirement that is still in progress. It has been adopted more in urban schools and higher education institutions in comparison to rural and secondary schools. Our study explores the evolution of M-learning, benefits, challenges, platforms, and various factors that affect mobile learning adoption. We have also discussed the existing models and frameworks for learning in higher education, university, *etc*. Hence, in this study, we have focused both on the positive and negative outcomes of all the previous studies to eliminate the issues and increase mobile learning adoption in the future. The main highlight of this paper is that we have presented various online platforms available for individuals, organizations, and enterprises for learning. These tools are as important as considering various other factors that have been discussed in previous findings. Moreover, a comparison table of various factors and conclusions of different researchers is shown. Furthermore, it has been concluded that the adoption of mobile learning technology must be increased in developing countries.

Keywords: Adoption, Classroom, COVID-19, M-learning 2, Mobile learning.

INTRODUCTION

Mobile technology has evolved rapidly over the last few years. Due to technological advancements, it has been widely used by society in various aspects. It is becoming diverse and has modified the way of communication,

---

[*] **Corresponding author Pooja Gupta:** Meerut Institute of Engineering and Technology, Meerut, Uttar Pradesh, India; E-mail: poojag2580@gmail.com

Vikash Yadav, Parashuram Pal & Chuan-Ming Liu (Eds.)

work, and tourism for people. Mobile learning [1] technology, in the form of tablets, mobile phones, and notebooks, is making our lives better than ever before.

It recreates meaning, importance, and various modes of learning. It is enriching our lives in every way. Thus, there is an increase in demand for lifelong learning by the people in the current era. Particularly, in the current scenario, people are using mobile phones more than personal computers for accessing pages, such as social media platforms that indicate that they are more prone to shift in a digital learning environment. In recent years, mobile learning has become popular due to the efficiency of the synchronous learning method. Thus, people are shifting from web-based learning to computer-based learning or mobile-based, with the enhancement in different technologies [1]. Technology has reformed the education system in many possible ways. Since 2000, a large number of people have been using mobile devices because these devices give rapid delivery and can be reached by everyone easily. According to statistics, mobile applications are being used by 1.2 million people all over the world. In 2017, it reached 2.7 billion. Then, the number of users has increased up to 3.5 billion in 2020. According to these statistics, it is only expected to climb up in the next few years. But the mode of teaching and learning is still traditional in many areas. Thus, this new mode of learning is less acceptable. It has been shown that innovative teaching and learning will help students in the skills development that they will need in future life and work.

M-LEARNING

M-learning is a growing trend. It is the fastest evolving learning technology in the current scenario. It is a type of learning that helps learners to learn independent of location and time. Different researchers from their perspectives have defined m-learning due to technological advancements; however, many definitions have lost their validity with time. So we define commonly used definitions in this study. Hidayat and Utomo [2] explained that portable learning is an electronic medium of information for learning. It provides the content from anywhere, anytime, and at any location globally. M-learning is an advanced version of e-learning. Electronic learning is the mode where learners are tethered to the desks, *i.e.*, learning requires being at a fixed place. E-learning does not give access to content and educational context across different locations at changing times. All these issues have been solved with the help of m-learning [3]. M-learning means learning that is changeable, *i.e.*, learning at different locations and at changing times is possible. These advancements have made mobile learning outperform other types of learning in various contexts. The term mobile learning or U-learning has been defined in different ways by different researchers as follows:-

It is called distance learning, a superset of e-learning and online education, using digital devices. Mobile learning has different names, like ubiquitous learning, M-learning, hand-held learning, U-learning, extension of e-learning, learning while mobile, portable learning, and personalized learning. It is available in all parts of society, including poor or rich and literate or illiterate, due to its easy accessibility. Besides its readiness, it gives individual personalization that helps learners learn independently of place, time, and communities. He [3] tried to meet all the requirements of m-learning in defining mobile learning. According to his theory, "Mobile learning is not just providing barrier-free information to the learners, it is also enlightenment that needs to be presented". Mobile learning tools that are used for teaching include mobile phones, tablets, podcasts, computers, e-readers, and laptops. Latest technology and tools access information with the help of mobile device, providing portability. Summing up, mobile learning can be generalized as the learning that allows anyone to access digital content, resources, platforms, websites, *etc.*, irrespective of predetermined location and changing time with the help of mobile technology.

MOBILE DEVICES

The term mobile device refers to an electronic device or gadget that can be used from anywhere. It is also called a hand-held computer. These devices are designed such that they can be carried anywhere and fit in your hand. Some mobile devices, like smartphones, cell phones, tablets, e-readers, personal digital assistant (PDA), and smartwatches, can be used to perform tasks in the same way as by desktop or personal computer. With the latest technology and trends, these portable devices are essential in the world. In modern life, the types of mobile devices that are used in mobile learning can be categorized as follows: -

- **Laptop**: There are some portable devices like laptops and notebook, which are commonly used in daily life. These devices have the same functionalities as that of a normal personal computer called PC.They are being manufactured with the help of advanced technology and their cost is high. These laptops are helpful in obtaining the information through various wireless technologies, such as USB cable, bluetooth, wireless network, and other infrared devices. Accessibility of content is independent of time and place from all over the world.
- **Tablet PC:** It is a portable and personal computer larger than a smartphone but small in size than a notebook computer. It is a type of device with 7 or 10.1 inch touch display with a user-friendly interface. It is used for viewing presentations, reading e-books, sharing photos, video-conferencing, and many more. It gives us an easy way of transferring the data with the help of the internet and memory device. There is a significant difference among different tablet pc models, such

as camera specifications, data connection speed, operating system and battery life span; however, they look similar in model.

- **PDA (Personal Digital Assistant):** It is also called a palmtop device or computer. Due to portability, we can connect this device remotely with the help of the internet. This mobile device acts as a personal data manager as it keeps the address or name of an individual. With the advancements in computer technology and electronics, the size of devices has become smaller, but their functionalities or features have been increased. This reduction in the size of devices has led to less usage of hardware and complexity, which is very beneficial. Devices produced with the high-resolution video cameras and global positioning system (GPS) are called smartphones.

- **Smartphone**: It is a device used for communication that has additional functions as compared to PDA. It provides an advanced screen display, camera, foldable smartphone, and different streaming platforms and applications [4]. A large amount of memory storage has been proven beneficial for various purposes. With the advancements in features of mobile phones, the number of smartphone users is increasing day by day.

- **Servers:** It is a computer that provides data or learning material to the other computer or learners. The data sent by the computer is called a server or host computer or master. Some servers facilitate many services, including DB, e-mail, file, SMS, proxy, servers, and many more.

- **Mobile phones:** Mobile phones have become an important mode of communication, and are used to send and receive messages, for calls, and learning by employing the latest development technologies. The latest 4G technology has increased the use of mobile phones with various additional features, like audio, videos, camera, display with high resolution, and moving pictures. These mobile devices integrated with 4G technology can be purchased at a low price. However, still, the screen size proportionally varies with the price of mobile phones. But the portability and accessibility make it worthwhile.

- **E-readers:** They are commonly known as e-book readers. They have the same design and structure as a tablet, but they are designed for reading e-books, online content, and downloaded books. Some examples of e-readers are Amazon kindle, kobo, and noble book. E-ink display enables the user to easily read the content than a traditional computer display. This helps learners to read even in bright sunlight, just like reading a regular book.

Other mobile devices: These are devices like x-box, media players, joy-pad, digital media receivers, game consoles, and video players. Some portable media players can download the apps and thus enhance their value. Apple's iPod touch is an I-phone without the phone.

EVOLUTION OF MOBILE LEARNING

Mobile learning has been revolving around in one form or another over the past many years. It advanced in the 1970s and spread widely in the mid-2000s across the world. Technology is mainly responsible for its inevitable development in our lives. The introduction and use of personal computers brought a revolution that enlarged the use of electronic devices by students and teachers for learning and teaching. Over time, the application of phones in education increased the scope of learning and teaching, but only the latest mobile technologies enable learning on the move. Compared to other technologies, m-learning is becoming more popular and developing day by day. M-learning has gained importance in the 21st century due to the unique features it provides over traditional classroom [5] environments. The earlier mode of teaching, a traditional classroom, has been formal in nature, which means learning within the classroom. It does not give mobility and portability to learners. This has resulted in the rise of mobile technology as a fundamental structure to support m-learning. M-learning is the newly adapted learning strategy, which is informal, *i.e.*, learning outside the classroom. It assists in learners' mobility, virtually anywhere and at any time, with the help of mobile devices. It provides special liberty to the students to resume their learning whenever and wherever they want. It does not limit the person to one place. Until recently, some problems might occur while learning in this way, such as the requirement of a cable to use the online-based learning platform, non-durable batteries, and lack of internet accessibility. These standalone benefits of m-learning have given rise to the use of mobile learning in the current scenario and a rapidly evolving research area by researchers. In the future, mobile learning seems to have wider scope in the area of education, teaching and learning techniques, with a large number of users in education and other fields as well. Table 1 shows a comparison table of e-learning and m-learning, considering the terminologies and various factors. It is evident that in the current scenario, with additional features and the evolution of e-learning, m-learning will be used everywhere in the world.

Table 1. Comparison table of e-learning *v/s* m-learning.

S. NO.	E-LEARNING	M-LEARNING
1.	It is a subgroup of mobile learning. It is distance learning using multimedia, which allows learners to access resources from their computer [6].	Mobile learning is an evolution of e-learning. It is also a type of distance education that allows learners to learn using mobile.
2.	It involves the use of fixed, wireless devices, such as personal computers.	It involves broadcast mechanisms, such as mobile phones, personal computers, cell phones, and personal digital assistants.

(Table 1) cont.....

S. NO.	E-LEARNING	M-LEARNING
3.	It is a mode of learning where the internet is accessed using telephone service.	M-Learning uses infrared rays to access the internet from anywhere and at anytime.
4.	In this type of learning, there is a face-to-face audio teleconference.	It is flexible and includes voice audio and video conferencing learning.
5.	It is the learning where users are tethered to desks, meaning learning is done at a fixed place.	M-learning allows learners to learn from anywhere, anytime, and at any location.
6.	This learning gives the user a lot of information and content such that it takes a long time to complete the course.	It gives users the accessibility to relevant information at a particular instant and time when needed.
7.	In this mode of learning, it has low level of communication channels protection.	Learners are able to connect with others with their own device, thus more protection is provided by learning.
8.	It is structured, useful, convenient, interactive, media-rich, broadband, and smart learning.	It gives spontaneity, informal, opportunistic and portable form of learning.
9.	It takes time to reach the internet site. Thus, it is slow in connectivity.	It takes no time because it uses a wireless connection to reach the internet. Hence, it is a fast mode of learning.
10.	It is the training given to a computer consisting of CD-ROM, an internet-based learning that helps in attaining personalization learning.	It provides resources, content, videos, audios, and platform to support individual learning and personalization.
11.	It is passive and asynchronous learning.	It is instant-based and synchronous learning.
12.	It consists of applications and methods, such as digital learning, implicit classrooms, web-based knowledge, and computer-based training. It delivers content using audio, video, satellite, internet, *etc*. It broadcasts information among individuals in offline mode only.	Mobile learning has various applications, such as m-learning in education, m-learning in sales, digital learning, and virtual classrooms. It delivers the content and information both offline and online.

Remaining paper is structured as follows:

In section 2 of the paper, m-learning components, benefits, challenges, and its applications are explained. In section 3, mobile learning and various mobile learning tools are detailed. The literature review and comparison table of research findings is presented in Section 4. At the end of the paper, the conclusion and future scope are given in Section 5.

COMPONENETS OF MOBILE LEARNING

There are five components of mobile learning, which are learner, teacher, content assessment and environment. Fig. (**1**) shows the interconnected components essential for m-learning.

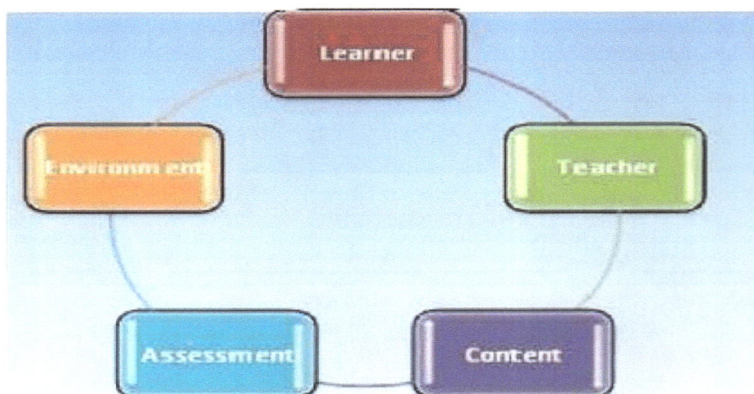

Fig. (1). Components of M-learning.

Learner: Learners play a central role in training, education and learning activities. All elements of m-learning serve the learner. Mobile learning is designed considering the learner's needs and interests. The only goal of mobile learning is to enhance the learner's skills in every aspect.

Services offered by mobile learning technology to the learners are as follows:

- 24 hours of content availability
- Self-learning
- Flexibility
- The easy way of communication
- More problem solving and discussion
- Collaboration among peer groups
- Study completion
- Access to new technology

Teacher: Teachers act as guides to learners using mobile learning. They learn and transfer the knowledge and content to the students using m-learning platforms. Teachers teach the students by audio, video classes, or notes in document form.

Services offered by mobile learning technology to the teachers are as follows:

- To provide large material lectures
- To encourage students to learn
- Performance evaluation and assessments
- To conduct quizzes and test
- Interaction with students

Content: M-learning provides the content in various forms, like online quizzes, interactive videos, audios, and the game to the learners. Content is precise that makes learning fun and complete in a given period of time. Content can be more enhanced with the use of graphics, charts, and diagrams to develop student interest in mobile learning.

Environment: In M-learning, an environment must be designed that gives a positive experience to learners. This includes student involvement, high-quality learning, content, and good scores. It allows students and teachers to interact easily by using discussion forums, private comments, or by sending an email. It gives students access to content, like assignments, quizzes, course material from anywhere and at any time. It provides online class sessions and interaction between students and teachers. It enables students to seek feedback. Moreover, it also provides a collaborative learning environment among peers.

Assessment: Evaluating performance is necessary for analyzing learning. M-learning allows the teachers to evaluate performance, record, and report the status of the students. Various online quiz assessments are assessed, thus providing feedback regarding their performance. This helps the learners to assess themselves in knowledge and skills. Assessment should not be used to discourage but motivate the students to take the course along with assessments.

BENEFITS OF MOBILE LEARNING

Mobile learning offers several benefits that shift education institutions, organizations, and companies towards it. Mobile learning allows users to gain knowledge outside the scope of a traditional classroom environment. Learning can be done on mobile devices or computers due to the portability and accessibility. It is becoming popular and widely used in the current scenario and will be in the coming years. Below are the benefits of mobile learning:-

1. **Accessibility to quality education:** This type of learning enables students from all across the globe to develop and learn collectively. There is no necessity to travel locally or internationally to get it. It gives access to all digital content on mobile phones virtually anywhere and at anytime. It also enables learners to learn the latest ongoing technologies via the internet using mobile devices.
2. **Better completion rates and higher retention:** M-learning offers chunk-sized and concise content. It is designed such that it encourages the learners toward course completion on time. This increases device usage and learning methods by students with a great experience.

3. **Learning path:** M-learning is integrated or inbuilt with device-based reminders and organizers for various organizations. Learners receive ongoing notifications and can check the status of their courses anywhere and at any time. They can resume their course whenever they want. Hence, this platform gives more personalization and continuous learning to learners.

4. **Multi-device support:** Multi-device support plays a key role in m-learning. In the M-learning environment, the course can be accessed on many devices ranging from mobile phones, personal computers, laptops, tablets, and many more.

5. **High engagement and motivation:** Various research studies show that there is an increment in learners when content is delivered using the mobile format, since mobile learning offers personalization that highly boosts learner engagement in learning. Moreover, its mobility and accessibility motivate the learners to learn anywhere and at any time. It also keeps the learners on track, resulting in more learning.

6. **Improve decision making:** Quick access to the small chunk-sized material often helps learners to understand the concepts and a chance to get connected to experts before the important meetings or before beginning tasks to improve decision making. Right decision making helps learners work effectively and increase productivity.

7. **Diversity in learning resources:** Mobile learning can be molded to different styles to increase engagement as follows:- learning through texts, quizzes, reading, audios, and videos, listening to podcasts, learning through apps, and using the online dictionary can all be incorporated flexibly into the content to suit varying lifestyles and can be done by surfing on the internet.

8. **Support self-paced learning:** People learn at different rates, and m-learning allows people to learn in their learning style at their own speed. In a traditional classroom, there will be some students who would not have learned the theories clearly or missed some classes but hesitate to ask for a re-explanation. In portable learning, rewinding and repeating the course contents give freedom to learners, and discussion forums and feedback give them the facility to clear their doubts until and unless their problem is resolved.

9. **Better performance:** Everybody likes a mode of learning which does not disturb their daily routine work. It requires any information that can be accessible while at work. The 24 hours availability of m-learning allows the learners to learn at any time. This will result in high performance and flexibility for learners. Employees often find learning useful because it increases their work performance.

CHALLENGES IN MOBILE LEARNING

Mobile learning has been found to be undeniably useful though it has some drawbacks as well that need to be considered for improvement in the future. Below are the major challenges faced by mobile learning that need to be tackled as follows:-

1. **Networking Problems:** M-learning faces several network issues, like connection stability, speed of internet, VPN request, network security, inadequate IT support, *etc.*, which need considerable effort for improvement. Indeed m-learning also supports the availability of material offline. But when there is an online learning network issue, it causes a barrier to learning.
2. **Risk of Distraction:** Mobile learning also creates some distractions and barriers to learning. Many students get distracted while learning if any notification occurs from social media platforms. It immediately enables the learner to switch the platform and leads to engaging in chatting, *etc*. These distractions waste a lot of time that can be used in some meaningful work.
3. **Software Problems:** Software is an application that runs on a device. Some factors will affect the performance of your device. These issues can be computability issues, not upgraded versions, regular system crashes, *etc*. They interrupt the smooth working of the device.
4. **Hardware Problems:** Unlike software, physical devices support hardware. But after a certain period of time, these physical devices are also worn out. The overuse of devices, dust, or lifespan are some of the reasons for worn out and failure of the devices. Hence, it affects the smooth working of the device too.
5. **Security Problems:** There is a need for improvement and enhancement in technologies and protocols that provide security and privacy in networked devices. It must be improved according to the use and requirements of mobile learning. Content and information are less secured and must be highly prioritized for security purposes.
6. **Screen Size:** The mobile screen is too small for interacting with teachers. Proper hardware is needed for learning and teaching. Another structure of content must be such that it can be viewed on all devices of different sizes. Many tools are designing screen-based content. Hence, a good response to learning can be achieved.
7. **Data Security and Privacy:** Before starting a mobile learning course, organizations need to aware people regarding the security challenges associated with mobile learning. An unmonitored mobile connection increases the risk of security threats. Therefore, it is necessary for people who wish to

undertake training courses that they must use their own devices to prevent their data from being exposed.

8. **Health Issues:** Continuous learning on mobile devices can endanger eyesight. Long hours of use of mobile devices can also cause several problems, like headaches, eyestrain, neck pain, backbone problem, *etc*. This can be avoided if it is not used continuously for long hours.

9. **Content Compatibility:** Different devices have different configurations and different standards. File size and formats that are compatible with laptops and personal computers lead to performance problems for mobile devices. Recreating content and adapting for mobile phones can delay the training program.

10. **Technical Challenges**
    i. Slow connectivity: Mobile devices suffer from slow connection due to network congestion, low bandwidth, and high latency.
    ii. Limited battery life: Mobile devices do not have longer battery time due to which work is left in the middle. Also, the charger available does not work on the go.
    iii. Adjustment to multiple operating systems: It causes difficulty in developing portals compatible with operating systems as mobile devices have different file formats, features, and operating systems.
    iv. Cost of investment: It means the cost incurred on mobile learning is high. Hence, it sometimes hits the budget for training programs.
    v. Work/life balance: It disrupts especially the life balance of mobile workers who face external and internal pressure to work effectively throughout the whole day. This lack of gap leads to a stressful environment.
    vi. Security: It is a major issue while learning as mobile security attacks are frequent and risk to confidential data of users. Therefore, learning platforms need encryption techniques to secure the data.
    vii. Bandwidth: It requires the bandwidth to be optimized based on the user network as different bandwidth is used for the various streaming processes. Screen size creates difficulty in creating content and is specific.

APPLICATIONS OF MOBILE LEARNING

In the 21st century, the extensive adoption of m-learning and mobile technologies has derived a vast range of domains. Three applications of m-learning are described in the below section as follows:

Online Learning and Blended Learning

One of the most widely used applications of m-learning is to create a space for complete online education and blended learning. A- blended learning environment is a union of virtual learning and traditional physical interaction between teacher and student. Essentially, in a traditional classroom, face to face interaction occurs, while online learning uses learning management system to deliver component that supplies facilities, such as quizzes, portable document file, discussion forums, schedule, and subject matter in a soft copy [7]. It allows delivering lectures, access to content, assessments, and feedback online with the students with the help of discussion forums and communicating with the instructor on the platform. The major benefit of this type of learning is to modify education into an unsynchronized or asynchronous experience.

Asynchronous learning means learners retrieve course content with the help of the online platform and learning management system (LMS) on their course. Moreover, the inference of blended learning will be discussed in the next subsequent subsection.

Game-Based Learning (GBL)

It is the process of applying relevant information or learning materials with the purpose of the involvement of users. This game-based learning has existed for twenty years. With technological advancements and pace, mobile technology plays a great role in advancing game-based learning. Many game panels can be accessed using mobile devices; the importance of including game-based learning in course layout structure has increased to improve students' learning and engagement, motivation, and course completion successfully [8]. The use of GBL showed a much higher level of student interest and engagement in learning. Thus, it can be a substitute for direct instruction among students.

Though still, it is the initial stage of GBL to be adopted in education. Hence, the development of a practical substitute for teaching is increasing with the progressing technologies.

Online Learning in Remote Areas

M-learning can provide training to the learners living in provincial and remote areas by connecting them with the internet globally [9]. There is a need to improve the broadband speed and connectivity in m-learning. In Canada, to improve broadband service, dollars have been spent on satellite technologies in provincial and distant areas [10]. Though poor students may not have easy access to information for online education in comparison to rich people. Thus, it will reduce the digital divide and give opportunities to students who are more intelligent and connected. However, using mobile technology, learners can access course programs taught by specialists from other schools synchronously or asynchronously in a shared classroom of hundreds of students [11]. It also connects different learners from the neighborhood and operates collectively on productive tasks.

MOTIVATION

The ongoing COVID-19 pandemic has resulted in lockdown all across the world. Each country is facing major crises in every sector, including healthcare enterprise, education, economy, and many more. Its major impact has been observed on the education sector as well. Globally, over 1.2 billion children are out of school as the COVID-19 outbreak intensifies. As a result, it has prompted education institutions to shift towards digital learning. Therefore, mobile learning adoption somehow will help to fulfill the gap created by the suspended classroom learning, whereby learning is done remotely on digital education programs. The digital training programs support learners not only just access the content but also involve them in online sessions and communicate with lecturers just like traditional teaching. These platforms give free access to their tools and technologies, thereby motivating learners to use them efficiently. M-learning has given us the facility to continue to work towards our target without an extended disturbance in an unimaginable tough time. As more and more learners will hold on to this mode of learning, the rise of mobile learning will continuesince the flexibility offered by online learning is unmatched.

Next, the major issue during covid-19 is communication when it is most essential. During the pandemic, m-learning allows for communication from anywhere in the world. The rise of mobile learning is in part due to the growing realization that learners are seeking high-quality information and learning experience in a more accessible format. M-learning allows learners to learn and improve their skills in a comfortable environment [39]. For example, m-learning courses can include simulation training. It will help students to focus on their work in an adaptable environment without feeling external pressure. Mobile learning is not less than traditional learning. Indeed it is another option for learners who may not feel much comfortable in a traditional classroom environment. It offers flexibility such that learners who are unable to balance their work or life schedule can easily access the learning. So, we are already exploring a world where virtual learning is valued and utilized on a broader scale. Although it is largely against our will, the situation requires that we adapt a broader approach to mobile learning.

MOBILE LEARNING TOOLS

In this section, we discuss various available mobile learning tools for learning and teaching. These mobile learning platforms or applications play a key role in learning and teaching nowadays. These tools aim to boost education effectiveness by shifting from obstruction to active knowledge, education, and the availability of interactive information to receivers, and desktop applications to both learners and educators. There are diverse learning and education materials in the program, through which educators can provide lectures to their own suitability. Hence, learners may have an easy access to education sources they require. This shows a stable association between training and learning [12]. Additionally, the platform gives a user-friendly interface and concise content to the learners. It gives easy accessibility by which learners can reclaim as much learning as possible. Hence, the program includes a complete method of education. These platforms are beneficial for teachers as well. Educators can also observe students' study, activity, assignments, preparation, tests, plus they can take the exam to achieve the scientific goals of the teaching process. They can enhance their pedagogy method based on the results and achievement of students in addition to the valuable feedback provided by students. Lastly, the program assists mobile learning by portable software, which is fully available for learners and educators to download and fix. These tools are depicted in Table **2** as follows.

Table 2. Details of mobile learning tools.

S. No.	Tools	Description	Advantages	Disadvantages
1.	Google classroom [13]	Digital learning management system for every individual.	Free to use, blended with g-mail, docs, sheets, slides, calendar, and material availability 24x7 and secure.	Non-availability of audio, video recordings, and uploaded work cannot be edited.
2.	Zoom [14]	Collaborative video conferencing cloud platform for individuals, institutions and organizations.	Free to use, high-quality audio and video, live interaction, noise reduction.	Less secure, limited bandwidth, slow performance due to CPU usage, time limit for meetings, and recordings can only be saved on computers.
3.	Google meet [19]	Collaborative platform with Google G-suite for educational institutions and organizations.	Free access to anyone with the Google account, secure, no time limits, and recording capabilities.	Disorganized whiteboard poll and survey options are not available.

(Table 2) cont.....

S. No.	Tools	Description	Advantages	Disadvantages
4.	Microsoft teams [14]	Collaborative with Microsoft office software.	Free to use, offline reading and writing message facility, unlimited audio, video sharing noise reduction in video calls.	Audio, video calling and sharing not supported by all browsers, less secure.
5.	Byju's [17]	Self directed learning content for competition exams and for class 1 to 12 students.	Free access for limited time, secure, free unlimited practice, test series, video lectures.	No real time interaction, no recordings, paid and expensive.
6.	Slack [14]	Collaboration platform available to everybody.	Easy set up, both free and paid, unlimited 1:1 video and voice calls, more file storage.	Less secure, scalability, architectural deficiencies, screen sharing unavailable in free version, message history limit in the free plan.
7.	Diksha app [15]	National platform for India by NCTE for students of classes 1 to 12	Free, secure, approx. 80000 content material, audio downloads.	Android OS above 5.0 is required.
8.	National Digital Library of India [15], [18]	Integrated platform for schools, higher education, also PHD level education by MHRD and Government of India.	Free to use, multilingual knowledge base, lab material availability and content access at anytime.	No offline material availability, no live video, audio classes.
9.	Umang app [15]	Government mobile application for primary and secondary school students.	Free to use, e-book availability, audio, videos available.	No real time interaction, no offline data availability.
10.	SWAYAM [15]	Massive open online course by government of India for class student 9 to 12 and post education.	Free and interactive, both offline and online data availability, user friendly, self assessments.	Easy dropouts of students, discussion problems, grading papers is difficult.
11.	Amazon chime app [16]	Communication platform for organizations	Open access, Screen sharing, quality software, support large enterprise.	Less used in small business, does not support mobile browsers.

LITERATURE SURVEY

O'Malley [20] described mobile learning as any mode of education that occurs when the student is not at a planned position, fixed place, or education that occurs when the student opts for education possibilities given by portable technologies. Traxler [21] explained that M-learning is perhaps being described as an educational procurement where the individual or authoritative technologies are handheld or palmtop tools. This description means that education will incorporate personal digital assistants (PDAs), mobile phones, and also their peripheral devices. Davis [22] was the first to introduce the technology acceptance model in 1986 to discover user support for movable learning employing this model. The technology acceptance model (TAM) is based on parameters that are perceived interaction and perceived easiness of usage. In this research, it adds an external variable perceived usefulness to the model for exploring the acceptance of mobile learning. Further, it has limitations of questionnaire responses from high students and very few by university students. Seyyedreza [23] in their study implement the mobile learning based education using the conceptual model by combining TAM and ml approaches in the Payamnoor University of Iran. A questionnaire was prepared for 351 students to assess the reliability of four factors like environmental characteristics, student behavioral characteristics, educational and technology infrastructure, education system failures with the ease of use of mobile learning for gender-based learning. Thus four hypotheses and eight sub hypotheses were prepared to show that there is a direct and positive relationship of all the four factors with the acceptance of ml and there is no difference between the Ml and acceptance of m-learning based on gender. HamidiHodjat [24] analyzed the determinants that affect the acceptance of Portable learning by distributing questionnaires among the 300 students of the IT department of K.N. Toosi University in Iran. Here, the author discussed the mobile service acceptance model (MSAM) using the TAM model by adding other factors like trust, context, and personal characters in it. Thus, the study determined that there is a definite correlation between PU and other factors for mobile learning adoption by the students. Bidin and Zidan [25] surveyed the technical factors that influence adopting mobile learning education and also discussed the benefits, challenges, and issues arising in mobile learning. This paper concluded that further issues based on academic performance need to be analyzed. Also, various challenges should be considered before the acceptance of mobile learning education. Yousef Mehdipour [26] explained the benefits and challenges of m-learning. The paper describes the current situation of mobile learning and its barriers to education. They discussed the analysis of mobile learning, differentiation of electronic learning and mobile learning, values, plus benefits, challenges, *etc*. It focused on the usage of portable learning where students work interdependently in groups or individually solve the work problems enhancing personalized learning. S. A & Economides [27] aimed their study at determining the factors that influence students in adopting mobile-based assessments. These assessments are done with the support of portable devices. A mobile-based Assessment acceptance prototype was proposed based on the technology acceptance model (TAM) by adding factors like Perceived Trust, Content, Cognitive Feedback, User Interface, Perceived Pervasiveness Value, and percentage variance on the Behavioral Purpose to utilize mobile-based assessments in high schools. Nikou and Economides [28] examine the different factors that influence the students' and educators' attitudes toward acceptance of movable learning in Higher Education University within OMAN and OAE of the Arab Gulf region. The implementation of mobile learning infrastructure develops a positive attitude towards its adoption in the country. Chuchu and Ndoro [29] proposed the conceptual design based on the TAM model to examine the learner's opinion towards the use of mobile applications used as learning tools in higher education of South Africa. This study showed a positive attitude towards the acceptance of portable learning programs, and the increased use of platforms increases the use of mobile learning in the institution. Alshurideh [30] proposed the model, which is an extension of the TAM model by adding important factors in it to study the attitude towards the use of portable learning programs based on the system quality and user interface leading to high user intention and the increased use of m-learning programs in UAE University. They emphasized the use of m-learning platforms of high-quality systems to provide a better outcome of the acceptance of mobile learning. Chavoshi and Hamidi [31] proposed a comprehensive model using the technology acceptance model (TAM) and unified theory of acceptance and technology model (UTAUT) to study the factors like technological, pedagogical, group, and personal problems to show the influence of students toward m-learning acceptance in Iran. They use demographic characteristics and factors in addition to government support factors to measure the receiving of portable learning amongst learners. This study uses an artificial neural network (ANN) to analyze results due to the high prediction power of acceptance of learning by students. Shamsuddin [32] used the STEEPV analysis technique to identify the factors and the UTAUT model to measure the level of m-learning acceptance in public university of Malaysia. This study showed that the technological factor is the most important factor among all the factors in influencing students to adopt mobile learning. Moreover, the attitude and behavior intention of students is an essential constituent in the increased level of mobile learning acceptance. Al-Adwan [33] proposed the empirical framework based on several previous models used for acceptance of m-learning. It aimed at investing the student's behavioral intention towards adoption in developing countries like Jordan in higher education. It studies the different factors that drive the user's attention to the adoption of m-learning. Though it is not implemented in Jordan, the usage of mobile devices is high and increases students' perception of the benefits of mobile learning. Kaliisa [34] proposed a theoretical framework as a UTAUT model by adding variables to it for calculating the variance of mobile technology use. This study reflects the students' attitude towards its use and challenges during m-leaning. It gives a deep insight into the review of m-learning adoption in developed and emerging countries like Australia and Uganda. Mobile learning is widely seen in developed countries like Australia more than in developing but it shows that students have a positive attitude towards using laptops for mobile learning. Gezgin [35] aimed to study the adoption of mobile learning by undergraduate computer science students in Turkish public universities using Mobile Learning attitude survey methods which determine the definite view towards the effectiveness of m-learning. Learners are more influenced by the user-friendly interface design and other benefits offered by it. The study showed that female students show more usability of m-learning than male students. More number of students are using m-learning who have mobile device ownership in comparison to others. Alhajri and Rana [36] in their study discussed the several challenges associated with mobile learning implementation. This study identified the positive attitude of both instructors and students towards m-learning in Kuwait HE institutions. Students and the instructors perspective towards the adoption of m-learning are welcoming and ready due to the knowledge about the benefits provided by it. However, it highlights many issues in implementation plus the major barrier is the socio-economic culture in Kuwait. Hafedh [37] proposed the neural network model based on the UTAUT model and TAM model by adding factors in these models to predict m-learning acceptance in developing countries. This study shows that perceived enjoyment is the major factor responsible for the enactment of mobile learning amongst learners in Oman [38]. Therefore, the use of virtual learning will be high among the students by developing mobile learning tools as per the needs of students. Research findings of existing approaches are given in Table 3.

Table 3. Research findings.

References	Factors	Research Findings/Conclusions
Alhajri, Rana (2016)	Gender, marital status, age, education, type of mobile device and frequency of use.	• All the factors show a positive influence of students and teachers towards mobile learning adoption.
Chuchu,Tinas-he, and Tinashe Ndoro (2019)	Perceived usefulness, (PU), perceived ease of use (PEOU).	• A positive relationship between PU and attitude • The positive relationship between PEOU and attitude. • The positive relationship between intention to use and attitude. • The positive correlation in intention to adopt and tangible use of m-learning.
Chavoshi, Amir, and Hodjat Hamidi (2018)	Social, pedagogical, technological, government support and individual issues.	• Government support shows a positive influence on students. • PU increases with a decrease in complexity. • PEOU increases with the increase in professionals and youth inclination towards mobile learning.

(Table 3) cont.....

References	Factors	Research Findings/Conclusions
Alshurideh, Said, Barween, Azza, Khaled (2019)	Content quality, custom state, service property, data attribute.	• The positive impact of all the determinants on the perceived easiness of usage and perceived usability. • High quality system increases the intention to use m-learning.
Stavros A. Nikou, AnastasiosA. Economides (2017)	(PEOU), (PU), perceived trus, mobile self-efficacy, Expediting Conditions (EC), cognitive feedback, social significance, mobile device anxiety, perceived ubiquity value, personal innovativeness, content, User Interface on Behavioral Intention to Use .	• The positive influence of PEOU, PU. • Social significance, mobile self efficacy, facilitating conditions, cognitive feedback, content, perceived trust, user interface has a positive influence on PEOU or PU. • Negative influence of mobile device safety on PEOU. • The perceived trust is the major factor that is added to determine the perception of students.
Kaliisa, Roger, Edward, and Julia Miller (2019)	Performance expectancy, social influence, country or culture background effort expectancy and facilitating conditions.	• Performance and effort have a positive impact on Australian students. • Social and facilitating conditions have a positive influence on Uganda students. • Country or cultural background is the most important determinant that makes a meaningful difference in the adoption of online learning among two countries.
Shamsuddin, Alina (2018)	Social, technology, economic, environmental, political values.	• The technological factors produce a significant positive impression on mobile learning adoption. • Behavioral intention values and performance expectancy increase the level of adoption of mobile learning among students.
Al-Shihi (2018)	Flexibility, social, efficiency, enjoyment, suitability, and economic learning.	• This study revealed that flexibility, social, and efficiency are the factors that are responsible for m-learning adoption. • Entertainment and efficiency have the highest priority in adopting m-learning. • Neural network approach helps in overcoming the simplistic nature of structure equation modeling.
Gezgin (2018)	Gender, mobile device ownership, area study.	• This study shows a more positive attitude of females towards its usability more than males. • Moreover the use of M-learning is high amongst the learners who have mobile device ownership than others.
Samsiah, and Azidah Abu Ziden (2013)	Mobile utility, ease of use, perceived enjoyment, performance	• M-learning usability is dependent on the academic performance of learners. • Mobile utility shows a positive attitude towards enjoyment.

CONCLUSION AND FUTURE SCOPE

The current COVID-19 pandemic has a meaningful impact on m-learning adoption that has led to the rise and growth of m-learning in education widely all over the world. In this paper, we have discussed various tools, benefits, and determinants that boost the learner's readiness to adopt m-learning technology. Our study reviewed the previous findings and identified a research gap that some factors from teacher's perspectives have not been considered in previous research. In a challenging time like covid-19, education issues, while teaching and adapting to digital learning, are a major challenge for some educators. The focus is more on students' attitudes than awareness of the benefits of portable learning among students and educators. The adoption of M-learning technology in developing countries has not been fully explored in countries like India. In the future, m-learning can be used in other areas like the banking and finance industry as a need to prevent financial loss from changing trends in the market. Moreover, m-learning will be valuable for educating health professionals and education sector.

CONSENT FOR PUBLICATION

Not applicable.

CONFLICT OF INTEREST

The author declares no conflict of interest, financial or otherwise.

ACKNOWLEDGEMENTS

Declared none.

REFERENCES

[1]   M. Sarrab, I. Al Shibli, and N. Badursha, "An empirical study of factors driving the Adoption of mobile learning in Omani higher education", *International Review of Research in Open and Distributed Learning,* pp. 331-349, 2016.
[http://dx.doi.org/10.19173/irrodl.v17i4.2614]

[2]   A. Hidayat, and V. Gayuh Utomo, "Open source based m-learning application for supporting distance Learning", *TELKOMNIKA (Telecommunication Computing Electronics and Control),* vol. 12, no. 3, pp. 657-664, 2014.
[http://dx.doi.org/10.12928/telkomnika.v12i3.104]

[3]   Ahmed Al-Hunaiyyan, Rana A. Alhajri, and Salah Al-Sharhan, "Perceptions and challenges of mobile learning in Kuwait", *Journal of King Saud University-Computer and Information Sciences,* vol. 2, pp. 279-289, 2018.
[http://dx.doi.org/10.1016/j.jksuci.2016.12.001]

[4]   İ. Göksu, and B. Atici, "Need for mobile learning: technologies and opportunities", *Procedia Soc. Behav. Sci.,* vol. 103, pp. 685-694, 2013.
[http://dx.doi.org/10.1016/j.sbspro.2013.10.388]

[5]   V. Yadav, "A Survey paper on wireless access protocol", *International Journal of Computer Science and Infoemation Technologies,* vol. 6, no. 4, pp. 3527-3534, 2015.

[6]   Z. Rimale, B.L. El Habib, and A. Tragha, "A Brief Survey and Comparison of m- Learning and e-Learning", *International Journal of Computer Networks and Communications Security,* vol. 4, no. 4, p. 89, 2016.

[7]   "Blended Learning", *Ontario: Ministry of Education,* 2013. Retrieved from http://www.edu. gov.on.ca/elearning/blend.html

[8]   Technavio., "Game-based Learning Market in the US – Increasing Popularity of Mobile Technologies To Boost Growth", *Business Wire,* 2018. Retrieved from https://www.businesswire.com/ news/home/20180303005017/en/Game-based-Learning-Market

[9]   C. Chen, "China to boost broadband speeds in rural areas to narrow education gap", *South Morning China Post,* 2018. Retrieved from http://www.scmp.com/tech/article/2133051/china- boostbroadband-speeds-rural-areas-narrow-education

[10]   K. Sasseville, "Government investing in space and satellite communications technologies to Improve access to broadband in rural and remote areas", Retrieved from https://www.newswires.ca/news-releases/government-investing-in-space-andsatellte.html

[11]   R. Valconi, "Principles and Applications of Mobile Learning and Technologies", *Technology and the Curriculum: Summer,* 2018.

[12]   Y. Zhonggen, Z. Ying, Y. Zhichun, and C. Wentao, "Student satisfaction, learning outcomes, and cognitive loads with a mobile learning platform", *Comput. Assist. Lang. Learn.,* vol. 32, no. 4, pp. 323-341, 2019.
[http://dx.doi.org/10.1080/09588221.2018.1517093]

[13]   https://en.wikipedia.org/wiki/Google_Classroom

[14]   https://www.forbes.com/sites/martingiles/2020/03/19/free-software-for-businesses-and-schools-covid-19/?sh=43fd000c752d

[15]   https://www.jagranjosh.com/articles/list-of-digital-learning-platforms-for-the-students-by-mhrd-and-

[16]   P. Miller, *Amazon Chime.,* 2020. https://aws.amazon.com/chime/?nc=sn&loc=0&chime-Blo--posts.sort-by=item.additionalFields.createdDate&chime-blog-posts.sort-order=desc

[17]   "Wikipedia contributors, "BYJU'S," Wikipedia, the Free Encyclopedia", *Accessed,* no. July, p. 1, 2020.

[18]   "National Digital Library of India", *Wikipedia, The free Encyclopedia,* 2020.

[19]   "Javier Soltero Vice President & GM, G Suite, Google Meet", https://www.blog.google/ products/meet/bringing-google-meet-to-more-people/

[20]   P. De Chazal, C. Heneghan, E. Sheridan, R. Reilly, P. Nolan, and M. O'Malley, "Automated processing of the single-lead electrocardiogram for the detection of obstructive sleep apnoea", *IEEE Transactions on Biomedical Engineering 50,* vol. 6, pp. 686-696, 2016.

[21]   J. Traxler, "Defining mobile learning", *IADIS International Conference Mobile Learning,* pp. 261-266, 2005.

[22]   L. I-Fan, M. Chang Chen, Y. S. Sun, D. Wible, and C-H. Kuo, "Extending the TAM model to Explore the factors that affect Intention to Use an Online Learning Community", *Computers & education 54,* pp. 600-610, 2010.

[23]   A. Seyyedreza, "Presenting mobile learning acceptance model in higher education", *2018 12ᵗʰ Iranian and 6th International Conference on e-Learning and e-Teaching (ICeLeT),* pp. 21-32, 2018.
[http://dx.doi.org/10.1109/ICELET.2018.8586688]

[24]   H. Chavoshi Amir, "Analysis of the essential factors for the adoption of mobile learning in higher

education: A case study of students of the University of Technology", *Telematics and Informatics,* vol. 35, pp. 1053-1070, 2018.

[25] S. Bidin, and A.A. Ziden, "Adoption and application of mobile learning in the education industry", *Procedia Soc. Behav. Sci.,* vol. 90, pp. 720-729, 2013.
[http://dx.doi.org/10.1016/j.sbspro.2013.07.145]

[26] Y. Mehdipour, and H. Zerehkafi, "Mobile learning for education: Benefits and challenges", *International Journal of Computational Engineering Research,* vol. 6, pp. 93-101, 2013.

[27] S.A. Nikou, and A.A. Economides, "Mobile-based assessment: Investigating the factors that influence behavioral intention to use", *Comput. Educ.,* vol. 109, pp. 56-73, 2017.
[http://dx.doi.org/10.1016/j.compedu.2017.02.005]

[28] M. Al-Emran, H.M. Elsherif, and K. Shaalan, "Investigating attitudes towards the use of mobile learning in higher education", *Comput. Human Behav.,* vol. 56, pp. 93-102, 2016.
[http://dx.doi.org/10.1016/j.chb.2015.11.033]

[29] T. Chuchu, and T. Ndoro, *An examination of the determinants of the adoption of mobile applications as learning tools for higher education students.,* 2019, pp. 53-67.

[30] M.T. Alshurideh, S.A. Salloum, B. Al Kurdi, A. Abdel Monem, and K. Shaalan, "Understanding the quality determinants that influence the intention to use the mobile learning platforms: A practical study", *International Journal of Interactive Mobile Technologies (IJIM),* vol. 11, pp. 157-183, 2011.

[31] A. Chavoshi, and H. Hamidi, "Social, individual, technological and pedagogical factors influencing mobile learning acceptance in higher education: A case from Iran", *Telemat. Inform.,* vol. 38, pp. 133-165, 2019.
[http://dx.doi.org/10.1016/j.tele.2018.09.007]

[32] A. Shamsuddin, E. Wahab, N.H. Abdullah, and A. Suratkon, "Mobile Learning Adoption in Enhancing Learning Experience Among HEI students",
[http://dx.doi.org/10.1109/ICEED.2018.8626923]

[33] A.S. Al-Adwan, A. Al-Madadha, and Z. Zvirzdinaite, "Al-Madadha, and Zahra Zvirzdinaite, "Modeling students' readiness to adopt mobile learning in higher education: An empirical study"", *Int. Rev. Res. Open Distance Learn.,* vol. 19, no. 1, 2018.
[http://dx.doi.org/10.19173/irrodl.v19i1.3256]

[34] Rogers Kaliisa, Edward Palmer, and Julia Miller, "Mobile learning in higher education: A comparative analysis of developed and developing country contexts", *British Journal of EducationalTechnology,* vol. 2, pp. 546-561, 2019.
[http://dx.doi.org/10.1111/bjet.12583]

[35] Deniz Mertkan Gezgin, and Meltem Acar Guvendir, "Mobile learning according to students of computer engineering and computer education: A comparison of attitudes", *Turkish Online Journal of Distance Education,* vol. 1, pp. 4-17, 2018.
[http://dx.doi.org/10.17718/tojde.382653]

[36] R. Alhajri, "Prospects and challenges of mobile learning implementation: A case study", In: *Journal of Information Technology & Software Engineering 6* vol. 5. , 2016, pp. 1-8.

[37] H. Al-Shihi, and S.K. Sharma, "Neural network approach to predict mobile learning acceptance", In: *Education and Information Technologies 23* vol. 5. , 2018, pp. 1805-1824.
[http://dx.doi.org/10.1007/s10639-018-9691-9]

[38] Abdulvahap Sönmez, Lütfiye Göçmez, Derya Uygun, and Murat Ataizi, "A review of current studies of mobile learning", *Journal of Educational Technology & Online Learning,* 2018.
[http://dx.doi.org/10.31681/jetol.378241]

[39] https://www.vectorsolutions.com/news-media/blog/role-of-mobile-learning-during-covid/

CHAPTER 8

Fuzzy Systems and Applications from an Engineer's Perspective (Fuzzy Textual Data Classification - Case Study)

Mohammed Abdul Wajeed[1,*]

[1] *Vasavi College of Engineering, Ibrahimbagh, Telangana, India*

Abstract: Soft computing has arisen as a standard presuming perspective; fuzzy ideas have advanced as imperative in the field of processing. The present chapter would expect to motivate and support the reader by giving all the necessary flavors empowering him to seek after and exude creative thoughts in the field of the fuzzy framework. The chapter presents the fundamental fuzzy ideas, including the operations performed on uncertainty sets. Fuzzy ideas and operations are contrasted with crispy sets for the better cognizance of the pursuers, specifically the naive. How the probabilistic and fuzzy frameworks (level of truthness) vary would be underscored with sufficient situations. Uncertainty, vagueness in the data, and historical crispy data when utilized later, would connect some vulnerability with it; an embodiment of such vulnerability and its need to consider in the processing is managed in detail. Different fuzzy membership functions commonly used are explored here. The underlying terminology (core, support and boundary) and its significance in the membership functions are explored. In the last segment of the section, text categorization (TC) application utilizing the fuzzy ideas in processing is investigated. The features in TC are transformed into fuzzy collections (soft, hard and blended) as feature reduction. Gaussian function is employed in the process of obtaining the fuzzy collections. Itemized steps during the time spent treating word-based data classification are talked about.

Keywords: Fuzzy Participation Functions, Fuzzy Systems, Soft Computing, Text Classification.

INTRODUCTION

The word computing is obtained from the Latin expression "computare" which intends "to Fig", "to tally" to "summarize", and "to think together". By and large, more exact word computing implies a "gadget that performs calculation".

---

*Corresponding author Mohammed Abdul Wajeed:Vasavi College of Engineering, Ibrahimbagh, Telangana, India; E-mail: drwajeed1@gmail.com

Vikash Yadav, Parashuram Pal & Chuan-Ming Liu (Eds.)

In view of the qualities of computing in writing, we find comprehensively two kinds of computing strategies.

Hard computing approach creates an ensured and deterministic exact outcome with pre-characterized positive control activities utilizing a numerical model or calculation. It deals with binary, crisp logic that requests precise, accurate data as input with a complete level of sureness. Hard computing maps the inputs provided into relating output by customary intelligence and requires an expository model. Yet, we are encircled with a serious level of vulnerability and commotion in input data. Hard computing, when applied to tackle certifiable issues with such vulnerability, devours a lot of calculation time and cost and is bound to give inaccurate outcomes. Soft computing is an advanced methodology speaking to the certitude that the human psyche has the capacity to store and handle data that can be loose and needs certainty. It manages rough models that are open minded toward imprecision, vulnerability and incomplete truth contributions, with serious level of vigor and are versatile to more extensive areas.

Few divergences among hard and soft computing are:

1. Hard computing is best for tackling the pure mathematical problems which are away from real world problems. Soft computing is better utilized in tackling certifiable real world issues as it is stochastic in nature. It is an arbitrarily characterized measure that can be investigated measurably, however not with accuracy.

2. Hard computing depends on binary logic and predefined own program like a mathematical examination using only bi-stable rationale. Soft computing depends on the model of the human psyche where it has probabilistic thinking, fluffy rationale, and utilizes multivalued rationale, and can advance its own program called as a model.

3. Hard computing needs careful contribution of the inputs and is consecutive; whereas, soft computing can deal with a wealth of information and handles different calculations which probably will not be definite in an equal manner.

4. Hard computing takes a great deal of time to finish assignments and is exorbitant while soft computing resistance of vulnerability and imprecision is assessed to accomplish Machine Intelligence Quotient (MIQ) and lower cost.

5. Hard computing is most appropriate for tackling numerical issues which offer some exact responses. Complete linearity among the inputs is given and corresponding output is obtained. Soft computing settles the nonlinear issues that

include vulnerability and uncertainty as it has human-like knowledge that can resolve the genuine issue.

In the current situation, both computing techniques are being utilized together in different ventures and alluded as hybrid computing frameworks with the point of creating profoundly steady frameworks.

For example consider a set, Tall Boys in class = {x | height(x) > 170 cms}. Here the height 170 is the property of the Tall boys set (for some nation).

In classical sets, the sets are characterized with crisp boundaries. Usually a classical set is known as an assortment of items which have a few properties recognizing them from different articles which do not have these properties.

Consider a population, students in a university whose statures are arranged in Table **1**. Regarding the classical definition of tall young boy set in a class, students Bhaskar, Cala and Falgu are tall students and students Anil, Dilip and Edi are treated as not tall students.

Table 1. The height of boys in a class.

Boy	Height
Anil	165
Bhaskar	172
Cala	175
Dilip	160
Edi	168
Falgu	178

Set of tall students T= { Bhaskar, Cala, Falgu} and set of not tall students NT = { Anil, Dilip, Edi}

$$\chi_T(e) = \begin{cases} 1 \ if \ e \ \in T \\ 0 \ if \ e \ \notin T \end{cases} \tag{1}$$

'χ_T' refers to the membership of tallness of the set T and e is the element in the set T.

The classical set cannot draw any relation among the elements in the set of tall students; same is the case with the set of not tall students, shown in Fig (**1**).

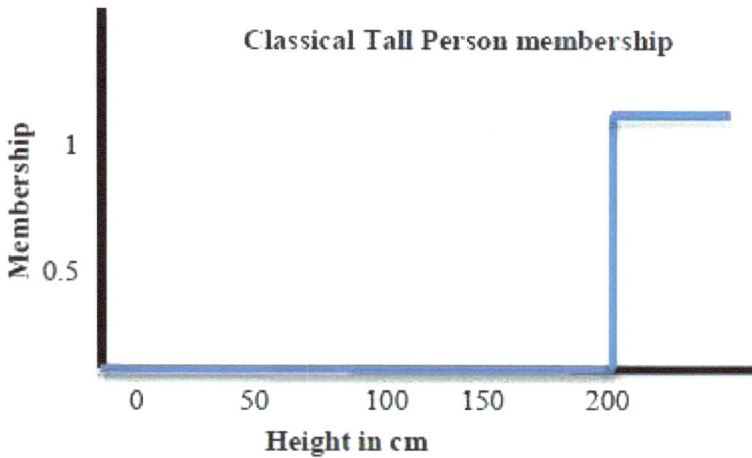

Fig. (1). Classical membership of tall persons in a class.

Introduction of Fuzzy sets can relate the elements in the sets; quantification is estimated in terms of participation (membership) values. The idea of Fuzzy set was presented by Lotif Zadeh in 1965 to deal with imprecise data [1]. Falgu is taller than student Bhaskar; it would be evident that student Falgu is relegated to a more prominent participation than the participation value of Bhaskar. Considering the genuine scenario that new students joining at later (any) stage whose tallness can be more than the stature of Falgu, it would be apparent that the participation estimation value of the new students should be bigger than the Falgu participation. This infers that the stature of the students is relative, the participation value should reflect the relativeness, and a value in the open interval 0 and 1(0,1) is assigned as participation value. A fuzzy set is a class with a continuum of participation grades [1].

Falgu would have a participation value near 1, however not equivalent to 1, giving extension to dole out the participation estimation of the students whose height is superior than Falgu and would likewise have participation value higher than Falgu's participation value.

$\mu_T(e)$ = {(Anil,0.5), (Bhaskar,0.9), (Cala,0.95), (Dilip,0.35), (Edi,0.85), (Falgu,0.98) }

The value associated with Anil is 0.5, which gives the participation value of the height property of the students.

Example 2: The ages of the individuals are given in Table **2**, determining whether the person is young or not.

Table 2. Individual ages.

Person Name	Age in Years
Iaan	28
Jai	18
Kamod	45
Laksh	16
Maan	22

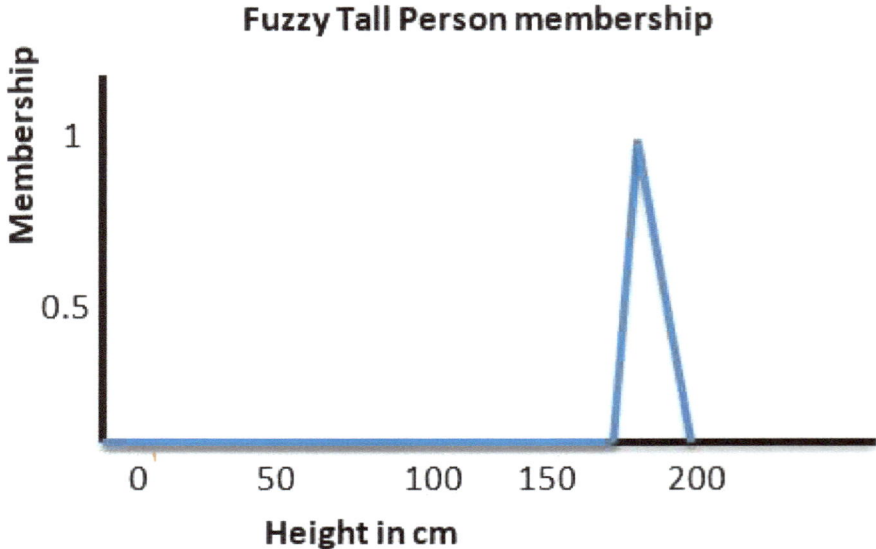

Fig. (2). Fuzzy tallest person participation values.

In the classical definition of youngness, an individual having an age lesser than 20 years is viewed as youthful. Elements in the set Young= {Jai, Laksh}, and on the other hand, elements in the set Not_ young= {Iaan, Kamod, Maan}, which is actually a complement of the set young. When a person attains an age that is marginally more noteworthy than 20, he is considered as not youthful any longer in the classical set, which is a little weird; the fuzzy set can deal with such circumstances with various membership values shown in Fig. (**3**).

$$\chi_Y\left(age\right) \ =\begin{cases}1 \text{ if age} \geq 20\\ 0 \text{ if age} < 20\end{cases} \qquad\qquad \textbf{(2)}$$

Classical Youngness membership

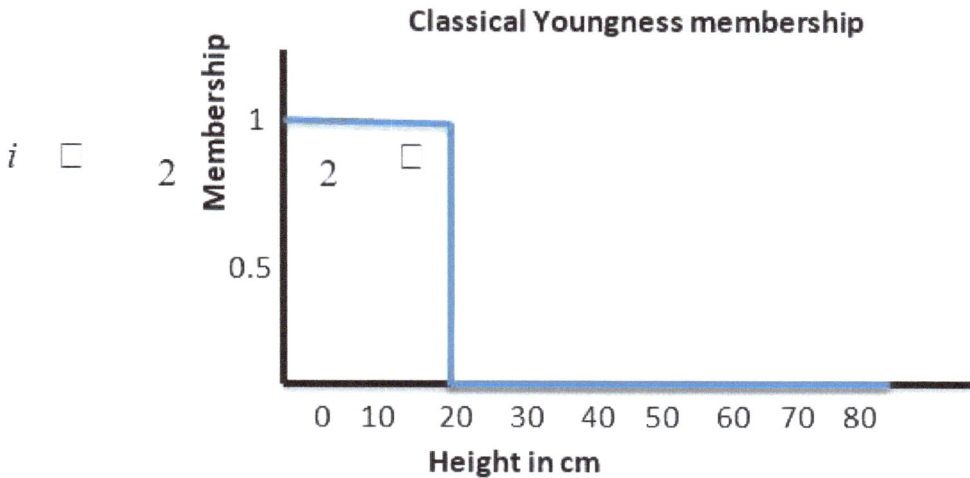

Fig. (3). Classical membership values for youngness.

To epitomize the participation of youngness modeled using the fuzzy sets, we need a mapping function that can make an interpretation of the interval [0,100] into [0, 1]. The commonly espoused function taking into consideration the above scenario is

$$\chi_Y(\text{age}) = \begin{cases} 1 & if\ 0 \leq age \leq 20 \\ \frac{40-age}{20} & if\ 20 < age \leq 40 \\ 0 & if\ age > 40 \end{cases} \tag{3}$$

In the above graph, the individual ages are given along the x-axis, and the corresponding youngness memberships are given on the y-axis. In the case where the application is patterned such that a person between the age 0 and 20 is assumed to have full participation for youngness and the participation gradually decreases between the ages of 20 to 40, any person who is above 40 years of age is treated as not any more young.

However, in the event that the application pattern needs to have the participation membership value distribution in an alternative manner based on the required participation value dispersion, the corresponding mapping function in the equation 3 is adopted to generate the corresponding graph.

Fig. (5) depicts the conversion of the crispy dataset into the corresponding fuzzy values. Consider a situation of categorizing the temperature into three categories (below average, average and above average), in the crispy system, at a particular instance of time, either the temperature is below average, average or above average. But in the fuzzy system, we have different participation values that are simultaneous, either below average and average or average and above average.

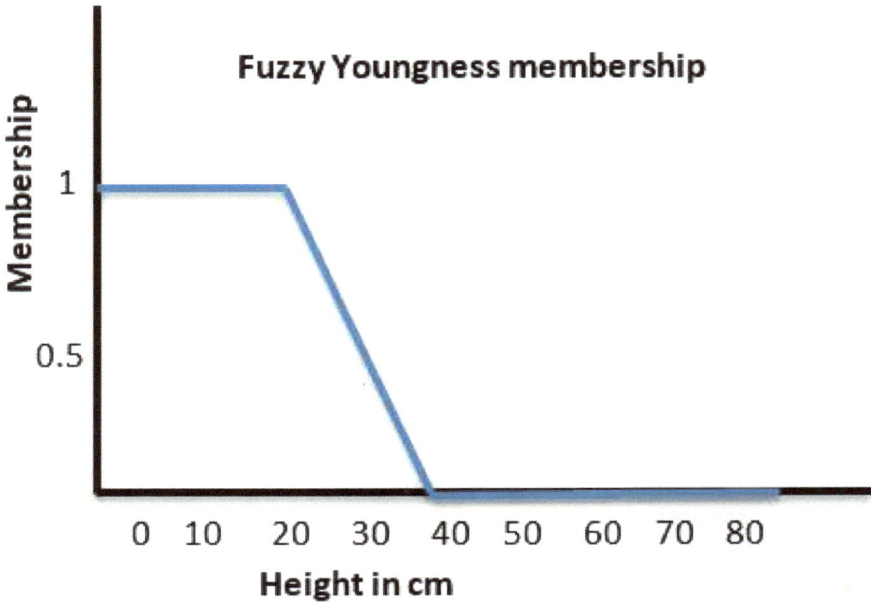

Fig. (4). Participation values for different individual ages.

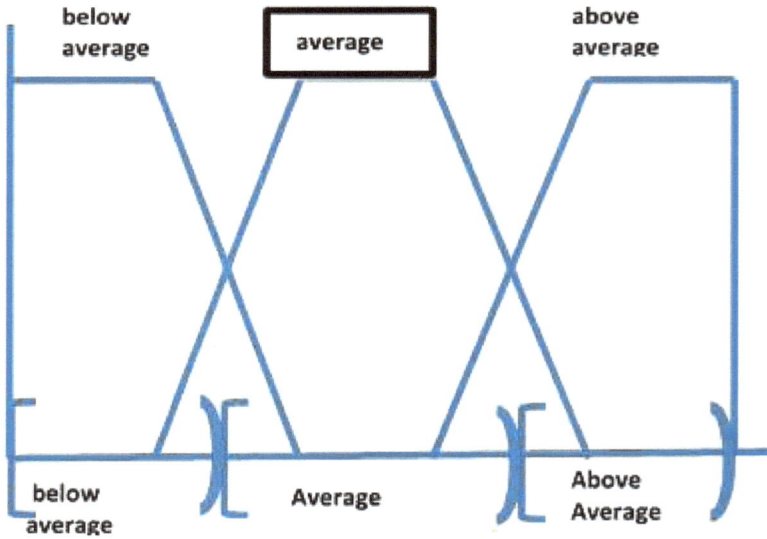

Fig. (5). Relation between the classical and fuzyy membership values.

Probability and Fuzzy Sets

Albeit fuzzy set participation membership value and probability work over a similar numeric reach [0,1], they are not equivalent [2]. Probability alludes to the opportunity of favorable events of an ideal occasion among all the conceivable number of occasions, and fuzzy alludes to the level of participation. Think about an opportunity of arbitrarily picking a student among the absolute number of students.

Consider a circumstance in a city where there are N number of individuals and the number of people considered as youngsters is Y, the probability of an individual being youthful is Y/N, *i.e.*, the more the numerator, the probability is bigger. But, the fuzzy number is the participation quantifying of an individual viable as youthful.

Participation Function Terminology

Since fuzzy frameworks are portrayed utilizing membership functions, it is clear and evident to characterize the terminologies related to it [3]. The terminology introduced in Fig. (**6**) is applicable to both discrete and continuous functions.

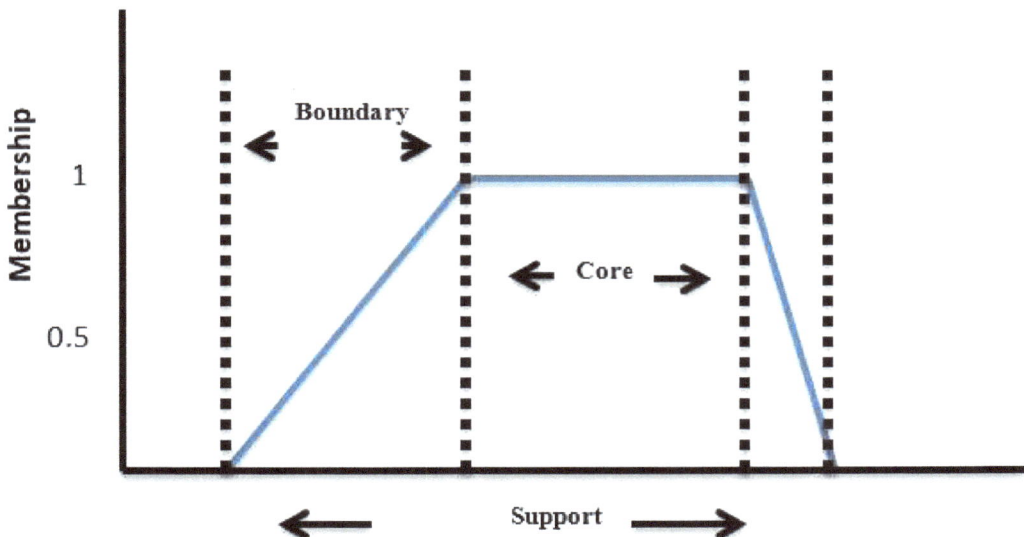

Fig. (6). Terminology related to membership functions.

The core of a participation function of a fuzzy set is the district of the universe described by complete and full enrollment. All in all, the core includes the components 'ele' of the set that has participation esteem $\mu T(ele) = 1$.

The support of a participation function of a fuzzy set is the area of the universe portrayed by nonzero enrollment; the support includes those components 'ele' of the universe with the end goal that $\mu T(ele)>0$.

The boundary of a participation function of a fuzzy set is the district containing enlistment regarding some place in the scope of 0 and 1. Normal fuzzy set refers to the fuzzy set where at least one element has a complete membership value. On the other hand, if no such element exists, then the fuzzy set is referred to as sub-normal fuzzy set. If there is only a single element that has the corresponding full membership, such an element is called the prototype or prototypical element.

The participation functions in Figs. (**2** and **4**) are referred to as ordinary participation functions. The counterparts for ordinary participation functions are generalized participation functions; they are used when the precise information about the participation values is not available but have interval-valued participation. Interval-valued fuzzy sets can be summed up further by permitting their spans to have fuzzy outcomes into type-2 fuzzy sets [4]. Commonly used generalized participation functions are triangular, trapezoidal, piecewise linear, Gaussian, *etc.* [5].

Gaussian Participation Function

Gaussian participation function is a summed up participation work whose enrollment esteems are communicated dependent on the condition given below

$$\mu_A{}^i(x) = \exp(\frac{(c_i - x)^2}{2\sigma_i{}^2})$$ **(4)**

c_i, σ_i denotes the center and width (variance) of the ith fuzzy set under consideration.

Operations on Fuzzy Sets

We have the following binary operations, *i.e.*, the operations which need two fuzzy sets [6], which may have different membership functions.

Intersection: Consider 1 and 2 scenarios as an example, the element in the set needs to be young and also should be tall; we perform the intersection operation on the two participation functions. The definition of the intersection of two fuzzy sets, namely young and tall, is given below:

$$\text{Young\_tall(ele)} = \text{minimum } \{ \text{ young(ele), tall(ele) } \}.$$ **(5)**

The intersection operation is used in the situation where we need the element suitable for both the functionality, *i.e.*, the elements should be tall as well as young.

Union: If we need to identify to which type of functionality an individual is suitable, among the two functionalities, namely in our case tall or young, the notion of use is union operation. The definition of the union of two fuzzy sets, namely young and tall, is given below:

$$\text{Either\_young\_tall(ele)} = \text{maximum}\{ \text{young(ele), tall(ele)}\} \tag{6}$$

Complement: It is the unary operation that can be applied on only one fuzzy set. Consider a situation we wish to obtain the set which is not tall, but we have the fuzzy set which has the participation value of being an individual tall; then we evaluate the difference between the participations of each element with unity (complete membership).

Inclusion: This operation is used in the situation where we wish to find out whether all the elements in a fuzzy set under a participation-1 are smaller than the participation-2 of another fuzzy set, then we say the fuzzy set under participation-1 is included in the fuzzy set under participation-2.

Text Classification

We provide the class label for a set of text_documents under training data to pattern a model which could give the class label of unseen text_document termed as Text Classification (TC) or word-based classification [7]. In the method of word-based data classification, the dataset from [8] is utilized. The dataset is a part of train and test involving 5485 number of documents in training D_{train} and 2189 number of documents in test D_{test}. The documents in the dataset are part of 8 class names. The chronicle in archiveset is slanted as the measure of text_document over different skewed classes. A text_document is a collection of locutions with some significant arbitrary length. For better comprehension of the reader, sample text_documents are provided in Table **3**.

Table 3. Sample documents for word-based classification.

T1: Machine learning techniques for anticipating lodging cost and climate expectation are depicted in detail.
T2: Statistical learning manages surmising relations among various characteristics.
T3: Reinforcement learning is one of the Practical Machine Learning tools which has gained huge success.
T4: Federated learning is also called collaborative learning, which is a new paradigm in machine learning.

Not dominant locution: In the pre-processing, stop words, additionally called not dominant locution, are eliminated as they have no critical part in the formulating technique for word-based classification, otherwise they would pre-dominantly downgrade the classification model. For *e.g.*, dominant locutions are it, in, an, on, so, but, the, *etc.*

Stemming: The subsequent stage in the pre-processing is stemming, which eliminates the prefix and suffix of the locutions. It is regularly applied in information retrieval systems with the objective of upgrading framework execution and is considered a features reduction technique. The popular stemming algorithm [9] is utilized for reducing the vocables.

Vocabulary Set (¥): It is the universal set (¥) comprising entire locutions from intact D_{train}, evacuating the not dominant locution such that it would diminish the number of locutions in the vocabulary set ¥, accordingly sparing system assets. After ascertaining the recurrence of the locutions, a suitable recurrence threshold is chosen; all locutions below the threshold are discarded from the vocabulary set.

Algorithm_1 for generating the vocabulary is given below.

Vocabulory_Generation

{

a. For different values of I varying from 1 through 5485 repeat till step c
b. Evacuate not dominant vocables from each document d_i
c. Execute stemming on all text in document d_i
d. Link (Concatenate) all the records into a solitary archive S
e. Produce the recurrence of each word by sorting it
f. Eliminate vocable whose recurrence is beneath the boundary (2 is chosen)

}

The vocabulary set ¥ for the model records demonstrated in Table **4** have 6 locutions. Locutions are machine, learn(ing), technique(s), statistic(al), reinforce(ment), and federal(ted) (remaining locutions are evacuated as not dominant), but the dataset under attention has 14,822 locutions in the vocabulary set. Word embedding is needed for the classification model to learn from the training data. The literary data should be transformed into mathematical form as the classifier anticipates mathematical form for accomplishing learning. Conventionally numerical vectors are generated for ease of the reader, and the basic binary vector generation is discussed.

$\overline{x}$ exemplifies binary vector, t_i refers to the locutions in vocabulary set ¥, D_j denotes the text_document, which essentially changes the literary information over to mathematical structure. C_i gives the recurrence of locution t_i in text_document d [10]. In vector type, the above-spoken form can be structured in the form below:

$$\overline{X_{ij}} = \begin{cases} 1 \text{ if } t_i \in D_j \\ 0 \text{ } otherwise \end{cases} \tag{7}$$

Table 4. Binary vector for sample documents.

-	D1	D2	D3	D4
Federal(federated)	0	0	0	1
learn(ing)	1	1	1	1
machine	1	0	1	1
reinforce(ment)	0	0	1	0
statistic(al)	0	1	0	0
technique(s)	1	0	0	0

In our consideration, the no. of locutions in vocabulary set ¥ is 14,822, and the total components in Xij→vector would be 14,822, with every component representing the jargon in the Vocabulary set ¥.

Instead of utilizing locutions as features, clusters, also called collections, are utilized as features, thus resulting in feature reduction by transforming the individual locutions, being framed into collections based on fuzzy participation, using the resulted collections as features.

TC attracts enormous dimensionality, which is termed as revile of dimensionality. As the order of the features included in TC is 15,000 as a rule, adapting to quite a tremendous arrangement of features is a problematic errand; additionally, the calculation cost is colossal. To assess the significance of each term concerning various class labels, locution_designs are obtained; in other words, it is the restrictive probability of different class labels given the locutions have occurred in the text_document. Text_documents have been parted across 'm' class labels. The likelihood of locutions befallen in all class labels is procured, is alluded as locutions_design $L_i = <l_{i1}, l_{i2}, l_{i3}, \ldots\ldots l_{im}>$. The locutions_design for every locution provides the effect of locutions superiority concerning every class label. Locutions_design of the locutions 'i' for the class label 'h' is acquired as structured in the below equation

$$l_{ih} = \frac{\sum_{r=1}^{n} d_{ri} * \partial_{rh}}{\sum_{r=1}^{n} d_{ri}} \tag{8}$$

'h' takes esteems for all classes shifting from 1 through m, and recurrence of the locution t_i in text_document d_r is represented by d_{ri}. The total number of text_documents is given by 'n'. The estimation of ∂_{rh} is acquired as structured below

$$\partial_{rh} = \begin{cases} 1 \, if \, d_r \in C_h \\ 0 \, if \, d_r \notin C_h \end{cases} \tag{9}$$

The locution_design matrix is of the order 14,822 x 8, which can be in agreement with the number of elements in the vocabulary set acquired and the number of class labels; thus, the text_document is split over.

A mix of supervised and unsupervised learning prototypes is employed in gathering the locutions into collections. By and large, the way toward acquiring collections is utilized in an unsupervised learning paradigm, which does not utilize the data of the class label. Utilizing the locution_designs and Gaussian function, which is a predominance in getting better collections, collections are obtained. Collections are shaped with the end goal that the closeness among the collections should be limited and intra-closeness of the collections must be expanded. During the time spent acquiring the participation of the locutions_designs in the current collections or in another collection, the average and eccentricity of the collections are utilized to acquire the finest worth nature of the collection.

Consider ψ be a collection comprising 'q' locutions_designs $L_1, L_2, \ldots .. L_q$. Let L_j = < $l_{j1}, l_{j2}, \ldots . l_{jm}$ >, j varying for all class labels (otherwords 1<=j<=q), be the locution_design, at that point the average of the collection ψ for different class labels is $\bar{L}$= <$l_1, l_2, \ldots \ldots . l_m$>, is characterized as

$$\bar{l_i} = \frac{1}{|\Psi|} \sum_{j=1}^{q} l_{ji} \tag{10}$$

'i' takes values varying from 1 through m, and the denominator in equation 10 gives the of components in the ith collection. The eccentricity $\alpha = < \alpha_1, \alpha_2, \ldots . \alpha_m>$ of each collection with regard to different classes is structured below in equation 11.

$$\alpha_i = \sqrt{\frac{1}{|\Psi|} \sum_{i=1}^{q} (l_{ij} - \overline{l}_{ji})^2} \tag{11}$$

'i' takes values varying from 1 through m; fuzzy comparability of a locutions_design L to each collection is characterized by gaussian participation function.

$$PN_{\Psi i}(L) = \prod_{j=1}^{p} \exp\left[-\left(\frac{l_j - m_j}{\alpha_j} \right)^2 \right] \tag{12}$$

The estimations of the participation (PN) in the above equation are limited in the span [0, 1], with i taking values varying from 1 through k and k denotes the number of collections obtained uptil now. A locution_design near the average of a collection 'i' gives the estimation value close to 1 in equation 12, treating the locution_design fundamentally the same as the collection 'i' to the collection in thought. If the estimation in equation 12 is close to 0, at that point, the locution_design is far inaccessible from a group 'i' in thought.

In light of the degree, which tells how far or close to the locution_design is to the worth obtained in equation 12, a new collection is made. By chance that the closeness of the locution_design is past the limit esteem constrained by the user, for all the current groups, another collection is shaped. The average of the new group is l =l_i, thus, the eccentricity and size, and lastly, the quantity of collection framed up to now are augmented by 1.

As shown in equation 13, locution_designs L participate in the current collection, where υ is the limit esteem.

$$\Phi = \begin{cases} 1 & if \ PN_{\Psi i}(L) \ \geq \ \upsilon \\ 0 & if \ PN_{\Psi i}(L) \ < \ \upsilon \end{cases} \tag{13}$$

By chance that the estimation of Φ is 1, at that point, locution_design L is added to the current collection 'i'; otherwise, another collection is made. If $PN_{\Psi i}(L) \geq \upsilon$, at that point, the locution_design L is added to the collection ψ_i, and the quantity of components in the collection ψ_i is expanded by 1; estimations of all collections are refreshed, for example, the average $\overline{l}$ i of the collection and eccentricity of the collection α_i . If $PN_{\Psi i}(L) < \upsilon$, at that point, another group is made with average mean as $\overline{L} = 1$, the eccentricity of the recently shaped collection as $\alpha = 1$ and the quantity of collections up to now made are moreover increased by unity.

All the locution_designs, total 'k' quantity of collection with associated refreshed average and eccentricity are obtained, and in vector notation are represented as $\bar{I} = <\bar{l}_1, \bar{l}_2 \ldots \bar{l}_n>$ and $\alpha = <\alpha_1, \alpha_2, \ldots \alpha_{nr}>$, respectively. Locutions_designs for every locution in the dictionary set are mapped into 'k' collections. The collections are treated as features during the time spent in word-based data classification.

Three kinds of collections are investigated, in particular soft, hard and blended in view of the participation of the locution_design in collections. In the event of hard collection dependent on equation 14, a locution_design L_j is permitted to be an individual from a solitary collection at some random occasion of time.

$$\Psi_i = \begin{cases} 1 & \max_{1<=i<=k} (\Psi_i(x_j)) \\ 0 & \forall\ k;\ k \neq i \end{cases} \tag{14}$$

In the event of a soft collection approach, the locution_design L_j is permitted to have a place with more than a single collection, so instead of considering the most extreme estimation of the condition in equation 14, likeness esteems for all the existing collections acquired are thought of.

Blended collection approach is investigated dependent on the given condition 15.

$$\Psi_i = (\Lambda) * H\Psi_i + (1 - \Lambda) * S\Psi_i \tag{15}$$

$H\Psi_i$ refers to hard-weighting collection and $S\Psi_i$ refers to soft-collection participation values. Estimation of Λ is client characterized, and is somewhere in the range of 0 and 1. In the event that Λ value is close to 0, at that point, the mixed-weighting collection approach agrees with the soft collection approach and in the event that Λ value is 1, at that point, the hard collection result concurs with mixed weighting collection.

Considering Λ esteem to be 0.1, the test results obtained are provided in Figs. (**6** to **9**) for varying values of K qualities on the X-axis, and classifier model exactness on Y-axis takes various estimations of Λ 0.5, 0.6 and 0.7. To control the number of collections shaped, distinctive estimations of Λ are thought of; the number of collections framed for the comparing edge esteem for values 0.5, 0.6, 0.7 is 14,12 and 10, respectively.

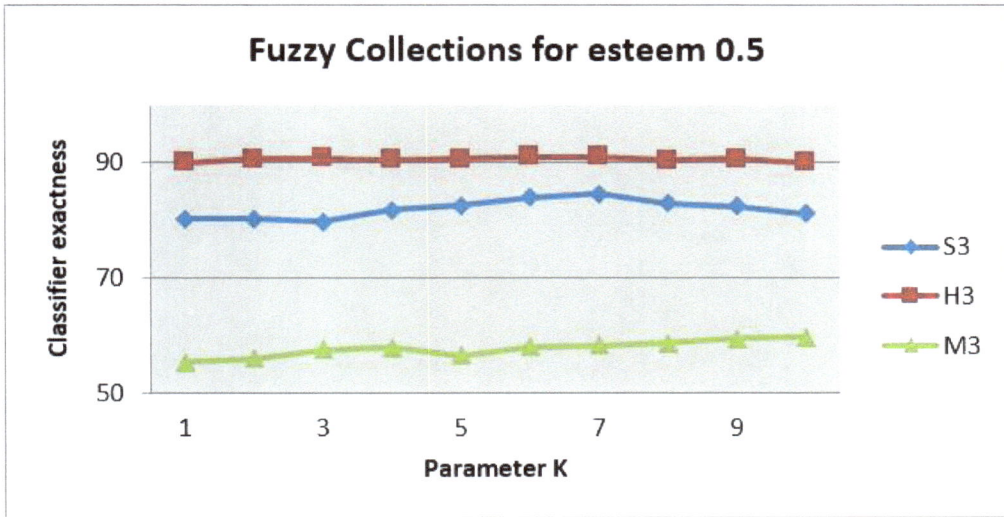

Fig. (7). Exactness of word-based classifier shifting values of K, 1 through 10 with 14 collections.

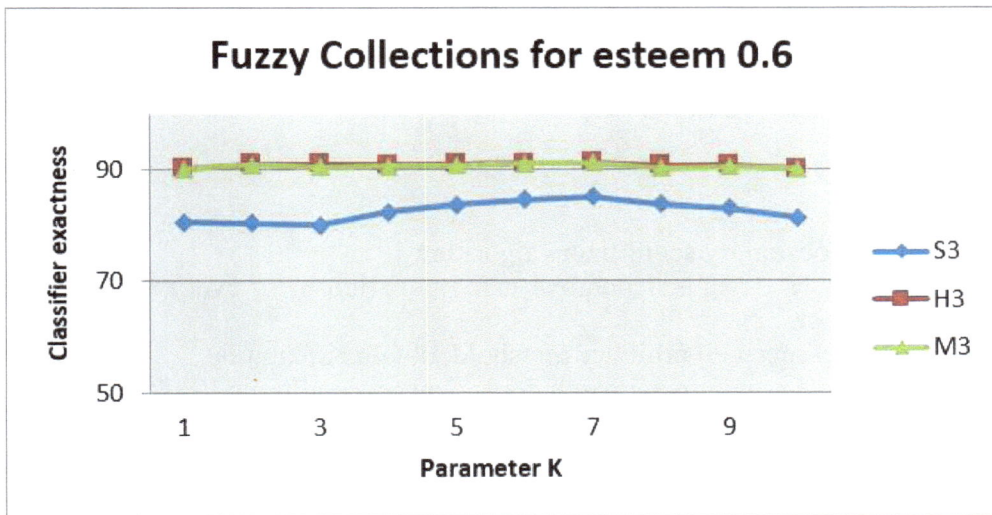

Fig. (8). Exactness of word-based classifier shifting values of K, 1 through 10 with 12 collections.

The test data is changed into locution_designs, and utilizing the obtained locution_designs, collections are acquired. The obtained collections are utilized as features, however, the class labels of D_{train} are deliberated. Conventional K-Nearest Neighbour algorithm is utilized in the word-based data classification with the features as collections.

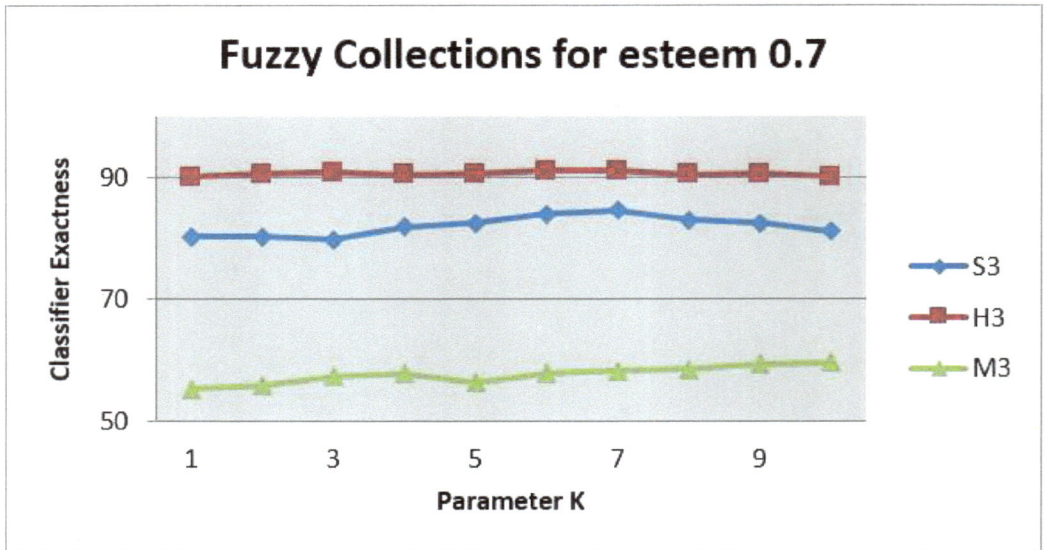

Fig. (9). Exactness of word-based classifier shifting values of K, 1 through 10 with 10 collections.

Algorithm-2 for generating fuzzy collections is given below.

Algorithm_2 Fuzzy_Collections

{

a. Create the vocabulary set utilizing algorithm 1.
b. Create vocable_designs dependent using equation 8 for every vocable in the vocabulary set.
c. Get K collections with arbitrary threshold, obtain K features.
d. Utilize diverse premium approach dependent on conditions 12, 14 and 15.
e. Produce the K features for D_{test}.
f. Process the resemblance in the train and test documents.
g. Repeat steps 8 through 10 for values shifting from 1 to 10 of k
h. Obtain the least K distance
i. Identify the majority of occurrences of a tie.
j. Produce the disarray framework and acquire classifier precision

}

In Fig. (**7**), a chart is presented, indicating the exactness of the classifier with various K value estimations on one axis in the K-Nearest Neighbor algorithm

[11], and the precision of the classification model on another axis for three sorts of assortments, in particular soft, hard and hybrid outcomes for limit esteem = 0.5.

For a better comprehension of threshold values varying from 0.5 to 07 stepping by 0.1, K values 1 through 10 are shown in Figs. (**8** and **9**).

The outcomes ascertaining the precision of word-based classifier for various premium approaches portray that for different K qualities, s1 is in a way better than s2 and s2 is in a way better than s3. Also, hard collection is superior to the soft collection. Exactness of the hard premium approach likewise increments with k qualities, with precision of both h1 and h2 collections nearly harmonizing, and h3 collection results show at first better exactness, and later it declines. Moreover, the precision of mixed weighting approach is the least.

The exactness of the fuzzy collections centered classifier precision for various estimations of K fluctuates from 1 through 10, for limit esteems 0.5, 0.6 and 0.7. S1 alludes to the soft collection's classifier exactness for edge esteem 0.5, acquiring 14 collections. H1 alludes to the hard collection, and m1 alludes to the blended collection for edge esteem 0.5, which plans the vocable_designs into 14 quantities of collections. S2, h2 and md2 allude to the collections shaped with edge esteem 0.6, which plans the whole vocable_designs into 12 quantities of collections. Also, s2, h2 and m2 allude to the collections shaped with edge esteem 0.6, which plans the whole vocable_designs into 12 quantities of collections. At the end, hard weighting approach for edge esteem 05 and 0.6 gives better precision.

CONCLUDING REMARKS

Fuzzy sets have become indispensable as the input to a system today has an uncertainty associated with it. Different fuzzy participation functions have been discussed in this chapter along with the common operations of fuzzy functions. In the concluding section, word-based data classification is discussed, which is applied to the fuzzy participation techniques.

CONSENT FOR PUBLICATION

Not applicable.

CONFLICT OF INTEREST

The author declares no conflict of interest, financial or otherwise.

ACKNOWLEDGEMENTS

Declared none.

REFERENCES

[1]   L.A. Zadeh, "Fuzzy sets", *Inf. Control,* vol. 8, no. 3, pp. 338-353, 1965.
       [http://dx.doi.org/10.1016/S0019-9958(65)90241-X]

[2]   B. Sanjaa, and P. Tsoozol, "Fuzzy and Probability", *International Forum on Strategic Technology,* pp.
       141-143, 2007.
       [http://dx.doi.org/10.1109/IFOST.2007.4798542]

[3]   M.K. Medynskaya, "Fuzzy set theory. The concept of fuzzy sets", *2015 XVIII International
       Conference on Soft Computing and Measurements (SCM),* pp. 30-31, 2015.
       [http://dx.doi.org/10.1109/SCM.2015.7190402]

[4]   C. Wagner, and H. Hagras, "Interpreting fuzzy set operations and Multi Level Agreement in a
       Computing with Words context", *2011 IEEE International Conference on Fuzzy Systems (FUZZ-IEEE
       2011),* pp. 2139-2146, 2011.
       [http://dx.doi.org/10.1109/FUZZY.2011.6007736]

[5]   T. Lei, P. Liu, X. Jia, X. Zhang, H. Meng, and A.K. Nandi, "Automatic Fuzzy Clustering Framework
       for Image Segmentation", *IEEE Trans. Fuzzy Syst.,* vol. 28, no. 9, pp. 2078-2092, 2020.
       [http://dx.doi.org/10.1109/TFUZZ.2019.2930030]

[6]   S.K. Kashyap, and J.R. Raol, "Unification and Interpretation of Fuzzy Set Operations", *2006
       Canadian Conference on Electrical and Computer Engineering,* pp. 355-358, 2006.
       [http://dx.doi.org/10.1109/CCECE.2006.277407]

[7]   P.R. Pal, P. Pathak, V. Yadav, and P. Ora, "Classification of Pruning Methodologies for Model
       Development using Data Mining Techniques", *Int. J. Eng. Adv. Technol.,* vol. 9, no. 2, pp. 2043-2047,
       2019. [IJEAT].
       [http://dx.doi.org/10.35940/ijeat.B3317.129219]

[8]   https://archive.ics.uci.edu/ml/datasets/reuters-21578+text+categorization+collection

[9]   tartarus.org/~martin/Porter Stemmer.

[10]   E. Leopold, and J. Kindermann, "Text Categorization with Support Vector Machines. How to
       Represent Texts in Input Space?", *Mach. Learn.,* vol. 46, no. 1/3, pp. 423-444, 2002.
       [http://dx.doi.org/10.1023/A:1012491419635]

[11]   S. Zhang, X. Li, M. Zong, X. Zhu, and R. Wang, "Efficient kNN Classification With Different
       Numbers of Nearest Neighbors", *IEEE Trans. Neural Netw. Learn. Syst.,* vol. 29, no. 5, pp. 1774-
       1785, 2018.
       [http://dx.doi.org/10.1109/TNNLS.2017.2673241] [PMID: 28422666]

CHAPTER 9

Efficient Resources Utilization of Containerized Applications Using TOPSIS

Mahendra Pratap Yadav[1,*], Harishchandra A. Akarte[2] and Dharmendra Kumar Yadav[2]

[1] *SRMIST NCR Campus, Modinagar, Ghaziabad, UP-201204, India*

[2] *Motilal Nehru National Institute of Technology, Prayagraj, Uttar Pradesh, India*

Abstract: Highly demanding services require an appropriate amount of resources to manage the fluctuating workload in cloud environment, which is a challenging task for cloud service provides over the Internet. Cloud providers offer these services to end-user with pay and use model, such as utility computing. The services are offered to end-user by a cloud provider in a shareable fashion over Infrastructure-as-a-Service. So, IaaS is a type of computing service on which third parties host their application on virtualized platforms, such as either VMs or Containers. Whenever some containers are overloaded or under-loaded, it may cause SLA violation, degrade performance, cosume maximum energy, and also cause minimum throughput and maximum response time. It also leads to minimizing the customer satisfaction level along with cloud providers, leading to the penalty. The services hosted on VMs or Containers are highly demanding services, and these highly demanding services are handled with the help of load balancing. Load balancing is a way to automatically transfer the incoming requests or load across a group of back-end containers. It improves the distribution of workload across multiple virtual machines. Traditionally, load balancing algorithms use one or two parameters to balance the load. In this paper, we used one of the popular optimization techniques, namely the Technique for Order of Preferences by Similarity to Ideal Solution (TOPSIS) algorithm to manage the incoming traffic with the multiple-criteria decision-making (MCDM) technique. When the proposed technique was compared with different other techniques, such as round robin, it was found that TOPSIS gives better performance in terms of efficient resources utilization. It also minimizes the average response time, which prevents the machine from getting overloaded.

Keywords: Cloud Computing, Container, Load Balancing, Service Elasticity, TOPSIS, Virtualization.

---

* **Corresponding author Mahendra Pratap Yadav:** SRMIST NCR Campus, Modinagar, Ghaziabad, UP-201204, India; E-mail: pratap2020@gmail.com

Vikash Yadav, Parashuram Pal & Chuan-Ming Liu (Eds.)

INTRODUCTION

In the current era, cloud computing is an emerging technology. Cloud computing has become an important aspect of IT industry as well as academia. Every organization has started to adopt cloud computing and replacing their traditional IT infrastructure. Cloud providers use three service models, namely Software as a Service (SaaS), Platform as a Service (PaaS), and Infrastructure as a Service (IaaS). Cloud providers use SaaS to provide access to complete applications as a service to end-users. They use the PaaS to provide a platform to end-users for developing applications or software over it. The most popular PaaS platforms are Google App Engine (GAE) and Azure [1]. Cloud providers use the IaaS platforms to provide an environment for end-users to deploy the application over a virtual environment. Cloud providers use virtual techniques to manage the workload dynamically. Using virtualization, cloud providers perform resource provisioning or de-provisioning [2]. Basically, when the users access the web service through the Internet, the cloud providers provide the computing resources based on the users' requirement.

The run time resources provisioning is allocated by the cloud providers using the elasticity characteristic of cloud computing to acquire/release the computing resources during runtime according to the demand of the application. Cloud computing provides device and location independence and simplifies the maintenance of cloud computing applications. It also increases the performance of the system as well as increases productivity. According to the NIST, cloud computing is defined as follows: "It is a model for enabling ubiquitous, convenient, on-demand network access to a shared pool of configurable computing resources (*e.g.*, networks, servers, storage applications and services) that can be rapidly provisioned and released with minimal management effort or service provider interaction" [3]. Cloud providers use virtualization techniques to build the environment for hosting the client application. Using virtualization, cloud providers create a virtual environment for different computing components, namely a computing server, storage server, database server, or operating system [4]. It also makes it possible to run multiple OS along with different applications over the same server at the same time. Virtualization provides more flexibility and efficiency for allocating computing resources.

Virtualization creates an abstract environment, which hides the system complexity between the users and system software and their internal component. Virtualization technique is commonly implemented through hypervisors or containers, or both [5, 6]. When the container is compared with hypervisors, it is a lightweight version of a hypervisor that allows a faster start time and minimum overhead. Cloud providers use virtualization to run multiple instances of computing resources (*i.e.*, virtual machine). For the most efficient and optimal use of these computing resources, cloud providers need a load balancer. Load balancer uses various load balancing algorithms that automatically transfer the incoming request over a group of services that are hosted by the application [7 - 9]. It improves the system response time and throughput for managing the huge workload of a group of servers. The load balancer uses various load balancing algorithms, namely First Come First Serve (FCFS), Round Robin (RR), Weight Round Robin, Modified Throttled algorithm, HAproxy, and Random algorithm [10]. These algorithms are used by cloud providers to assign the incoming network traffic to different cloud servers that are virtually available in a distributed environment. Although these load algorithms are used by researchers, still they are facing some challenges, like efficient system resource utilization, system reliability, communication delay, and assigning the incoming traffic to the underutilized VM or Container, which have not been addressed efficiently in the existing literature survey so far. The primary objective of the load balancing approach is to optimize the computing resource utilization, increase the system throughput, minimize the system response time and also avoid the overload due to the single or multiple node failure. Therefore, the question is how to allocate the incoming traffic to virtual machines that are available in IaaS to maintain SLA. The SLA violation between providers and subscribers is the major challenging task over IaaS and also is the cause of reduced customer satisfaction [11]. Reducing customer's satisfaction may impact in terms of penalty, such as customers' loss over providers. The cloud providers use the available information of each container over an IaaS, which will be used for improving system performance, managing the network traffic over system, and enhancing the system performance. Cloud providers use various methods to monitor the system and collect the relevant information about nodes that will be used by the cloud provider for broadcasting the traffic, centralizing polling through the monitoring agent. The monitoring agent mechanism is used for collecting information about the various nodes to find out efficient resource utilization and enhance node efficiency. The monitoring tool has the autonomy to collect different information related to containers, such as CPU and memory utilization, unutilized CPU and memory capability, load balancer transmission rate, *etc*. However, in this chapter, we have used the multiple agents' mechanism to gather all related information related to container in the IaaS environment and optimize resources utilization and cost optimization. We have used multiple-criteria decision-making (MCDM) [12] technique for load balancing in the cloud IaaS environment by using monitoring agents that forecast the incoming traffic to containers with distinctive characteristics so that they gain desired achievement.

The rest of paper is organized as follows: In section 2, the proposed work has been described. In section 3, background and related technology have been given. Section 4 presents the literature review for the work. In section 5, the solution to the problem has been proposed. In section 6, the experimental setup has been discussed. In section 7, the result analysis has been presented, and the last section (*i.e.*, Section 8) concludes the work along with future directions.

MOTIVATION

We tried to search all the metrics regarding running containers and requests that can be potentially used to tell the state of the system. We found that response time produced by logs of the load balancer can be a very good metric to gain insight into the current load on the system. We decided to scale horizontally according to the response time of live requests to the web server. In HA Proxy, the requests are transferred on the basis of only one criterion or no criteria, like in round robin, there is no criteria, while in least connection, only criterion used is the no. of requests being fulfilled by each container. So we decided to use multiple criteria before deciding to forward the request to get better results. So, on this basis, we ranked the alternatives. We used TOPSIS algorithm to decide this ranking. After this ranking, top containers were weighted more when forwarding the requests.

BACKGROUND RELATED TECHNOLOGY

In this section, we have discussed the background and related methodology that are used to perform the load balancing through the multiple criteria decision-making (MCDM) technique.

Load Balancing

This technique is used by cloud providers to receive the incoming traffic and transfer the incoming traffic among available servers. It is also used to enhance the system performance by transferring larger processing loads into smaller processing nodes Fig. (**1**). Load balancing is used for fair allocation of incoming traffic and efficient utilization of computing resources so that providers achieve maximum system performance and user satisfaction. By using it, cloud providers gain maximum throughput and minimum response time. The processing workload is shared among a group of machines rather than relying on a single server to handle every request. CPU load, amount of memory, and other parameters are combined together to calculate the load of the machine. The major objectives of the load balancing algorithm are to provide service availability, system performance, and flexibility [13]. Fig. (**1**) shows the basic architecture in which it transfers the incoming request from clients to over different servers.

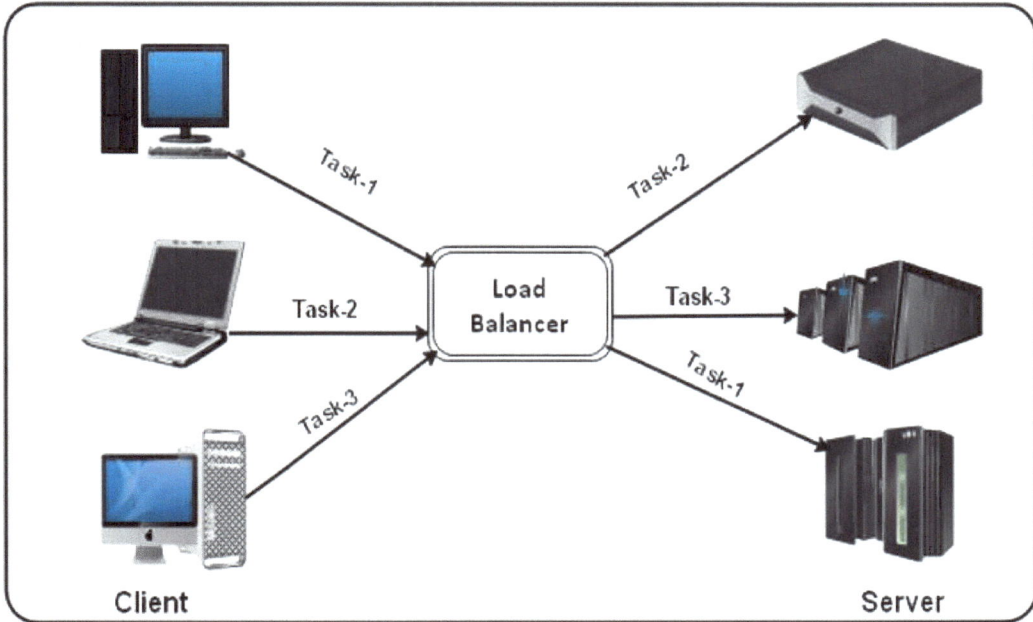

Fig. (1). Load balancing approach.

Load balancing algorithm is classified into two types, namely static and dynamic load balancing algorithm. In the case of static, it basically defines the system design or implementation. The static load balancing mechanisms divide the incoming traffic over all the servers that are available in the cluster. In the case of dynamic load balancing, it only considers the system's current state based on the system statistic load balancing decision. The dynamic approach is very effective in using remotely located distributed systems, such as cloud computing.

Containers

It is a virtualization approach that is used in the modern cloud environment. Cloud providers use the container to host the client application over the cloud data center. Containers and VMs both are used by cloud providers and their goals are similar, *i.e.*, to isolate an application and all its dependencies making a self-contained box of container that can run parallel. Moreover, containers and VMs both are used to remove the limitation of physical hardware; both are allowed cloud providers to use their computing resources efficiently along with cost-effectiveness and energy consumption. VM in comparison to Container is lightweight, stand-alone, executable package of a piece code that includes all dependencies files that are needed to run it, such as code, runtime, system tools, system libraries, and settings. Fig. (**2**) shows the basic difference between the VM and container. Unlike a VM, which is used by a cloud provider to provide hardware virtualization through which they hide internal system structure, a container provides OS level virtualization through kernel feature by abstracting the user space. In VM, an additional operating system (*i.e.,* guest operating system) is needed on which the applications deploy. The hypervisor is installed over the host operating system. There are various hypervisors, namely, Xen, KVM, VMWare *etc.,* which are used by cloud providers to provide virtualization. However, for the container, host OS kernel feature is used to provide the virtualization. There are various tools, namely Docker, Rocket, OpenVZ, *etc.,* which are used by cloud providers to provide the container-based virtualization. All these tools are available for all platforms.

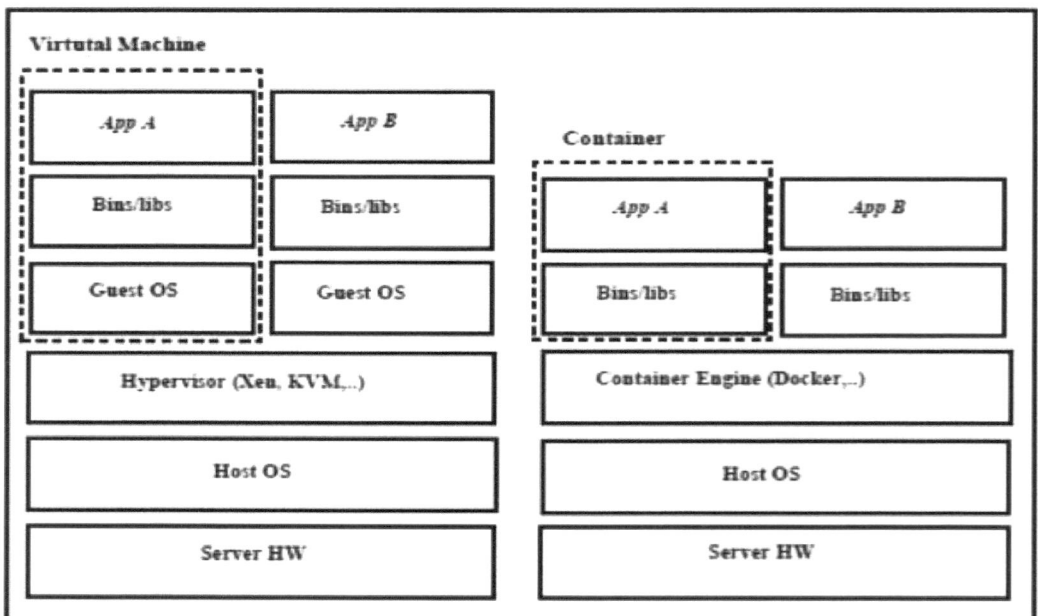

Fig. (2). VM *v/s* Container.

Docker Swarm

Docker Swarm is an open-source software orchestration tool used to perform the clustering and schedule the Docker containers. Cloud administrators and developers use the Docker swarm to manage the cluster Docker nodes running the virtual system. In container technology, clustering is an essential feature of a cloud environment that consists of a group of systems that host different applications or the same application over a different machine. In the cluster, Docker Swarm enables if failover has occurred due to one or more nodes going down with the workload and also manages the workload with the help of a load balancer. A Docker Swarm cluster also provides the ability to easily scale up and down the number of containers and the number of resources needed by each container as computing demands change. A Container Orchestration System is used to manage running containers by providing features, like health checks, scaling the number of containers, and rolling updates of s/w across containers. Containers in a swarm are called nodes. Some nodes work as manager nodes, while some nodes work as worker nodes. The manager node assigns the units of work called tasks to worker nodes to manage the workload.

Multi-Criteria Decision Making

While taking a single criterion into consideration, decision making [14] is intensely inherent as we have to select the substitute with the higher preference rating. When decision-making estimates other possibilities with multiple criteria, various problems, similar to weights of criteria, the dependence of preference, and conflicts of criteria appear to make the problems difficult and need to overcome by additional refined methods. When dealing with MCDM issues, the remaining move is to find out how many different parameters or criteria remain in the problem and how to grasp the problem in an efficient way. The decision-making process consists of a series of steps:

1. To identify the problems.
2. Construction of preferences.
3. Preferences evaluation.
4. Deciding the excellent alternatives.

After that, we need to gather the appropriate information or data values in which the preference of Decision Making can be effectively reacted upon and considered. Further work builds a set of possible strategies or alternatives in order to assure that the main objective will be founded. Through these things, the further step is to select an appropriate mechanism that helps to evaluate and improve all the possible available alternatives or strategies. The MCDM procedure consists of 5 steps:

1. Define what is the nature of the problem.
2. To construct a system hierarchy to evaluate it.

3. Select an appropriate model for effective evaluation.
4. With respect to each alternative of every attribute, obtain performance score and relative weights.
5. Find out the best alternative based on the synthetic utility values, which are the concentricity of the value with their relative weights, and performance scores on behalf of alternatives.

Docker

It is simply an open-source tool that is used for packing, shipping, and running applications along their dependencies to run within containers. More formally, Docker is a platform that uses the kernel feature of Linux to perform OS-level virtualization. It is also known as containerization. Docker uses Linux kernel features, such as namespaces and control groups, to build containers on top of the host operating system. A Docker container wraps an application's software (*i.e.*, base image) along with their dependencies that are required to run as application. It helps to enable flexibility and portability on where the application can run. Docker reduces development complexity by allowing finding, downloading and starting images of containers that were created by other developers very quickly and conveniently. Docker enables true independence between cloud provider's infrastructure and applications developers along with IT professionals to unlock their potential and creates a model for better innovation and collaboration.

HA Proxy

HAProxy is freely available open-source software. It provides a high availability load balancer to manage the workload. It acts as a proxy server for TCP layer as well as for HTTP layered-based applications. The primary objective of HAProxy is to optimize response time, minimize resource utilization, maximize throughput, and avoid the service unavailability along with overloading over a single machine. HAProxy balances the requests by default in round robin mode between the container nodes hosting the server. When the Docker/Kubernetes node receives the request, the HAProxy performs load balancing between the containers of each server. We use it as software-based load balancer. By default, HAProxy consists of the following algorithms.

a. **Round Robin:** HAproxy uses the round-robin as a default algorithm. Load balancer transfers the incoming traffic in a round-robin fashion. It manipulates how frequently the server is selected, compared to other servers.

b. **Static Round Robin:** It is similar to round-robin in which the load balancer transfers the incoming network traffic over the server according to their weights. Unlike round-robin, switching the server's weight on the fly is not a choice.

c. **Least Connections:** In this approach, the load balancer uses the least-connection algorithm to transfer the incoming network traffic to those servers that have minimum numbers of active connections. It is used by cloud providers when the active links need a long session.

d. **Source:** The source load balancing algorithms select servers to transfer the incoming traffic based on the hash of the source IP, *i.e.*, available servers' IP address. It is one approach that assures that a user will equate to the corresponding server.

Apache HTTP Server Benchmarking Tool

It is a dummy workload generated tool that generates a massive amount of network traffic. It is used to benchmark the network traffic over Apache Hypertext Transfer Protocol (HTTP) server. Apache benchmark tool is used to design a hypothesis of how the current Apache server handles the incoming request. It mainly shows how many requests per second the servers build through the Apache benchmarking tool. The general syntax to run the apache to generate the request is ab -k -c 350 -n 20000 example.com/. It uses three parameters:

a. **Concurrency**- The number of parallel requests generated at a time. By default, the benchmarking tool generates one request at a time. It is denoted by c.

b. **Requests**- Number of requests generated by the apache server in a benchmarking session. It is indicated by n.

c. **Keep Alive-** It is enabled by k (it indicates that we desire for the test to use the Keep-Alive header from HTTP and sustain the connection).

RELATED WORK

Several researchers have contributed, and still, many researches are continuing work in the area of cloud environments considering the various load balancing techniques and task scheduling algorithms. For the purpose of load balancing, some of the authors use popular scheduling techniques, like Round Robin and FCFS. The authors have proposed an algorithm [15], which analyzes the load balancing techniques performance for the cloud computing environments. Many accepted load-balancing algorithms have been compared, considering various metrics like throughput, complexity and speed. But, at last, according to them, no existing examined algorithm fits all the prescribed techniques of load balancing. In a research work [16], a specialized innovative algorithm has been proposed, in which the technique of natural selection strategy by applying Genetic Algorithm is used. In this algorithm, a fitness function is specifically defined in terms of the cost related to the execution of instruction and the cost incurred due to delay. The delay cost is an estimated amount as a fine, which needs to be paid to the customer by the Cloud service provider when the actual time for finishing a job is higher than the predicted deadline promised by the cloud service provider.

For finding a global optimum processor for a job in a cloud, a genetic algorithm is proposed as a technique of load balancing for cloud computing. But only one parameter of Overall Average Response Time is considered for comparison with other algorithms. Also, calculate fitness function after encoding chromosomes as binary strings has not been calculated. Authors have proposed another algorithm for self-organization based on a nature-inspired algorithm with a decentralized honeybee algorithm-based technique of load balancing [17]. Global load balancing aspect is achieved by means of local server actions. The system performance is improved by increasing the system divergence without increasing the throughput even though system size increases. This is appropriate in case of a situation where a diversified population of cloud-based service types is needed. Once again, the authors have proposed an ant colony algorithm-based and complex network theory-based new algorithm for load balancing mechanism for an association of open cloud computing [18]. This association uses the restricted periphery and is free from scaling aspects with a complicated network for achieving superior load balancing. As this technique overthrows heterogeneity and also is adaptive to changing environments, it is impressive in fault tolerance and also has better scalability, which improves the existing work of the system.

In a research paper [19], the authors have performed ultra-modern load balancing techniques. The paper also surveyed the requirements for the design and implementation of suited load-balancing algorithms considering cloud service environments. The modern derivative of load balancing technique has been proposed that evaluates based on appropriate metrics. They also concluded that modern systems of load balancing concentrate on saving energy with its pros and cons. Another algorithm [20] has tabulated the mostly adapted load-balancing mechanisms in the area of distributed systems, along with technologies like grid, cluster and cloud systems. They have also presented a very well extensive analysis of various algorithms used in load-balancing along with several indicators of efficiency, like throughput, response time, and migration time. Another algorithm [21] has reviewed load balancing problems, together with Artificial Bee Colony (ABC), Ant Colony Optimization (ACO), Particle Swarm Optimization (PSO) and Genetic Algorithms (GA). The accomplishment of Ant

Lion Optimizer (ALO) has also been introduced as a powerful algorithm for a cloud computing environment, and which is required for providing the end results in load balancing. The authors have discussed a nature-inspiration based decentralized algorithm called honeybee-based load balancing algorithm for the sake of self-organization [22]. This algorithm also achieves load balancing across a heterogeneous environment using local server actions. It calculates the current workload of the machine and then decides if the VM is overloaded or underloaded. It makes the grouping of VM according to the machine workload. The important complication of the said algorithm is that the throughput is not increased when the size of the system increases. This algorithm is appropriate in those conditions when a divergent population of service types is needed. The advantage of the said algorithm is that the performance of the system improves with the increase in the diversity of the system.

Primarily, human-defined components in the systems are concerned with scheduling difficulties. Earlier, researcher scientists in this field have moved significantly to the programming of modeling and also handling ambiguous system information. Hwang and Yoon [23] introduced TOPSIS optimization. This type of strategy is used for finding out advantageous options, which are known to have the smallest interspace from the Positive Ideal Solution (PIS) and also the largest interspace from the Negative Ideal Solution (NIS) [24]. The TOPSIS approach is more efficient, robust, and easy to implement when we compare it with various MCDM models. In TOPSIS, the benchmarks and substitutes are tremendous in number. TOPSIS mechanism has an enormous influence in actuality while solving the decision-making issues. It also works efficiently while solving the issues considering different applications [25].

PROPOSED APPROACH

TOPSIS is a multi-criteria-based decision analysis approach. It works on the concept of the compromise solution, *i.e.*, the chosen alternative should have the shortest geometric distance from the positive ideal solution (PIS) and the longest geometric distance from the negative ideal solution (NIS). It simply compares the set of alternatives by identifying the weights of each criterion (CPU, RAM, *etc.*), and then it normalizes the score of each criterion; after this, the geometric distance between each alternative and ideal alternatives is calculated, which provides better score in each criterion [26]. In TOPSIS, we make an assumption that the criteria are monotonically decreasing or increasing. We have also used the normalization technique to normalize the matrix. TOPSIS allows tradeoffs between alternatives and criteria, where a negative result obtained from one criterion can be negated by a good result in a further criterion. Here, we use two types of normalization, linear normalization and vector normalization. Fig. (**3**) shows the various steps that are used in the TOPSIS algorithm [27]. We made a container of load balancer using TOPSIS, which takes attributes (like load, memory, *etc.*) of all the running containers into account. And after this, we used the TOPSIS algorithm (*i.e.*, algorithm 1) to get the rank of all the containers, and on the basis of the rank, we sent the incoming traffic to the containers.

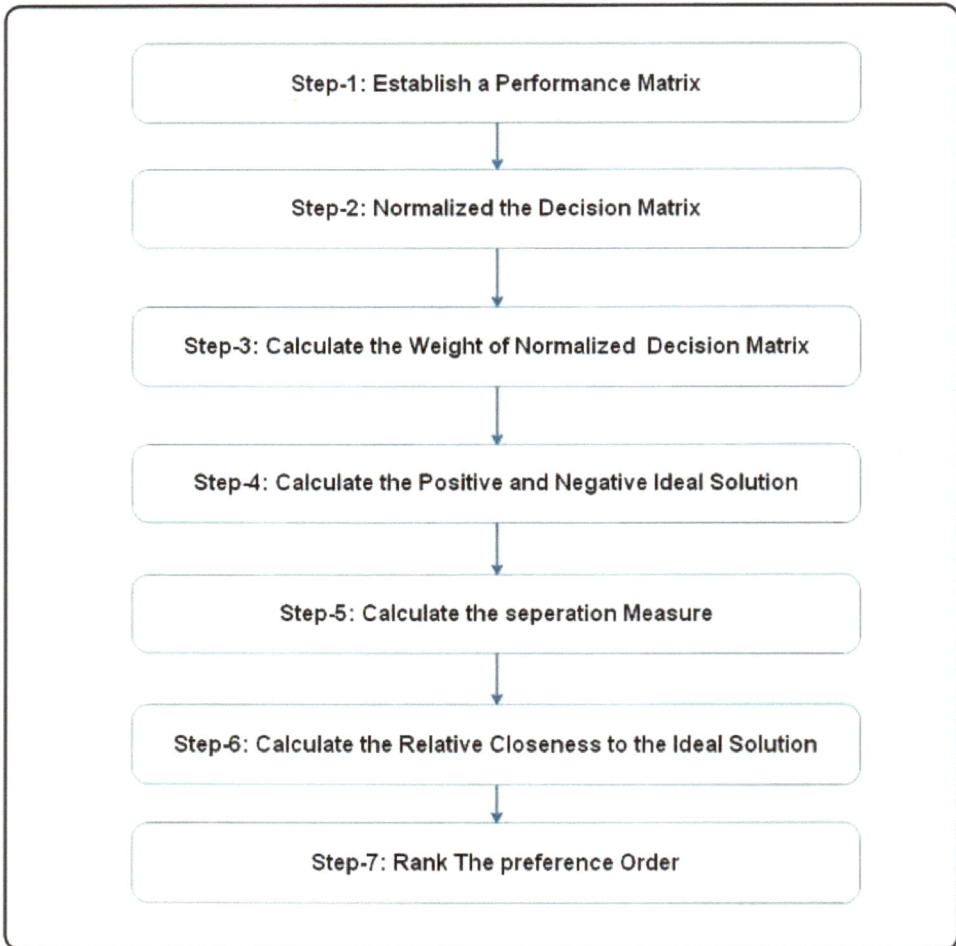

Fig. (3). Steps of the TOPSIS process.

TOPSIS Algorithm: TOPSIS algorithm consists of the following steps to construct a rank matrix as follows:

Step 1: To create an initial evaluation matrix. It consists of 'a' alternatives and 'b' criteria. It intersects each alternative and criteria given as $M_{i.j}$; therefore, we have a matrix $(M_{ij})_{a*b}$

Step 2: The created matrix $(M_{ij})_{a*b}$ is normalized and forms another matrix $R = (R_{i.j})$ with the help of the normalization method.

$$R_{i.j} = \frac{M_{i.j}}{\sqrt{\Sigma_{i=1}^{a} M_{i.j}^{2}}} \; i = 1, 2 \ldots a \text{ and } j = 1, 2 \ldots b \tag{1}$$

Step 3: Here we have applied the weighted normalization on matrix- $s_{i.j} = R_{i.j} \cdot w_{j}$; and i = 1, 2, 3,…a; j = 1,2,3,….b. Where W_{j} is the original weight and w_{j} is expressed as

$$w_j = \frac{W_j}{\Sigma_{k=1}^{b} W_k} , j = 1, 2, \ldots . b \tag{2}$$

Step 4: Now we have determined the worst alternative (X_{worst}) and the best alternative (X_{best}):

$$X_{worst} = \{(\max(s_{i.j}| i = 1, 2, \ldots, a)| j \epsilon J_-)_1 (\min(s_{i.j}| i = 1, 2, \ldots, a)| j \epsilon J_+)\}$$

$$\equiv \{s_{worst.j}| j = 1, 2, \ldots, b\} \tag{3}$$

$$X_{best} = \{(\min(s_{i.j}| i = 1, 2, \ldots, a)| j \epsilon J_-)_1 (\max(s_{i.j}| i = 1, 2, \ldots, b)| j \epsilon J_+)\}$$

$$\equiv \{s_{best.j}| j = 1, 2, \ldots, b\} \tag{4}$$

Where

$J_+ = \{j = 1, 2, 3, 4,, \ldots . .b|j\}$ is associated with criteria with a positive impact, and

$J_- = \{j = 1, 2, 3, 4,, \ldots . .b|j\}$ associated with criteria having a negative impact.

After that, we calculate the Euclidean distance

Step 5: In this step, we have calculated the Euclidean Distance(Ed) for the ideal best and ideal worst:

Euclidean Distance for ideal best:

$$Ed_{i.best} = \sqrt{\Sigma_{j=1}^{b}(s_{i.j} - s_{best.j})^2} \; i = 1, 2 \ldots a \tag{5}$$

Euclidean Distance for the ideal worst:

$$Ed_{i.worst} = \sqrt{\Sigma_{j=1}^{b}(s_{i.j} - s_{worst.j})^2}\, i = 1, 2 \ldots \text{a}$$
(6)

Step 6: Now we have calculated the performance rank score of each alternative:

$$Rs_{i.west} = \frac{d_{i.worst}}{d_{i.worst} + d_{i.best}} \quad 0 < Rs_{i.worst} < 1, i = 1,2,3, \ldots \ldots \ldots$$
(7)

Where

Rsi.best=1 if and only if the alternative solution has the best condition; and

Rsi.worst=0 if and only if the alternative solution has the worst condition.

Step 7: Ranking process is evaluated based on the ranking score, *e.g.*, $Rs_{i.worst}$ (i = 1, 2, 3,……a).

EXPERIMENTAL SETUP

The proposed model has been implemented using the python programming language. There are different libraries imported to perform the experiments. Main python libraries, which we have used are Pandas, Matplotlib, Statsmodels, and Numpy. We have also used the Docker API to simulate the behavior of the Docker Container. The configuration of the systems is as follows: System Processor-i7, x64-based processor; CPU Speed- 2.40 GHz; RAM- 12 GB; Hard Disk-1TB; OS- Ubuntu 16.04.

Build Image

Create the image of our load balancer using the Docker file. To use Ubuntu [28] as the base image, run the following command to create a custom image of the container.

docker build -t [REPOSITORY[:TAG]] [PATH].

In the Docker file, we specified the commands to install the necessary software on the base image. We have installed Docker and python on top of our Ubuntu image to create the load balancer container. We further installed some extra libraries like python library for Docker engine API [28] inside the running container. Once the container was conFigd to our liking, we committed the state of the container, *i.e.*, we created a new image from our container's changes using the command:

docker commit CONTAINER [REPOSITORY[:TAG]]

Now we have a Docker image of our load balancer with all necessary software installed. Now we pushed the image of our load balancer to the Docker hub registry using the command:

docker push IMAGE[:TAG]

Docker Compose

To deploy the services on the swarm and specify the initial configuration of the containers, we use the Docker compose file and command:

docker stack deploy -c [DOCKER COMPOSE FILE] STACK

In this Docker compose file, we specify the services. For each service, we specify the replicas, *i.e.*, initial no. of containers and resource limits for CPU and memory. Using docker-compose.yml, we created 2 services:

a. The first service is our Node.js web app. We specified the service port as an environment variable. Note that no port is exposed since all requests are routed through the load balancer container. We also specify an initial number of replicas, memory limit and CPU limit of this container.
b. The second service we create is of our load balancer, whose image we created in the previous step. The TOPSIS algorithm is implemented inside this container. It also mounts the /var/run/docker.sock file (in the volumes field) so that this container can access the current information about the containers. This is the file load balancer that needs to get various attributes of the running web containers in its network. These attributes are used by TOPSIS to load balance the requests. We expose port 8080 since this container will receive and respond to all external requests by forwarding the request to the web server containers. While deploying, we put this container on the manager node.

Now we have the above two services running on our system, one of the load balancer and the other of the web server. These two services can interact with each other using an inbuilt overlay network. External requests are entirely handled by the load balancer container, including load balancing, forwarding and fulfilling the requests. So, only the load balancer container has exposed ports.

Create Docker Swarm

The network, the services, and all the containers are collectively called a stack. To create our web stack using node server and load balancer containers, we used the Docker stack command and Docker compose file as mentioned above. When we hit http://127.0.0.1:8080, we get the container id in the response, and we can see it in the form of a different id for every few requests. These requests are handled by a load balancer container in the swarm. These requests are forwarded to web server containers based on ranking produced by TOPSIS Algorithm in the load balancer. So, the first few requests are forwarded to top-ranked container, and then the next few to the container next in ranking; in this way, the requests are fulfilled and load balanced.

Workload Generation

The workload generation was made using "ab" tool (apache bench). ab -k -c 200 -n 2000 http://127.0.0.1:8080/ By issuing the command above, we will be hitting http://127.0.0.1:8080/ with 200 simultaneous connections until 2 thousand requests are met. It will be done using the keep-alive header to simulate a real web request. After benchmarking is finished, it produces some stats, which tell us how well the site performed under stress, like average response time, the number of requests handled per second, *etc*.

Plotting Results

Gnuplot is a portable command-line-driven graphing utility for Linux. The number of containers and response time are sampled in an interval to generate plots set style line 1 lc rgb '#0060ad' lt 1 lw 2 pt 7 ps 1.5 plot 'plotting_data.dat' with lines points ls 1.

RESULT ANALYSIS

Figs. (**4**, **5**) show the memory and CPU utilization of systems, respectively. When the TOPSIS algorithm is compared with the round-robin, the incoming request is effectively managed through the TOPSIS approach. The available servers are efficiently ranked according to their computing resources, such as Memory and CPU. When the TOPSIS approach is used for load balancing, it efficiently manages the network traffic and the Memory and CPU utilization of every container with the comparison of the round-robin.

Average Memory Utilization

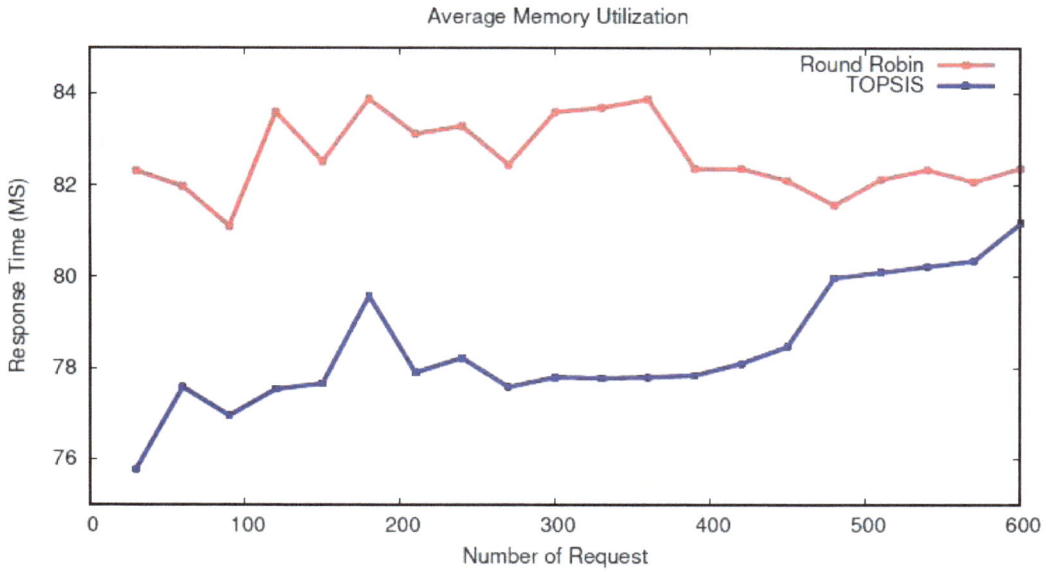

Fig. (4). Average memory utilization of TOPSIS and with round-robin.

Average CPU Utilization

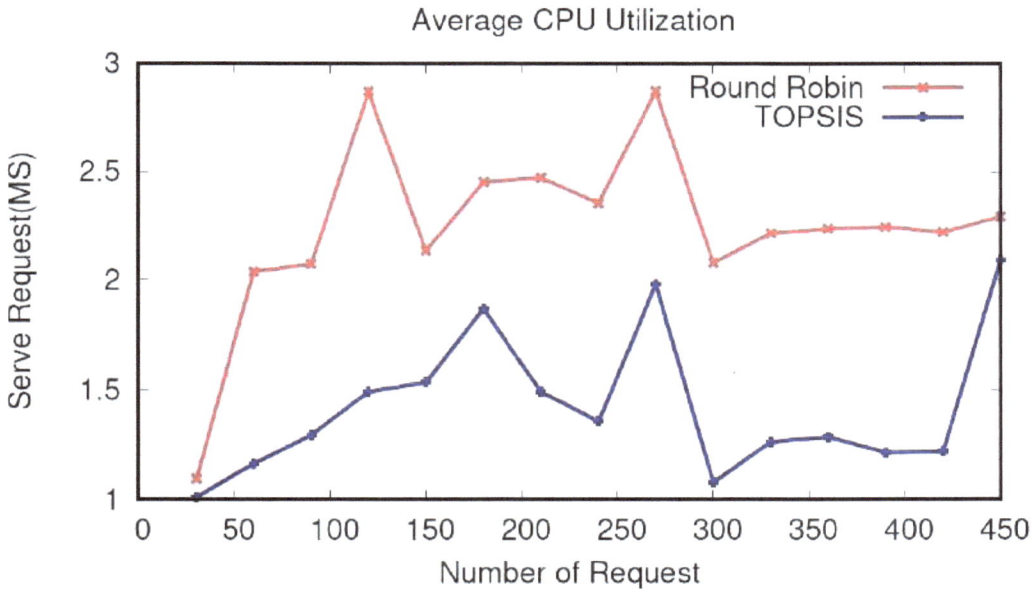

Fig. (5). Average CPU utilization of TOPSIS and with round-robin.

Fig. (**6**) is a plot of the number of requests *v/s* time elapsed with the TOPSIS algorithm and round-robin algorithm. It clearly displays the contrast between the two. The information about the time per request was obtained from the feedback of the Apache benchmark tool after all requests were completed. To ensure valid testing of both algorithms in the same environment, we implemented round-robin algorithm in python and forwarded the requests similar to what we did with the TOPSIS algorithm. We got comparably better results when we used "ab" with the TOPSIS algorithm when requests were large. The system was able to handle 68.35 requests per second with the TOPSIS algorithm, while only 57.54 requests per second were handled when we used the round-robin algorithm. The average response time of all requests at the end of the Apache benchmarking was 14.631 ms with TOPSIS versus 17.380 ms with round-robin when 6500 requests were sent. This clearly displays that the current system is able to use resources more efficiently. Most of the results were very close, but when the number of requests increased, TOPSIS was able to get better response time due to better ranking of containers.

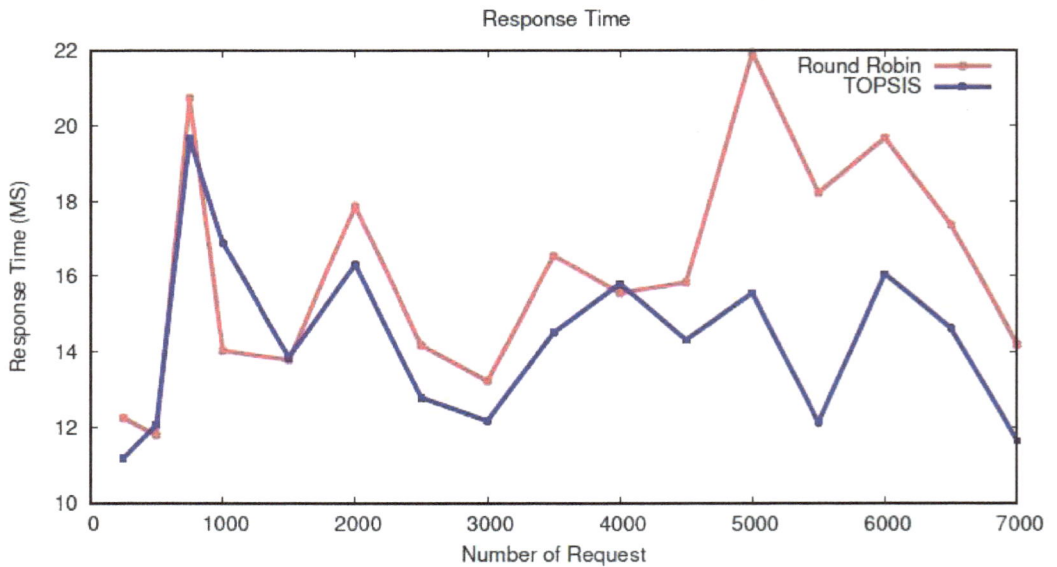

Fig. (6). Response time of requests with TOPSIS and with round-robin.

CONCLUSION

The proposed approach explored the rank-based TOPSIS algorithm for load balancing of web requests. It aims to optimize the time and resources needed to fulfill the web requests to increase the efficiency of the system. With the proposed approach, we got better results in terms of overall response time when the number of requests was high. When the number of requests was low, we got almost the same results because a low number of requests fulfilled immediately, and TOPSIS did not have any major advantage with an updated ranking. When we tested the system with more number of requests, TOPSIS algorithm updated the ranking optimally and forwarded the requests accordingly. We got comparably better results with TOPSIS as compared to round robin. In future work, we can use other MCDM techniques from operations research, like FTOPSIS (Fuzzy TOPSIS) and VIKOR (VlseKriterijumska Optimizacija I Kompromisno Resenje). We would like to extend this work to use a hybrid approach that changes the load balancing algorithm according to the current configuration. Furthermore, the proposed work needs to be more extensively tested on different orchestration systems, like kubernetes, mesos, *etc.*

CONSENT FOR PUBLICATION

Not applicable.

CONFLICT OF INTEREST

The author declares no conflict of interest, financial or otherwise.

ACKNOWLEDGEMENTS

This research was supported/partially supported by Visvesvaraya PhD Scheme for Electronics and IT, Ministry of Electronics and Information Technology, Government of India. The authors thank their colleagues from Motilal Nehru National Institute of Technology Allahabad, Prayagraj, India, who provided insight and expertise that greatly assisted the research, although they may not agree with all of the interpretations/conclusions of this paper.

REFERENCES

[1]   R. Buyya, C.S. Yeo, and S. Venugopal, "Market-Oriented Cloud Computing: Vision, Hype, and Reality for Delivering IT Services as Computing Utilities", *10th IEEE International Conference on High Performance Computing and Communications,* pp. 5-13, 2008.
       [http://dx.doi.org/10.1109/HPCC.2008.172]

[2]   S.S. Manvi, and G. Krishna Shyam, "Resource management for Infrastructure as a Service (IaaS) in cloud computing: A survey", *J. Netw. Comput. Appl.,* vol. 41, pp. 424-440, 2014.
       [http://dx.doi.org/10.1016/j.jnca.2013.10.004]

[3]   Q. Zhang, L. Cheng, and R. Boutaba, "Cloud computing: state-of-the-art and research challenges", *J. Internet Serv. Appl.,* vol. 1, no. 1, pp. 7-18, 2010.
       [http://dx.doi.org/10.1007/s13174-010-0007-6]

[4]   M. Armbrust, A. Fox, R. Griffith, A.D. Joseph, R. Katz, A. Konwinski, G. Lee, D. Patterson, A. Rabkin, I. Stoica, and M. Zaharia, "A view of cloud computing", *Commun. ACM,* vol. 53, no. 4, pp. 50-58, 2010.
       [http://dx.doi.org/10.1145/1721654.1721672]

[5]   B. Jennings, and R. Stadler, "Resource management in clouds: Survey and research challenges", *J. Netw. Syst. Manage.,* vol. 23, no. 3, pp. 567-619, 2015.
       [http://dx.doi.org/10.1007/s10922-014-9307-7]

[6]   A. Hameed, A. Khoshkbarforoushha, R. Ranjan, P.P. Jayaraman, J. Kolodziej, P. Balaji, S. Zeadally, Q.M. Malluhi, N. Tziritas, A. Vishnu, S.U. Khan, and A. Zomaya, "A survey and taxonomy on energy efficient resource allocation techniques for cloud computing systems", *Computing,* vol. 98, no. 7, pp. 751-774, 2016.
        [http://dx.doi.org/10.1007/s00607-014-0407-8]

[7]   G. Galante, and L.C.E. de Bona, "A Survey on Cloud Computing Elasticity", *2012 IEEE Fifth International Conference on Utility and Cloud Computing,* pp. 263-270, 2012.
        [http://dx.doi.org/10.1109/UCC.2012.30]

[8]   S. Soltani, P. Martin, and K. Elgazzar, "A hybrid approach to automatic IaaS service selection", *Journal of Cloud Computing: Advances, Systems and Applications,* vol. 7, no. 1, pp. 1-18, 2018.

[9]   S-M. Han, M.M. Hassan, C-W. Yoon, and E-N. Huh, "Efficient Service Recommendation System for Cloud", *ICIS '09: Proceedings of the 2nd International Conference on Interaction Sciences: Information Technology,* pp. 839-845, 2009.

[10]   V.R. Kanakala, V.K. Reddy, and K. Karthik, "Performance analysis of load balancing techniques in cloud computing environment", *2015 IEEE International Conference on Electrical, Computer and Communication Technologies (ICECCT),* pp. 1-6, 2015.
        [http://dx.doi.org/10.1109/ICECCT.2015.7226052]

[11]   Z. u Rehman, F. K. Hussain, and O. K. Hussain, "Towards Multi-criteria Cloud Service Selection", *2011 Fifth International Conference on Innovative Mobile and Internet Services in Ubiquitous Computing,* pp. 44-48, 2011.

[12]   H. Qian, H. Zu, C. Cao, and Q. Wang, "CSS: Facilitate the cloud service selection in IaaS platforms", *2013 International Conference on Collaboration Technologies and Systems (CTS),* pp. 347-354, 2013.
        [http://dx.doi.org/10.1109/CTS.2013.6567253]

[13]   K. Dasgupta, B. Mandal, P. Dutta, J.K. Mandal, and S. Dam, "A Genetic Algorithm (GA) based Load Balancing Strategy for Cloud Computing", *Procedia Technol.,* vol. 10, pp. 340-347, 2013.
        [http://dx.doi.org/10.1016/j.protcy.2013.12.369]

[14]   M. Randles, D. Lamb, and A. Taleb-Bendiab, "A Comparative Study into Distributed Load Balancing Algorithms for Cloud Computing", *2010 IEEE 24th International Conference on Advanced Information Networking and Applications Workshops,* pp. 551-556, 2010.
        [http://dx.doi.org/10.1109/WAINA.2010.85]

[15]   A.A. AlKhatib, T. Sawalha, and S. AlZu'bi, "Load Balancing Techniques in Software-Defined Cloud Computing: an overview", *2020 Seventh International Conference on Software Defined Systems (SDS),* pp. 240-244, 2020.
        [http://dx.doi.org/10.1109/SDS49854.2020.9143874]

[16]   E. Jafarnejad Ghomi, A. Masoud Rahmani, and N. Nasih Qader, "Load-balancing algorithms in cloud computing: A survey", *J. Netw. Comput. Appl.,* vol. 88, pp. 50-71, 2017.
        [http://dx.doi.org/10.1016/j.jnca.2017.04.007]

[17]   G. Baranwal, and D.P. Vidyarthi, "A cloud service selection model using improved ranked voting method", *Concurr. Comput.,* vol. 28, no. 13, pp. 3540-3567, 2016.
        [http://dx.doi.org/10.1002/cpe.3740]

[18]   M. Rahul, and V. Yadav, "A Survey on State-of-the-art of Cloud Computing, its Challenges and Solutions", *International Conference on "Recent Trends in Communication & Electronics (ICCE-2020),* 2020.
        [http://dx.doi.org/10.1201/9781003193838-105]

[19]   Z. Yue, "A method for group decision-making based on determining weights of decision makers using TOPSIS", *Appl. Math. Model.,* vol. 35, no. 4, pp. 1926-1936, 2011.
        [http://dx.doi.org/10.1016/j.apm.2010.11.001]

[20]   Arabnejad H., and Barbosa J.G., "Multi-workflow QoS-Constrained Scheduling for Utility

Computing", *2015 IEEE 18th International Conference on Computational Science and Engineering,* pp. 137-144, 2015.
[http://dx.doi.org/10.1109/CSE.2015.29]

[21]   Y. Chen, D.M. Kilgour, and K.W. Hipel, "Screening in multiple criteria decision analysis", *Decis. Support Syst.,* vol. 45, no. 2, pp. 278-290, 2008.
[http://dx.doi.org/10.1016/j.dss.2007.12.017]

[22]   Z. He, and W. Jiang, "An evidential dynamical model to predict the interference effect of categorization on decision making results", *Knowl. Base. Syst.,* vol. 150, pp. 139-149, 2018.
[http://dx.doi.org/10.1016/j.knosys.2018.03.014]

[23]   H. Ching-Lai, "Methods for Multiple Attribute Decision Making: Methods and Applications", *Lecture Notes in Economics and Mathematical Systems,* pp. 58-198, 1981.

[24]   C. Kao, "Weight determination for consistently ranking alternatives in multiple criteria decision analysis", *Appl. Math. Model.,* vol. 34, no. 7, pp. 1779-1787, 2010.
[http://dx.doi.org/10.1016/j.apm.2009.09.022]

[25]   M. Aghajani Mir, P. Taherei Ghazvinei, N.M.N. Sulaiman, N.E.A. Basri, S. Saheri, N.Z. Mahmood, A. Jahan, R.A. Begum, and N. Aghamohammadi, "Application of TOPSIS and VIKOR improved versions in a multi criteria decision analysis to develop an optimized municipal solid waste management model", *J. Environ. Manage.,* vol. 166, pp. 109-115, 2016.
[http://dx.doi.org/10.1016/j.jenvman.2015.09.028] [PMID: 26496840]

[26]   D.L. Olson, "Comparison of weights in TOPSIS models", *Math. Comput. Model.,* vol. 40, no. 7-8, pp. 721-727, 2004.
[http://dx.doi.org/10.1016/j.mcm.2004.10.003]

[27]   Available from, py.readthedocs.io/en/stable/

[28]   Available from, https://docs.docker.com/con g/containers/resource constraints/

CHAPTER 10

Increasing Performance of Boolean Retrieval Model by Data Parallelism Technique

Mukesh Rawat[1,*], **Preksha Pratap**[1], **Manan Gupta**[1] and **Hardik Sharma**[1]

[1] *Department of Computer Science and Engineering, Meerut Institute of Engineering & Technology, Meerut, U.P., India*

Abstract: Information retrieval (IR) is to identify documents of non-uniform behavior that fulfill information requirements from the huge repository (maintained in computer systems). Different models have been defined to retrieve/fetch information. For example, the **Boolean** model, the **Statistical** model, which focuses on the vector space and probabilistic retrieval, and the **Linguistic and Knowledge-based** retrieval models. The Boolean model is defined as the "perfect match" model. If the queries are not accurate, they retrieve/fetch some irrelevant documents. This is called the *precision (p) rate*, which is the proportion of the relevant retrieved documents. The Boolean method provides good techniques to elaborate or concise a query. The Boolean method works well for the search process because of the clarity between the concepts. The *Boolean retrieval* model processes the queries in which terms of the queries are in the form of Boolean expressions, that is, in which terms of the user query combined with AND(&), OR(||), and NOT(!) operators. The model views documents in the form of inverted indexes. The key concept of an inverted index is to maintain a *dictionary* of terms. For every term, there is a collection of documents in which the term occurs. Posting is a collection of documents in which a term occurs. The list is known as the *postings list* (or inverted list), and all the postings lists are collectively called *postings*.

But as the number of documents is increased, the postings of documents are also increased, and processing these documents becomes time-consuming; so to resolve this problem, a multithreaded model is proposed in which the postings list is broken down into different chunks and processes, due to which Boolean operation between postings in accordance with Boolean query becomes faster. Using this data parallelism technique, the performance of the Boolean Retrieval Model is increased.

Keywords: Boolean retrieval, Inverted index, Postings, Posting list.

---

[*] **Corresponding author Mukesh Rawat:** Department of Computer Science and Engineering, Meerut Institute of Engineering & Technology, Meerut, U.P., India; E-mail: mukesh.rawat@miet.ac.in

Vikash Yadav, Parashuram Pal & Chuan-Ming Liu (Eds.)

INTRODUCTION

Information Retrieval

Information retrieval is rapidly becoming the dominant form of information access. The Information Recovery Program is a part of any communication system. It is part of Information Science, which studies the activities related to retrieval of information. The aim of information retrieval is to provide the right information in the hands of the right user(s) at the right time. Retrieving information means to find some information resources that are relevant to some required information from a larger database of all kinds of information (relevant as well as irrelevant) (Fig. **1**) [1]. This search can be based on metadata or on complete text. We can describe this process as:

Store ➡ User ➡ Requirements of the user ➡ Search mechanism ➡ Dissemination.

Fig. (1). Process of Information Retrieval.

All kinds of structured as well as unstructured data (which does not have a clear and easy-to-read structure for computer like random data stored in a disk with no classifications) and information problems beyond the above specified definition may also be covered in information retrieving [2]. Unstructured data is just the opposite of structured data, for example, a relational database used by organizations to maintain their records of employees and products and their specific details. But actually, no data can be regarded as completely unstructured, especially if all the text data is in a linguistic structure of human languages. Even the text documents (considered to be unstructured) are somewhat structured by headings and paragraphs or by highlighting or explicitly marking them in bold/underline, and more such techniques like using bullets, points or inserting code in between [3]. IR can also be used for analyzing "semi-structured" searches like searching a document where the title has HTML and the body has 'table' in their contents, so both values are structured in terms of title and rest of the body, but still unstructured as all data lies in the form of plain text. Information retrieval program also includes support for users to browse or filter document collection(s) or even process a set of already retrieved documents [4].

Clustering is similar to the arrangement of books on a bookshelf according to some specific topics. In a large set of documents and files, it means to come up with a good grouping (formation of clusters) of these documents according to the topic(s) and their contents. According to a given set of topics or information requirements, or categorical needs (such as the relevancy of a product to someone who has an interest in some other product), classification decides in which classes, every set of documents should be grouped. An approach to classify them is to manually classify some documents and then let the program automatically classify all the new documents that join in. Information retrieval systems can be distinguished on the basis of the scales at which they operate [5]. Mainly three scales are useful for distinguishing; these are discussed below:

1. *Web search*: the system searches a massive amount (billions) of documents stored in all (millions) accessible computer machines across the world. Issues faced here are the need to gather document files (for indexing), low efficiency of present systems to work at such a huge scale, handling the exploitation of hypertext and dodging the tricky manipulation of data and document content (attempt to fool the search engine) by site providers in order to trend their site in search engines, and use the commercial importance of the internet in their favor.

2. On the other hand, there is *personal information retrieval*. Nowadays, consumer operating systems have a built-in information retrieval system to personalize data for the user. IR for emails management system provides searching feature and also text classification: spam detection/junk mails, and automatically classifies each mail so that they can directly be put into respective classified directories. Distinctive issues faced here are managing the various kinds of documents on a typical PC (personal computer), building a search system that is lightweight (takes less space and time) to reduce loads on owners' PC, and does not require any kinds of maintenance [6].

3. Then there is *enterprise, institutional, and domain-specific search* lying between the above-discussed points. Here, retrieval may be provided for collections, such as a company's confidential documents, patents, or research articles on various topics. In such a case, these documents are to be stored on a centralized file management system(s), which is implemented on some machines dedicated to provide search for this collection [7].

MAJOR I.R. MODELS

Mainly, the following models are used to retrieve information: **Boolean** retrieval model (BRM), **Statistical** retrieval model (includes probabilistic retrieval model and the vector space retrieval model) and the **Linguistic and knowledge-based** retrieval models.

• Statistical Model:

The *probabilistic* and *vector space* models are the two good examples of this statistics-based approach. These models use information from stats like the term frequencies, and check the relevancy of a document according to a given condition or query.

Though both of them differently use the term 'frequency', both produce a ranked list of documents according to their relevancy with the query [8]. Although these statistical-retrieval models solve some limitations present in Boolean methods, they too have some problems associated with them.

• Boolean model:

The BIR (Boolean model of information retrieval) methods are a classical type of information retrieval methods, but still the first and most adopted one. Today, these are used by many IR programs because of their core advantages.

• Linguistic and knowledge-based:

In its simplest form, a user enters the keywords that are needed to be searched; these keywords are searched in the inverted indexes of each document's keywords. In other words, this approach is based solely on the concept whether the exact word (specified in the searching query) is present or absent in the document. If found, it collects this document in its result; else, it ignores this document and checks another. Clearly, due to its inability to understand the true meaning of word(s) in the query, this approach may not consider some relevant documents to be a good output and ultimately fail. This problem is well handled and tried to be completely removed by a smarter approach in *Boolean and Statistical information retrieval methods* [9].

But still, methods like morphological, syntactic and semantic analysis [Lancaster and Warner 1993] can also work to defeat this problem and retrieve information much more effectively after being integrated into Linguistic and knowledge-based approaches.

In a morphological analysis, the presence of parts of speech (nouns, verbs, adverbs, adjectives *etc.*) in the query is analyzed that helps to identify the root and affixes of word(s), and then syntactic analysis parses complete phrases. Based on some semantic relationships between words, the linguistic methods finally resolve the words' ambiguities and produce possible synonyms or quasi-synonyms. Developing a good and sophisticated retrieval system based on linguistic features of the language is difficult as it needs knowledge of complex structures and basics of semantic information and retrieval implementation of the language. Therefore, this approach needs much more advanced techniques, such as AI (Artificial Intelligence) or expert system techniques [10].

Boolean Retrieval Model

The term "information retrieval" may have a very broad meaning. But, to define it, we can say Information *retrieval* (IR) is searching material (of various unstructured features) from large collections to fulfill an information need. For query processing, there can be two possible outcomes, TRUE and FALSE;"exactly-matched" retrieval is the simplest form of ranking. Boolean Operators (specified in query) like AND, OR, NOT or proximity operators are used for matching the relevant documents.

The advantages of the model are as follows:

1. It gives predictable outputs.

2. Relatively low complexity, and hence easier to understand.

3. Can be integrated with various other features.

4. Effective process management as many documents are eliminated accordingly.

The disadvantages of the model are as follows:

1. Dependency on user for efficiency.

2. Simple query input is usually not very efficient.

3. Complex queries cannot be handled easily.

Narrowing and Broadening Techniques

We can describe a Boolean query on the basis of 4 terms: coordination type and its degree, its proximity, degree of stemming and field specifications in terms of word or string specifications. To formulate or reformulate a query, informed choices should be made by the user, according to these 4 dimensions, for this query to be sufficiently broad or narrow as per the requirement of the information. Usually, broadening techniques raise the recall but lower the precision, while narrowing techniques raise the precision but lower the recall. Ideally, all queries can be reformed and achieve the desirable precision and recall, but usually, it is not easy to achieve both simultaneously [11]. All the four terms in the query (re)formulation have some particular operators, out of which some tend to give the narrowing effect, while others give a broadening effect. For each operator with one type (narrow/broad) of effect, there can be one or more inverse operators which give the opposite effect [12].

Smart Boolean

Traditional Boolean retrieval techniques include some disadvantages (as mentioned above); to cover up those, we have discovered a newer method, called Smart Boolean [12]. This method helps the users in constructing and modifying a Boolean query and make better choices through the four dimensions of query's character. It explains some of the best possible ways to convert traditional Boolean retrieval methods into a much more user-friendly and effective technique for information retrieval.

Extended Boolean Models

Various methods have been (and are being) developed for extending the traditional Boolean model to terminate some issues like:

1. The Boolean operators can be very rigid (strictly according to the rule) without an extended development that can soften them.
2. There is no provision for ranking the results in the standard Boolean model (unlike statistical frequency methods).

Extended methods provide users the relevanct documents with the query so as to provide a basis for ranking of results.

INVERTED INDEXING

Now, we consider a scenario to familiarize ourselves with the dimensions of various kinds of problems that we might need to face in realistic situations. Let's say we have 1 million documents containing all kinds of data, and each of them is approx. 1000 words long. Here, *data* can be whatever units about which we are making a retrieval system (for example, individual memos). Data collection is the grouping of a huge amount of data on which we have to apply our retrieval system (sometimes referred to as *corpus*). Let's assume that it takes 6 bytes per word (plus space and marks) on an average, then the size of this data collection is more than 6 GB. Possibly there can be about 500,000 different terms present in these documents. These numbers are common while handling real problems and might vary in magnitude when we implement the system in reality [13].

The inverted *index* is the first major idea for information retrieval. Actually, this term (*inverted index*) is redundant; the parts of the document are always indexed backwards from the term. But still, in IR, '*inverted index*' (also known as 'inverted file') has evolved as a standard term. Fig. (**2**) below presents the basic idea of inverted indexing.

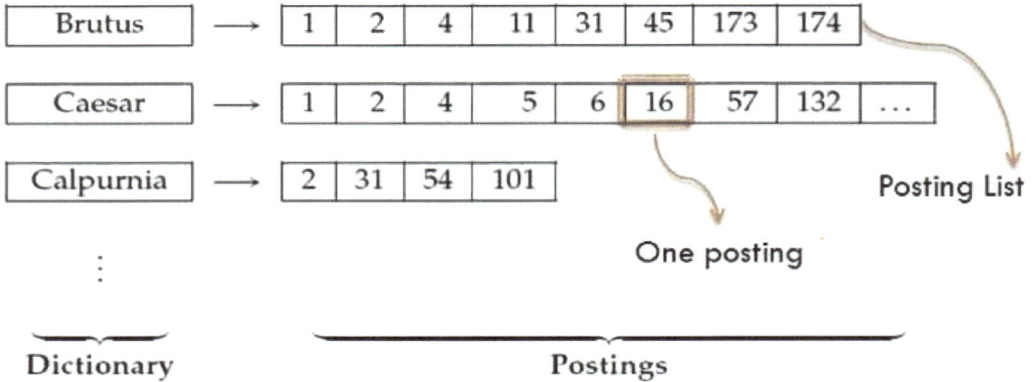

Fig. (2). Basic idea of inverted indexing.

First, a dictionary containing some terms is maintained (also known as *vocabulary*). Now, for each key in the dictionary, a list of documents in which this term occurs is maintained. Conventionally, a *posting* refers to each item present in this list that holds that the term has occurred in this document (and, later often, the positions in the document). This list is called a *postings list* (also known as an *inverted list*), and the postings lists altogether are known as *postings*. Now, each list is sorted by its document ID, while the whole dictionary containing terms can be sorted alphabetically [14].

Increasing Performance of Boolean Retrieval Model Using Data Parallelism Technique

Information retrieval (IR) is to identify documents of non-uniform behavior that fulfill information requirement from the huge repository (maintained in computer systems). Different models have been defined to retrieve/fetch information. For example, **Boolean** model, the **Statistical** model, which focuses on the vector space and probabilistic retrieval, and the **Linguistic and Knowledge-based** retrieval models. The Boolean model is defined as the "perfect match" model. If the queries are not accurate, they retrieve/fetch some irrelevant documents. This is called the *precision (p) rate*, which is the proportion of the relevant retrieved documents. The Boolean method provides good techniques to elaborate or concise a query. The Boolean method works well for the search process because of the clarity and exactness with which relationships between concepts can be represented. The *Boolean retrieval* model processes the queries in which terms of the queries are in the form of Boolean expressions, that is, in which terms of the user query are combined with AND(&), OR(||), and NOT(!) operators. The model views documents in the form of inverted indexes. The key concept of an inverted index is to maintain a *dictionary* of terms. For every term, there is a list of documents in which the term occurs. Each item in the list, which records that a particular term is present in a specific document, is called a *posting*. The list is known as the *postings list* (or inverted list), and all the postings lists are collectively called *postings*.

But as the number of documents is increased, the postings of documents are also increased, and processing these documents becomes time-consuming; so to resolve this problem, a multithreaded model is proposed in which the postings list is broken down into different chunks and processes, due to whichperforming Boolean operations between postings in accordance with Boolean query becomes faster. Using this data parallelism technique, the performance of the Boolean Retrieval Model can be increased [14].

Issues and Challenges of BRM

It is effective to use Boolean Retrieval Model for information retrieval, as the Boolean operation is performed between the postings lists. But these things become much more complex when the size of the postings list increases; it takes much longer time for performing the Boolean operation between the postings. So, there is a need for an enhanced BRM that can reduce the time complexity of Boolean operation between the postings lists.

In this chapter, we suggest a Multithreaded Data Parallelism Model to reduce the complexity of Boolean operation b/w the postings list.

WORKING OF THE PROPOSED BOOLEAN MODEL FOR IR

Sequential Execution of this Model

Here, the search is implemented sequentially (word by word). In the picture below, the word 'JAMES' is searched first, and then the word 'JOHN' is searched among the documents named D1, D2, D3, D4, D5, D6, D7, D8, D9, D10; the names of those documents have been scored which have the exact word present in them in the respective postings list. In the third step, the intersection of JAMES' posting list and JOHN's posting list is found out. Here, D4 and D5 are the common postings so it returns the list of documents which contain both the words, JAMES and JOHN (Fig. **3**).

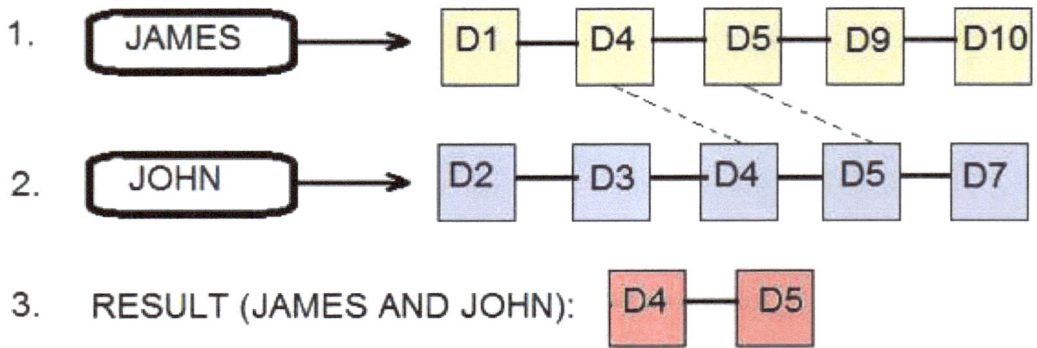

Sequential Apporach

Fig. (3). Sequential search.

Module – 1. Storing Files

Theory: Storing files module is the first part of both sequential as well as the parallel sequential model. The purpose of this module is to first find out the directory whose path is given and where all the documents files lie at. Then it one by one picks up all the files and puts their content into a Tree-Map (data structure), and also it does the same for the search file where all the words (query's data) to be searched are present. By this means, it speeds up the searching logic and the controller never has to go back to the secondary memory again and again for every document to be loaded to primary memory for searching.

Algorithm

1. Initialize a fixed variable FOLDER_PATH storing directory's path.

2. Paths.get (FOLDER_PATH): loads up the path of directory.

3. Initialize a Tree-Map, say "linesOfFiles": to store files' names and their content.

4. Initialize a Tree-Map, say "freqOfWords": to store searched words corresponding to files.

5. Initialize a Dictionary named "word": to store frequency of each word that is to be searched.

6. Initialize an ArrayList named "fileNames" to store names of files in directory.

7. For each directory Stream in Files.newDirectoryStream (Paths.get (FOLDER_PATH))

A. Add files path into "fileNames" as its name.

8. For each file in "fileNames"

A. Initializing the String List named "lines".

B. lines = Files.readAllLines(folderPath.resolve(file))

9. Initializing an ArrayList of String type named "st" to store searching words.

10. Initializing a FileReader for "SEARCH_FILE_PATH".

11. For each line of above file

A. Put each word in "st" ArrayList

12. Finish

Module – 2. Data Pre-processing

Theory: Symbol Remover and Queuing algorithm comes second in sequential model, right after the storing files. Its work is also very straightforward, which is just to reduce the time taken for searching out the result; what this model does is that it removes off all the common grammatical words like are, is, the and so on, along with all the punctuations which would make our task more difficult to find out our desired word. It also eliminates the next line characters, *i.e.*, new line characters, and replaces them with a space.

Algorithm

1. For each file in "linesOfFiles".

A. Initializing a dictionary "word" to store searched words along its frequency.

B. For each word 'temp' in "st"

i. Initializing d = temp as LowerCase.

ii. Initializing counter i to 0.

iii. For line as 'line' in "lines".

a. line = " " + line (Add space in beginning of each line).

b. line = line as LowerCase.

c. For each character c in 'line'.

I. If c is other than alphabet or number,replace it with space (' ').

d. For each line containing d.

I. Increase counter i by 1.

iv. Put searched word 'd' along with its frequency 'i' to 'word'.

C. Put file name "fileName" along resulted dictionary "word" to "freqOfWords".

2. Finish

Module – 3. Creation of Indexes and Posting lists (String w)

Theory: Creation of Indexes means finding out the result throughout the directory along with their frequencies. And posting list is the storing of each result as a recorded list with each file along with the filename. Basically, what is taking place here in this model is that it first retrieves throw content of all the files and reads the content word by word and matches them with the required word; if it is matched up, the frequency variable is upgraded and this process continues till every file is being retrieved out from TreeMap. It then stores up the result in the form of a dictionary attached with the respective file name as tag.

Algorithm

1. Initializing an Integer array of size to that of Dictionary "word".

2. Fill the array with 0.

3. Initialize counter 'i' to 0.

4. For each word "t" in "st".

A. Initialize d to t in lower case.

B. For each file "fileNames" in "linesOfFiles".

i. Initialize counter c to 0.

ii. For each line 'line' in "fileNames"

a. Add " "(space) on before and after the line.

b. Convert line to LowerCase.

c. For each 'line' contains "d"

I. Increase counter c by 1.

iii. If counter is greater than 0.

a. Increase value of countNode at index i by 1.

b. Putting the "fileNames" into ArrayList "InsertFile".

C. Increase counter i by 1.

D. Put word "t" and ArrayList "InsertFile" to Dictionary "InsertNode".

5. Finish.

Module - 4 Boolean Intersection

Theory: Intersection itself tells us what is common among two or more things. So, this intersection module basically checks out the common nodes that entered query has, that is, it gives the name of the nodes (files) containing that particular query. This module uses up an ArrayList to store the resulted file names. It traverses through each entity presented in the dictionary "InsertNode", and then matches the entity's Node list with the previously stored one.

Algorithm

1. Creating a String arrayList "result" of the size of Dictionary "word".

2. Initializing "result" to first key's value (list) of "InsertNode".

3. For each key's value (posting list) "p" in "InsertNode".

A. Set "result" (list) to the intersection of "result"(self) and "p" (this posting list of words).

4. Result is stored in 'result' arraylist containing names of files that contain all the words that were searched.

5. Finish.

Parallel Execution of BRM

Theory: This Parallel Sequential Model for searching of Boolean Retrieval Model basically works on the basic principles of Multi-threading. Here we, let's suppose, have to search out any two literals, so what we do is that we create a new thread for each search. So, for two searches, there are two threads for this. And these two threads will work out like they both start at the same time, let's suppose t1, and end up approximately together, depending upon their search through the directory. In this way, rather than searching them one by one, we found the result for both only at the cost of one's execution time (Fig. **4**).

Consider the picture below; there are two words, 'JAMES' and 'JOHN' to be searched along the entire range of documents named D1, D2, D3, D4, D5, D6, D7, D8, D9, and D10. For achieving actual parallelism, we split the searching into 2 threads T1 and T2, through multi-threading. T1 will handle the process of searching 'JAMES' while T2 will do the same for 'JOHN'. After searching is done and we have documents with occurring keywords in their respective posting lists, the second step is to find the intersection of these two posting lists of JAMES and JOHN, similar to the sequential approach. Documents with both JAMES and JOHN are D4 and D5. See how this method only took 2 steps instead of 3, which is the main reason for reduction in net time taken by the approach.

Algorithm

Create two Threads for executing two word's searching in parallel

1. Retrieve all file names from folderPath to FileNames.

2. Put the contents of each file having their names in FileNames into linesofFiles.

3. Read the file containing words to be searched and store content in searchWords.

4. For each entity in linesofPath (filename, lines)

a. For each item in searchWords (search word)

i. Convert this word into lower case.

ii. Initialize a counter to 0.

iii. For each line in lines

A. Convert this line into lower case

B. For each character of this line: Check if character is other than alphabet or a number, replace it with a space (' ').

C. For this line check if this search word is present, if present, increase the counter by 1.

iv. Put word along with its counter as its value into wordDictonary.

b. Put filename and wordDictionary into freqofWords.

5. Set i=0

6. For each word in searchWord.

a. Convert word into lower case.

b. Assign the following code to an idle thread.

c. For each lines of LinesOfFiles (filename, lines).

i. Initialize counter to 0.

ii. For each line in lines

A. Convert line into lower Case

B. For this line check if this search word is present in lines

I. Increase the counter by 1.

II. Terminating the current loop

C. If Counter is greater than 0

I. Increase counterNode by one.

D. Generate the results of each word stored in searchWord along with its counterNode value.

E. Increase the counter I by 1.

7. Run the intersection module (discussed earlier in sequential approach) to produce the results.

8. Finish.

RESULT ANALYSIS

In Table **1**, the names and number of keywords of the document files used for testing this model are shown. The maximum number of files used at once for testing is 30. 'Keywords fetched' refers to the number of meaningful words (not the grammatical words) present in the document.

Table 1. Description of document file used for testing.

Document Name	Number of Keywords Fetched
Doc1.txt	34
Doc2.txt	40
Doc3.txt	47
Doc4.txt	33
Doc5.txt	52
Doc6.txt	41
Doc7.txt	67
Doc8.txt	55
Doc9.txt	62
Doc10.txt	49
phy_unit1.txt	4396
phy_unit2.txt	3679
phy_unit3.txt	2158
phy_unit4.txt	4841
phy_unit5.txt	5416
phy_unit6.txt	5122
phy_unit7.txt	4067
phy_unit8.txt	3690
phy_unit9.txt	2903
phy_unit10.txt	2235
chem1.txt	5811
chem2.txt	4962
chem3.txt	4608
chem4.txt	4380
chem5.txt	3795
test.txt	153
aml.txt	1206

(Table 1) cont.....

Document Name	Number of Keywords Fetched
index.txt	114
index copy.txt	114

Table **2** shows how the average posting lists' size changes when the number of documents and dictionary size vary. The numbers of documents used for testing differ from 30 to 20. Dictionary size means the number of words searched in one query. Average posting list size refers to the average calculated by division of each posting list's size (each word's occurrences) and the number of words searched in that query.

Table 2. Average posting list size.

No. of Documents	Dictionary Size	Average Posting List Size
30	5	7
30	8	5
30	4	8
25	4	7
20	4	5
20	3	8

Output Screen Shots of Program

Table **3** shows time taken for BRM in sequential execution. Boolean Query refers to the operation (AND here) and operands used for the particular test. Time taken gives the time elapsed while execution of the programs in milliseconds.

Table 3. Time taken for BRM in sequential execution.

No. of Documents	Dictionary Size	Ave. Posting List Size	Boolean Query	Time Taken (ms)
5	2	2	work AND doctor	23.45
10	2	4	Man AND Woman	28.94
15	2	4	Classification AND acting	44.23
20	2	6	Hello AND create	56.87
25	2	10	Functions AND practice	63.14
30	2	4	Culture AND local	88.42

Input: "understanding thermodynamics applications" (Fig. **5**)

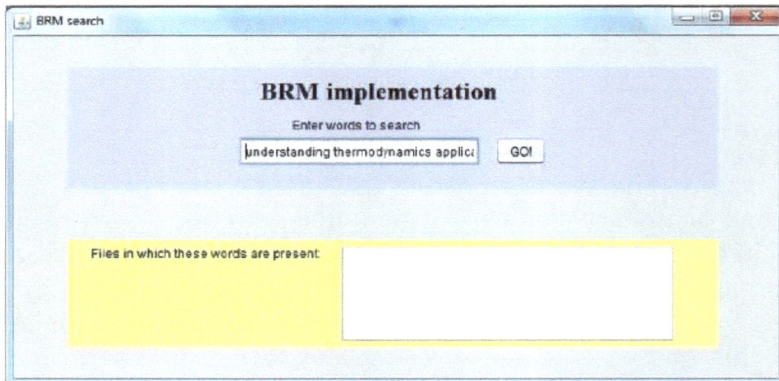

Fig. (5). Screenshot after implementation.

On clicking the "GO!" button;

Output: "phy_unit3.txt", "chem5.txt" (Fig. **6**)

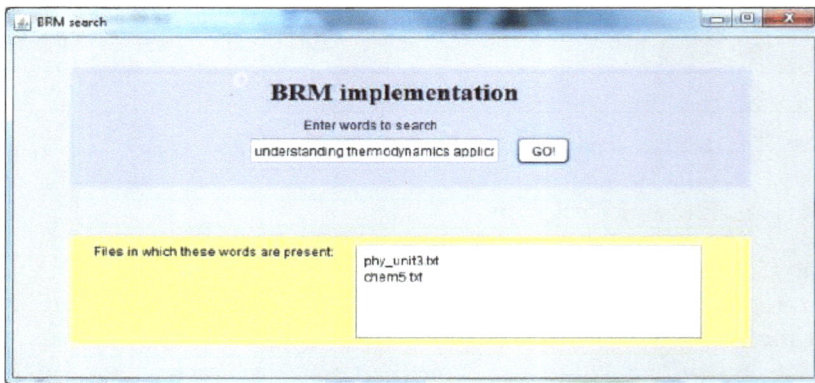

Fig. (6). Screenshot after implementation.

Table **4** shows the time taken for BRM in parallel execution via multi-threading.

Table 4. Time taken for BRM in parallel execution via multi-threading.

No. of Documents	Dictionary Size	Ave. Posting List Size	Boolean Query	Time Taken(ms)	No. of Threads Created
5	2	2	work AND doctor	16.09	2
10	2	4	Man AND Woman	19.17	2
15	2	4	Classification AND acting	28.44	2

(Table 4) cont.....

No. of Documents	Dictionary Size	Ave. Posting List Size	Boolean Query	Time Taken(ms)	No. of Threads Created
20	2	6	Hello AND create	33.91	2
25	2	10	Functions AND practice	39.55	2
30	2	4	Culture AND local	51.28	2

In Fig. (**7**), it is shown how time taken differs in a sequential and parallel approach.

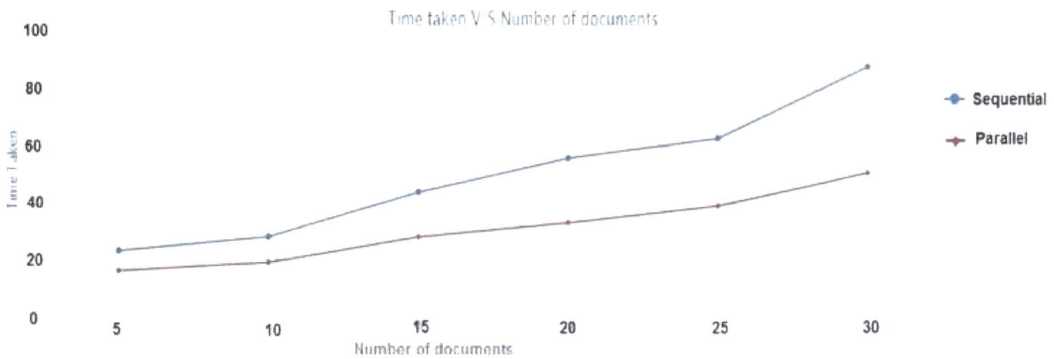

Fig. (7). Difference of time taken using a sequential and parallel approach.

Analysis

Correct identified documents $\rightarrow$ C

Wrong identified documents $\rightarrow$ W

Non-identified documents $\rightarrow$ M

Precision

Precision tells about the fraction of the retrieved documents that are actually relevant to the user's information need.

$P = C/ (C + W)$

Recall

Recall tells about the fraction of the documents that are relevant to the query that is successfully retrieved.

$R = C / (C + M)$

F-measure

F-measure is the fraction that gives both precision and recall equally weighted. Its value varies from 0 to 1.

$F = 2 * P * R / (P + R)$

Table **5** shows the values of different parameters like precision, recall and F measures.

Table 5. Representation of Precision, Recall and F-measure.

No. of Documents	C	W	M	P	R	F
5	1	0	0	1	1	1
10	3	0	0	1	1	1
15	3	0	1	1	0.75	0.86
20	4	1	1	0.8	0.8	0.8
25	6	1	2	0.85	0.75	0.79
30	2	0	1	1	0.67	0.8

In Fig. (**8**), F-measure is shown as the number of documents change.

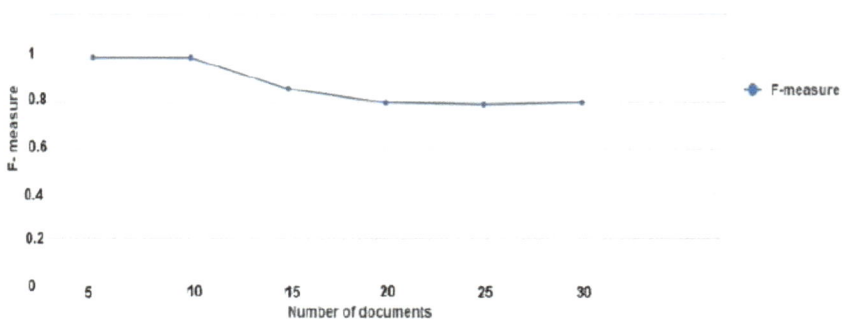

Fig. (8). Representation of F-measure.

CONCLUSION

This enhanced Boolean Retrieval Model (BRM) focuses on retrieving information much faster than previously discussed methods. Proposed parallel execution of Boolean operations enables quicker calculation of results, unlike sequential methods. In this paper, multithreading using java 8 is used, but other methods like

Hadoop's MapReduce or any distributed processing systems with multi-core processing architecture can implement the model on the basis of the above discussed algorithm. Implementation of sequentially executable algorithm is much easier for general multi-purpose PCs, but due to unavailability of multiple CPUs, it is impossible to achieve actual parallelism unless there is an interconnected multiple processor architecture present within the system. But even if such multi-processing environment is unavailable, the model would still work in sequential mode but with reduced speed. This multiple environment support allows users independency over any type of structure, while its best performance (in terms of speed) can be seen on multi-core processing architecture. For example, in the above algorithm, only 2 threads are used for processing each posting as the testing data was smaller in comparison to real-life data; for huge data input, the number of threads may be increased up to the number of processors available. Proportionally, the speed will vary with number of threads, *i.e.*, increasing number of threads will increase the speed (or decrease the time taken by each processor to complete the search).

Today, time is considered to be the most precious asset. So, the priority of the system is to reduce the time complexity to as low as possible over space conservation. Future scope of this work may include compression techniques to reduce the memory used in the execution of the program. The space required for each thread to search a word increases with the number of documents available for search; if documents are huge in number or heavy by size, each thread will take up large spaces to execute searching. In such cases, it may be needed to construct a technique that compresses or manages the present data in such a way that it takes minimum space on primary memory without exploiting the time complexity of the proposed system.

Applications of the proposed model (for information retrieval) can be search engines (web), recommendation systems, digital libraries, email/file management, social media searches, news retrieval, *etc.* In a web search engine, this model can be used as a module that takes a preprocessed input (*i.e.*, reduction of words that may have the same meaning or adding words very relevant to the user input, *etc.*) to reduce the ignorance of some relevant documents which have the word in other forms as it is an exact match based model (it searches the word for its exact match in documents). Spam detection in email management is another major possible application of this model as it will return all those documents which contain all spam recognized words; in this case, a Boolean model may reduce false accusations of spam on a genuine document, hence increasing its performance than other methods. Another example of its use is news retrieval; for multiple agencies like news channels, it is a daily task to study very old news for investigation and reports; this model will provide the exact search for such tasks even before the user blinks again.

CONSENT FOR PUBLICATION

Not applicable.

CONFLICT OF INTEREST

The author declares no conflict of interest, financial or otherwise.

ACKNOWLEDGEMENTS

Declared none.

REFERENCES

[1]   A. Z. Broder, ""On the resemblance and containment of documents," Proceedings", *Compression and Complexity of SEQUENCES 1997 (Cat. No.97TB100171),* pp. 21-29.

[2]   J. Cho, H. Garcia-Molina, and L. Page, *Efficient Crawling through URl,* 1998.

[3]   E. Stephon, "The TREC-9 filtering track final report", *Voorhees EM, Harman DK (eds) 9th text retrieval conference (TREC-9),* 2001.

[4]   Z. Andrei, ", "Algorithmic Aspects of Information Retrieval on the Web"", In: *Handbook of Massive Data Sets,* Kluwer Academic Publisher, 2002, pp. 3-23.

[5]   S. Lawrence, and C.L. Giles, "Searching the world wide Web", *Science,* vol. 280, no. 5360, pp. 98-100, 1998.
    [http://dx.doi.org/10.1126/science.280.5360.98] [PMID: 9525866]

[6]   "The Anatomy of a Large Scale Hypertextual web Search Engine", *Proceedings of World-Wide Web,* 1998.

[7]   G. Pandurangan, Prabhakar Raghavan, and Eli Upfal, "Using Page Rank to Characterize Web Structure", In: *Computing and Combinatorics. COCOON 2002. Lecture Notes in Computer Science,* O.H. Ibarra, L. Zhang, Eds., vol. 2387. Springer: Berlin, Heidelberg, 2002.

[8]   M.R. Henzinger, "Algorithmic Challenges in Web Search Engines", *Internet Math.,* vol. 1, no. 1, pp. 115-123, 2004.
    [http://dx.doi.org/10.1080/15427951.2004.10129079]

[9]   R. Monika, *International World Wide Web Conference,* vol. 33, Elsevier Science: Amsterdam, pp. 295-308, 2000.

[10]   K. Bharat, and A. Broder, "A technique for measuring the relative size and overlap of public Web search engines", *Comput. Netw. ISDN Syst.,* vol. 30, no. 1-7, pp. 379-388, 1998.
    [http://dx.doi.org/10.1016/S0169-7552(98)00127-5]

[11]   A. Sharma, and V. Yadav, "Impact of Morphology on the performance of Search Engine while retrieving information in Hindi Language", *International Journal of Advanced Trends in Computer Science and Engineering,* vol. 9, no. 4, pp. 4182-4188, 2020. [IJATCSE].
    [http://dx.doi.org/10.30534/ijatcse/2020/02942020]

[12]   C.W. Cleverdon, and J. Mills, "The testing of index language devices", In: *Spärck Jones K, Willett P (eds) Readings in information retrieval,* 1997, pp. 98-110.

[13]   L. Page, S. Brin, and R. Motwani, *The Page Rank Citation Ranking: Bringing Order to the Web, Technical Report.* Stanford Infolab, 1999, pp. 3-4.

[14]   C.E. Buckley, and L. Darrin, "Bias and the limits of pooling", In: *SIGIR '06, 29th annual international ACM SIGIR conference on research and development in information retrieval,* Dumais ST, Efthimiadis EN, Hawking D, Järvelin K, Eds., New York, 2006, pp. 619-620.

SUBJECT INDEX

9 781681 089690